Youth Unemployment and Joblessness

ADAPT LABOUR STUDIES BOOK-SERIES

International School of Higher Education in Labour and Industrial Relations

ADAPT (www.adapt.it) is a non-profit organisation founded in 2000 by Professor Marco Biagi with the aim of promoting studies and research in the field of labour law and industrial relations from an international and comparative perspective. Our purpose is to encourage and implement a new approach to academic research, by establishing ongoing relationships with other universities and advanced studies institutes, and promoting academic and scientific exchange programmes with enterprises, institutions, foundations and associations. In collaboration with the **Marco Biagi Centre for International and Comparative Studies** (www.csmb.unimore.it), ADAPT set up the International School of Higher Education in Labour and Industrial Relations, a centre of excellence which is accredited at an international level for research, study and postgraduate programmes in the area of industrial and labour relations.

Youth Unemployment and Joblessness: Causes, Consequences, Responses

Edited by

Alfredo Sánchez-Castañeda, Lavinia Serrani and Francesca Sperotti

CAMBRIDGE SCHOLARS

PUBLISHING

Youth Unemployment and Joblessness:
Causes, Consequences, Responses,
Edited by Alfredo Sánchez-Castañeda, Lavinia Serrani and Francesca Sperotti

This book first published 2012

Cambridge Scholars Publishing

12 Back Chapman Street, Newcastle upon Tyne, NE6 2XX, UK

British Library Cataloguing in Publication Data
A catalogue record for this book is available from the British Library

ISBN (10): 1-4438-4056-4, ISBN (13): 978-1-4438-4056-9

TABLE OF CONTENTS

Chapter Two: The Transition from Education to the Labour Market: What Makes for Better Transitions?

Chapter Three: The Transition from Education to the Labour Market

Chapter Four: Future Scenarios for Young People

LIST OF ILLUSTRATIONS

LIST OF TABLES

FOREWORD

TAYO FASHOYIN

The current global unemployment problem presents a particularly difficult labour market experience for young workers. The ILO estimates no less than 40% of all unemployed people are young. As available knowledge indicates, young people are disadvantaged in finding employment, especially in rigid labour markets. There are several factors, such as their relative lack of skills, unstable labour market experience and discrimination, which contribute to the difficulty usually faced by young people entering the labour market. Thus, unemployment among young people has become a major policy challenge for governments and employers in the 21st century. The fact that during this period countries have to deal with sluggish growth and economic activities has pressured public policy into creating opportunities for economic growth and employment. There is no shortage of ideas and policy initiatives for addressing the daunting challenge of youth employment, but the need for a comprehensive policy approach which combines dedicated strategy for youth employment must also include measures addressing systemic and institutional impediments to the sustainability of policies for the employment of young people. In addition to ensuring that young people stay in school longer, public policies must also create the enabling environment and avenues for skills acquisition and real work experience among young workers. Clearly, there is a strong case for governments and other stakeholders to put in place policies that encourage or motivate employers, particularly in the private sector, to recruit young workers, through various forms of public and private initiatives that are dedicated to the promotion of youth employment. There are many programmes of this kind across countries, but one that has the potential of creating the foregoing enabling environment is the devising of innovative apprenticeship schemes that depart from the traditional apprenticeship, which has proved inadequate in meeting the labour market expectations of prospective employers and young people. The present issue of the ADAPT LABOUR STUDIES BOOK-SERIES, *Youth Unemployment and Joblessness: Causes, Consequences, Responses* is dedicated to the employment challenge facing young people, but also to the focus and extent of responsiveness of policies, both public and private, in tackling this global challenge of our time. Apart from sharing comparative experiences on policies, practices and trends, the volume seeks to contribute to a wider understanding of the scale of the challenge of youth employment.

UNDERSTANDING THE CAUSES AND THE CONSEQUENCES OF YOUTH UNEMPLOYMENT AND JOBLESSNESS

ALFREDO SÁNCHEZ-CASTAÑEDA, LAVINIA SERRANI AND FRANCESCA SPEROTTI

For national governments and international organizations worldwide, youth unemployment and joblessness remain major issues. Undoubtedly, the global economic crisis has further exposed the fragility of the youth in the labour market. Between 2008 and 2009, the number of unemployed youth increased by an unprecedented 4.5 million; at the end of 2010, there were an estimated 75.1 million young people in the world struggling to find work – 4.6 million more than in 2007. Moreover, the number of youth who are not in employment, education or training is on the rise in most countries. These alarming trends, alongside recent youth-led political unrest, the persistent lack of job opportunities and ineffective programmes for school-to-work transitions, call for action on the part of political and social institutions at national and international levels.

In an awareness of the seriousness of the foregoing questions and consequences that ensue, the present volume aims to provide some valuable insights into these issues, compiling contributions of academics, researchers and practitioners who participated in the ADAPT-UNAM International Conference, *Youth Unemployment and Joblessness: Causes, Consequences, Responses* which took place on 29-30 August 2011 in Mexico City (Mexico).

The range of solutions provided in this volume is the result of the distinctive features of each national geopolitical context, but also of the interdisciplinary approach through which these topics are analyzed. Indeed, given the undergoing changes in the world of work, youth unemployment and joblessness are issues to be dealt with by different subjects such as economics, labour law, education, sociology and industrial relations. However, the set of proposals put forward does not imply the absence of shared views. On the contrary, there is broad consensus on the urgent need of investing in training and skills development as the main levers to fight unemployment and overcome the current mismatch in the labour market.

Equal attention should be paid to the shift from education to work, which in many countries proved to be a complex process, affected by variables such as the length and quality of the education received, national traditions, the state of the labour market, and economic and demographic issues. In considering different flexible forms of work, apprenticeship appears to be one of the most effective tools for ensuring a successful transition, and also the integration between education, training, and employment. Indeed, apprenticeship provides for a win-win solution: securing the transition towards employment for young people with appropriate skills, as it is up to the employer to train young workers, while eventually reducing labour costs. Such a reduction in labour costs is another positive effect for employers and not necessarily a direct consequence of training.

In view of the above, the set of proposals examined in the present volume is intended to gain a better understanding of the causes and the consequences of youth unemployment and joblessness, and to disseminate the main findings discussed over the ADAPT-UNAM International Conference.

YOUTH AND THE LABOUR MARKET WORLDWIDE: THE CURRENT SCENARIO

YOUTH, UNEMPLOYMENT AND EDUCATION

HÉCTOR-HUGO BARBAGELATA

1. Introductory Remarks[1]

The difficulty in finding employment as a means for securing a livelihood experienced by young people is an ongoing issue, along with the sense of frustration arising from failing to meet their work expectations. Indeed, youth unemployment has always been one of the major concerns of governments, and this is exhibited—among other things—by the rate of migration reported in different regions.[2]

Nevertheless—and unlike the past—the question is given more relevance[3] and wider media coverage, also because of the impact of youth unemployment.[4] As a result, although unemployment for young people is not a recent issue, it has gained unprecedented significance, calling for an in-depth study of the several facets to be dealt with, in order to address the matter and determine adequate solutions.

There is broad consensus that inadequate training—or the lack of training more generally—is one of the reasons why[5] young people struggle in their search for employment. Accordingly, the focus should be on reviewing the functioning and structure of the education system in a number of countries. In this regard, special attention should be paid to the

---

[1] Translation from Spanish by Pietro Manzella.

[2] Naturally, the migration process involves people of all ages. However, the majority of immigrants are young people who have left their places of origin in search of new job opportunities.

[3] According to a survey carried out in September 2011 on occasion of the Tunza Conference for children and youth in Bandung, Indonesia, almost 40% of those unemployed are young people in the 15-24 years age group.

[4] The UGT Global Bulletin No. 76/2011 issued a document titled *The Fight of Young People*, according to which "young trade union leaders would meet in Singapore on the 27th and 28th of September 2011 to discuss the serious difficulty faced by the youth in finding a job".

[5] The lack of correspondence between adequate training and job opportunities has recently been highlighted by the spokesperson of the General Council of the Judiciary, Gabriela Bravo.

provision of effective training and education, in order to meet the needs of young jobseekers, their parents, the employers and society. On this subject, one should also consider the positive impact resulting from the supportive role of the family, as well as the discouraging effects on young people ensuing from uninvolved parents in terms of advice and guidance.

Another issue that is gaining considerable attention at the moment, as regarded as thorny and complicated to deal with, is that of young people in the 15-18 years age group who are not in employment nor in education or training (NEETs).

At the time of discussing measures to tackle unemployment, considering gender issues is likewise important, also in modern and more developed societies. This is even true in cases of women performing better than men in terms of educational attainment.[6] Of equal significance is the difficulty faced by people with disabilities in securing employment, even though national legislation usually provides protection to this category of workers.[7]

On the basis of what has been pointed out so far, it can be argued that the issue of youth unemployment has an international dimension and presents some common features, although different circumstances in cultural and economic terms are clearly to be taken into account. In this sense, national newspapers refer to young people struggling to find a job, and this news is usually accompanied by some relevant statistics. Further, data and comments are routinely provided on the percentage of early-school leavers in any grade, or repeating students in primary and secondary education—due to a lack of commitment or inadequate support—the reasons of which are often unclear. As already stressed, although acknowledging the relevance of an investigation carried out at an international level, it is necessary to highlight the nuances of national and local differences and put forward some proposals to limit the scope of the issue and minimise its effects.

Compounding the picture is the problem of children who are employed in different tasks[8] despite their young age. Their rights are violated and,

---

[6] Surveys provided in the press seem to uphold this statement. In Uruguay, 65% of students enrolled in the University of Montevideo are women, yet the number of female jobseekers is twice as high as the number of males looking for a job (Source: *La República*, Montevideo, 28 September 2011, 17)

[7] In many countries, the law provides that a number of positions in the public sector should be reserved for people with disabilities. Nonetheless, many cases of non-compliance with these provisions have been reported.

[8] The majority of national legislation and international labour laws provide that children under the age of 15 are not allowed to work. Unfortunately, the inspection

what is worse, they are not able to enjoy their childhood in a light-hearted fashion. This crucial point— the fulfilment of children rights—has been the subject of a number of provisions, particularly at an international level.[9] Children are employed—especially in rural areas—in family-run farms and contribute to the livelihood of their family. In other cases, however, they are engaged in activities concerning waste collection and recycling, with the latter that is regarded as one of the most dangerous forms of child labour.[10] The need to help their family, alongside the efforts of parents to provide children with prosperity and adequate levels of education at a later stage of their life, seem to somehow justify the recourse to child labour and the negative consequences that ensue. Nonetheless, this is not always the case, as these children are often deprived of their rights, and they are not allowed to access education, with a serious impact on their lives.[11]

At an international level, organised crime-related activities represent another major challenge to cope with. For instance, sexual exploitation of youth through prostitution is a widespread phenomenon in many countries, the seriousness of which is amplified by adults engaged in sex tourism. These practices are closely connected to other forms of exploitation—e.g. trafficking of human beings and slavery—which concern above all individuals under age.

In the context of this paper, aside from the foregoing questions, it seems worth pointing out another aspect. Indeed, tackling youth sexual exploitation is just one of the problems, as only in a few cases can jobs children are engaged in be labelled as legal and decent.

This section has provided an outline of some of the obstacles faced by young people of working age at the time of seeking work. Far from comprehensive, this first part has drawn attention to the factors that can affect the search for a job in a serious and inconvenient way, causing

---

systems monitoring the compliance and enforcement of such provisions are often insufficient and, to some respects, ineffective.

[9] This aspect is stressed in par. 1, Art. 32 of the International Convention on the Rights of Child issued by UNICEF as well as in the legislation of some countries, such as in the last paragraph of Art. 162 of the Code on Childhood and Adolescence of Uruguay. The document makes provision for the well-being of both children and adolescents.

[10] Art. 3 of ILO Convention No. 182 on the Worst Forms of Child Labour.

[11] A case which is worth mentioning is the one concerning talented kids who play sports, particularly soccer. Their parents conclude contracts with overseas institutions which legally bind their children—who are very young and usually do not complete secondary school—to practice for these teams. This situation *de facto* leads only to the father enjoying the advantages of the agreement.

children under age to carry out working activities that are unappealing. After this descriptive section, an investigation of the most practical aspects related to vocational training that might help boost employment among the youth now follows.

2. Vocational Training: Recent Developments in Academic Programmes and Legislation

A major innovation in the field of education which is increasingly met with approval is the scope for students to change and select different academic courses, with a view to making school more engaging. This is particularly the case of junior high school, where priority is given to educational paths that smooth the transition into the labour market.

Unfortunately, the commendable attempt on the part of the legislator to stimulate children's interests in education—by way of reforms or new programmes—did not provide the expected results. If anything, such an effort has become a source of confusion in terms of the objectives to be met, above all in reference to students' actual needs, guidance provided, and the levels of commitment, *de facto* facilitating the admission to the following grade and not contributing to further education.

The review of academic programmes in junior high school in order to ease access to the labour market has been, to varying degrees, more promising. Numerous courses that focus on practical and technical skills have been established, also with a view to fill in the gap between institutions providing general education and technical schools, and stimulate the students' interest in these kinds of studies.

As said, the task to review the school system appears to be an arduous one. The complexity lies in the duration of the academic year, as it is not workable to provide for additional courses or lengthen the school day to carry out practical activities without negatively affecting the management of courses of a more general nature. Indeed, the classes providing knowledge labelled as "general"—e.g. Philosophy, History, Social Sciences, Music and Arts—are still attached great importance in the process of imparting knowledge to young students, with this set of circumstances that makes the rethinking of the school system more challenging. Furthermore, the extension of school hours, in principle regarded as a reasonable alternative to the reduction of general education course material, would shorten the time needed to study, an activity that is to be carried out individually and that cannot be replaced by in-class joint activities. Aside from that, planning so many activities at the beginning of the academic year inevitably reduces the scope for students—mainly teenagers—to put forward proposals on their own initiative.

One should also consider that reforms of this kind usually concern technical institutions in disadvantaged areas, thus widening the social gap between those who enrol in schools where general education is prioritised and young people receiving vocational training. In other words, students engaged in training activities will have access to fewer job opportunities and will not be adequately prepared to attend university.

The same holds true for vocational training provided by programmes other than those included in traditional education.

With regard to legislation governing education, a comparative analysis of the laws regulating vocational training in a number of countries revealed some common features, with special reference to contractual arrangements providing for the alternation of theory and practice:[12]

- as for vocational training in a strict sense, national legislation usually gives priority to on-the-job learning, although this could have an impact on general education.
- In considering new ways to promote training contracts, it emerges that there is a limited use of this contractual scheme, as preference is given to apprenticeship contracts. This state of affairs leads to a high level of precariousness, because frequently young workers hired through this employment relationship do not maintain their jobs at the end of the apprenticeship period.
- In order to boost youth employment, employers are provided with incentives and financial support at the time of hiring apprentices. For instance, workers under this contract are paid less than permanent employees performing the same tasks, with employers that have a number of benefits also with regard to social contributions and training costs, which are partly or totally borne by the state.
- These contractual schemes are intended to ease the access to the labour market, although they seem to overlook the quality of education provided, which in most of the cases binds holders to undesirable positions.
- In a number of countries, the age group of those who can enter into these contracts is increasingly widening, moving beyond the

[12] In this connection, a more detailed study is provided in Barbagelata, H-H. 2002 (second ed.). *Formación y legislación del trabajo.* Montevideo: Cinterfor/ILO. The English version is available for the first edition: Barbagelata, H-H. 1997. *Training and labour legislation.* Montevideo: ILO, Poliform-Cinterfor.

traditional notion of "young". For instance, in Belgium vocational training can be provided to young people in the 18-25 age group, while in Italy the age cohort is 19 to 31 years old and—in some cases—these contracts also apply to people of the age of 35.

- Although contractual arrangements which provide vocational training are employment relationships *per se*, they often fall within the labour law sphere.
- The same holds true for social security benefits, in the sense that the law hardly provides protection against occupational injuries and work-related diseases.
- Finally, governments that have given priority to apprenticeship have also devised other forms of training and education.

On the basis of the above considerations, it is not difficult to imagine, with the exception of those countries where traditional vocational training- particularly apprenticeship- is well established, that young people are not interested in entering this form of work. This has led countries with traditional forms of training to adapt their legislation to make it more appealing.

3. Concluding Remarks

1) In social terms, youth employment has always been a thorny issue, but nowadays it has acquired considerable relevance as it affects an increasing number of young people worldwide.

2) At the time of addressing the problem of unemployment among youth, it is also pivotal to review traditional paths in education in order to supply adequate training.

3) In exploring different education systems, the attempt to attract the students' interest in education has emerged, with special reference to technical subjects. This attempt proved difficult in practical terms, and the outcomes reported are often unsatisfactory.

4) Whereas adequate education and training facilitate access to better positions on the part of young people under normal economic conditions, doubts are cast on the effectiveness of training programmes in times of crisis.

5) Notwithstanding the seriousness of unemployment for the youth, special attention should also be given to the precarious nature of their occupations, e.g. young people working in family-run companies.

6) Governments and employers worldwide are mostly concerned with initiatives aimed at providing the young with in-company training, often overlooking the side effects of these policies.

7) Domestic laws often set forth several incentives for employers that provide in-company training.

8) In a number of cases, job-training contracts envisage limited to no forms of protection in terms of health and safety at the workplace and social security benefits.

9) As a result, those who take no interest in education do not think that these employment arrangements supply on-the-job training, thus resulting in an alternative to traditional schooling.

10) In sum, the search for measures to tackle youth unemployment and the consequences that ensue is a challenging task to national governments, educational bodies, experts of social sciences, and more generally to those who are attentive to the needs of their communities.

References

UGT. 2011. "The Fight of Young People," *UGT Global Bulletin*, No. 76.

Barbagelata, H-H. 2002 (second ed.). *Formación y legislación del trabajo.* Montevideo: Cinterfor/ILO.

—. 1997 (first ed.). *Training and Labour Legislation.* Montevideo: ILO, Poliform-Cinterfor.

YOUNG PEOPLE IN WORLDWIDE LABOUR MARKETS: STRUCTURAL WEAKNESSES AND VARIOUS FORMS OF SCHOOL-TO-WORK TRANSITIONS

FRANCESCA FAZIO

1. A *Caveat* to Youth Labour Markets most Revealing Indicators and Peculiarities

It is common practice for the media to treat the problems faced by the youth—usually those between the ages of 15 to 24 years old—in the labour market by only considering youth unemployment indicators. This approach, although useful, is not sufficient to provide a complete understanding of the condition of young people in the labour market. Indeed, the number of young who actively seek employment is not an exhausting indicator, nor alarming, especially if one looks at both the structural features of young people in the labour market and the Italian labour market *per se*. With regard to the first *caveat*, economic literature has discussed the topic extensively, with scholars who have tried to explain, in both theoretical and empirical terms, the high rates of unemployment among the youth, particularly if compared to adults (two to four times higher). One reason for this is that young people, usually hired under fixed-term contracts, are most affected by the "super-cyclical" trend of the labour market. Their unemployment rate is more sensitive to the economic cycle than that of their adult counterparts, for making them redundant is easier and less expensive. Further, young people are usually less experienced and possess lower levels of job tenure. In this sense, the smaller investment in human capital in terms of general and special knowledge provided to young workers will translate into a lower cost at the time of terminating their contract. Such a situation can also be explained in consequential terms, taking account of two main aspects. First, as a reaction on the part of young people to the deterioration in labour market prospects, that is determined by the decision to postpone their entry into the labour market and to increase their investment in human capital.[1] Secondly, as the fact that young people stay in their parental home longer, with this state of affairs that is both the cause and the consequence of the difficulty in the labour market. If labour demand is considered, a significant number of studies have pointed out that young people experience discrimination at the time of applying for a position, because of their lack of experience and the uncertain nature of their career path.

In many respects, the transition from school to work of young people is marked by certain constraints in the labour market—which involuntarily lead to an alternation of periods of employment and unemployment—and by the explicit attempt on the part of school leavers to move between jobs in order to benefit from occupational guidance, and look for their preferred occupation, personal and professional growth, to satisfy their desire to "shop around" and in search of the best match for themselves..[2]

For a number of reasons, the unemployment rate *per se* represents a partial—and rather static—tool to assess the condition of the youth in the world of work. First off, low unemployment rates should not be necessarily seen as problematic or negative, provided that alternative employment opportunities and a sufficiently dynamic labour market are provided. This is because unemployment in this case would be the result of the latency period between two jobs. Furthermore, these statistics leave out inactive and discouraged people, that is those who are not in employment, nor are they engaged in any job search. A more complete picture can be obtained by examining trends in employment and unemployment—in order to get an idea of the labour force participation rate of young people—and above all the NEET rate (i.e. the share of youth not in Education nor in Employment or Training), a true social emergency that deteriorates the occupational future prospects and postpones the emancipation of young people from their parental households.[3] It is likewise important to assess the trend of human capital utilisation for this category of workers and their levels of education, through the employment rates and data on their educational attainment. With regard to Italy, the interrelation between the foregoing structural difficulties and the features

[1] Blanchflower, D. G., and R. Freeman. 2000. *Youth Employment and Joblessness in Advanced Countries.* Chicago: University of Chicago Press and NBER.

[2] Clark, K. B., and L. H. Summers. 1982. *The Dynamics of Youth Unemployment*, NBER Chapter 2, 72.

[3] Card, D., and T. Lemieux. 1997. "Adapting to Circumstances (The Evolution of Work, School, and Living Arrangements among North American Youth)," NBER Working Paper No. 6142.

of the domestic labour market resulted in an even more problematic shift from school to work. The Italian labour market is a two-tier one, with people living in the southern regions that face economic backwardness and difficulty in comparison with those living in northern Italy. The difficulties experienced by young people are even more pronounced, with southern Italy that along with Spain is ranked among the last positions in Europe with regard to youth employment. Accordingly, the last *caveat* is therefore related to the unemployment rates in the South, which are higher in comparison with the rest of the country. Notwithstanding structural differences in economic terms and job creation, the incidence of the informal sector plays a role and should be considered as an important cause of youth unemployment in the South.

2. The International Dimension: Stylised Facts

Starting from the 1990s, young people in industrialised countries have been facing unprecedented difficulties in entering the labour market. This situation culminated in the recent economic crisis and caused youth unemployment rates to increase and double those of adults, with this trend that is estimated to remain steady also for the years 2011 and 2012.

Fig. A-1. Youth and Adult Unemployment Rates (%) and Ratio, 2010.

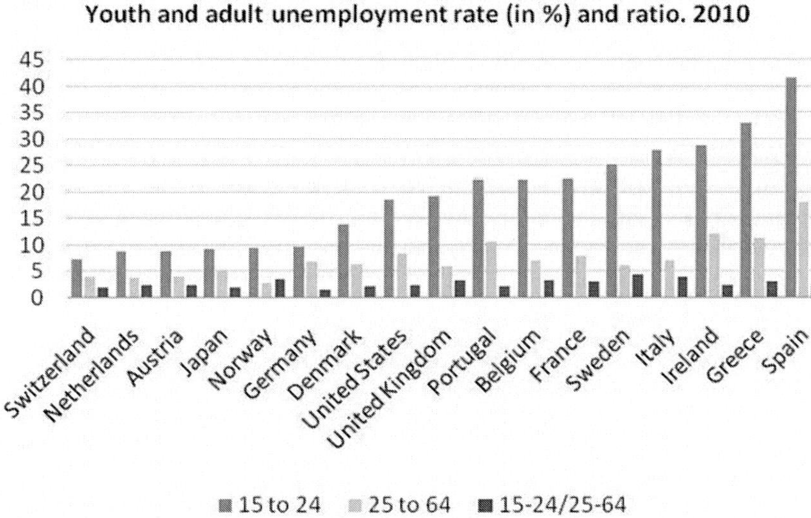

Source: Elaboration on OECD data.

Fig. A-1 shows the rates of unemployment for youth and adults, as well as the ratio of youth-to-adult unemployment in several OECD countries in 2010.

As previously pointed out, young people are more likely to remain unemployed compared to their adult counterparts in all the countries surveyed. On close inspection, however, one might note that the rate of youth unemployment differs considerably from country to country: 7% in Switzerland, 8% in The Netherlands, and up to 41% in Spain. In 2010, Italy reported one of the highest youth unemployment rates in Europe, after Spain, Greece and Ireland. Such a variation among countries is also mirrored in the adult unemployment rates, as the result of structural and macroeconomic differences among the national labour markets and economies. There are, however, some exceptions.

In this sense, if one looks at the ratio of youth-to-adult unemployment rates—which measures the gap between the two groups—what emerges is that Italy stands at the bottom of the pile, confirming the divergence in the employment outlooks between the youth and adults in this country.

On the contrary Germany—and to a lesser extent Switzerland—where the dual system of apprenticeship applies, youth unemployment rates are almost the same as those of adults. Here, young and adult jobseekers have the same probability of being unemployed, while in Italy young people are four times more likely to be in employment than those aged 24 and over. This situation is dependent upon differences in national economic conditions and the legal institutions governing the labour market, such as policies, taxation, industrial relations system and the Employment Protection Legislation.[4]

With regard to Employment Protection Legislation (EPL), the statistics of which are provided by the OECD under the rubric of strictness of employment protection,[5] it is interesting to compare Italy and Germany, especially considering the debate on the Italian labour market dualism between "overprotected adults" and "youth with no safeguards", which

---

[4] Scarpetta, S. 1996. "Assessing the Role of Labour Market Policies and Institutional Settings on Unemployment: A Cross Country Study," OECD Economic Studies 26:43–98. Bassanini, A., and R. Duval. 2006. "Employment Patterns in OECD Countries: Reassessing the Role of Policies and Institutions," OECD Economics Department Working Papers, 486. Paris: OECD Publishing.

[5] According to the OECD, there are four forms of employment protection: overall, regular work, temporary work and collective dismissals. The higher the index, the stricter the institution governing the use of one of these forms, and the more rigid the labour market.

further stresses the importance of apprenticeship for young people in a two-tier labour market.

Indeed, there are some schools of thought which attribute the difficulty faced by young atypical workers in finding stable employment to the different levels of employment protection, which is higher for adult workers. This is because whereas insiders in the labour market already benefit from a well-established system of social protection, outsiders view the flexible forms of work as a tool to find stable jobs, even though those hired under flexible contractual arrangements might run the risk of remaining in fixed-term contracts for a long time. One of the instruments to mitigate the effects of such dualism is apprenticeship. In this respect, the strictness of employment protection in Germany with regard to adults is higher than in Italy—in 2008, according the OECD it was 2.85 and 1.69 respectively. With regard to temporary jobs, that is the use of fixed-term contracts, the strictness of employment legislation is lower (1.96 and 2.54, respectively). In Germany, the difference between the levels of employment protection granted to young and adult workers does not make it more difficult for the former to find and retain a job, which is tantamount to saying that this state of affairs does not produce a dualistic labour market. This is evidenced by the fact that the unemployment rates for the two categories of workers are almost the same, upholding the importance of apprenticeships in easing the transition to work in markets with high levels of protection, particularly in regular employment.

Evidently, the difference in the pace of growth between Italy and Germany is a decisive element to be considered. In Italy's case, economic growth is reported to be low, as is the rate of job creation and turnover, and the new recruits are the first to be penalised by this situation. The reform that was introduced in Italy to tackle the debt crisis and to stimulate growth (Legislative Decree No. 138 of 13 August 2011 "Further urgent measures for financial stabilisation and growth"), provided for a new form of flexibility, which empowers actors of collective bargaining to deviate from statutory law and to conclude company-level agreements which laid down special provisions with regard to dismissals.

This form of flexibility is intended to reduce the dualism—which is typical of Italy—between "super-protected adults already in employment" and "precarious young people" who are forced out of the labour market, and supplement the reform on apprenticeship that previously took place to stem youth unemployment and boost employability. However, and as already pointed out in the introductory section, taking account of the unemployment indicators on an exclusive basis risks providing a partial explanation to the issue.

Fig. A-2. Employment Rate, Schooling Rate and Activity Rate (%), 2010.

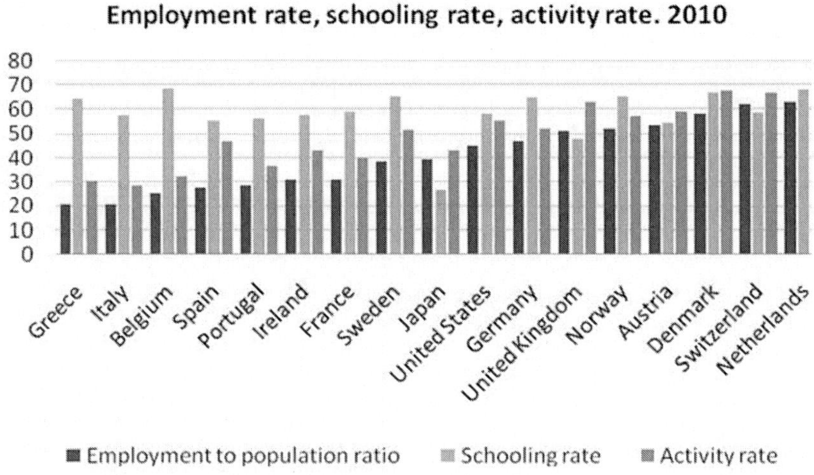

Source: Elaboration on OECD data.

A comparative analysis at an international level shows some other distinctive traits of the Italian labour market. Fig. A-2 considers two additional elements that are associated with unemployment, namely employment and schooling rates. The focus is also on the labour force participation rate, which is the sum of the number of people employed and unemployed divided by the population aged 15 to 24 years old. In many cases, the total amounts to more than 100%, because it might happen that a young person is—or claims to be—either a student and a worker. This is actually very common in the Netherlands, where students are also engaged in part-time or full-time jobs.

On the contrary, Italy has low levels of employment. At the aggregate level, out of a total population of 62 million people, those employed are barely 22,800,000 with 44.2% of them that are over 15 years old.

The low employment rate mostly affects young people. Indeed, in 2010 they reported an employment to population ratio of only 20%, the lowest among the OECD countries after Greece and 14 percentage points less than the UE-27 average (34%). In France it was 30%, in the UK and Germany 47%, and in Denmark and the Netherlands it peaked to 56.6% and 62.6%, respectively. The sum of employed and unemployed people divided by the youth population provides higher levels of youth activity in the labour market. The activity rate of 15-24 year olds in Italy is much lower than that in the rest of the OECD countries, that is 28.3% in 2010.

This indicator—only Greece fared worse—was not offset by higher schooling rates, which was indeed lower than many other countries too. Accordingly, in 2010, 57.7% of young people in Italy were in education, and 28.3% were active in the labour market, meaning that at least[6] 13.8% of youth did not study, nor did they work or look for a job (the NEETs). In absolute terms, they are reported to be 842,000 but only if one considers young people until 29 years old, that is more than 2 million. One youth out of five in Italy does not study nor work.

Table A-1 outlines the situation of young Italians compared to both European and OECD countries, confirming the negative Italian trend and offering new insights resulting from the temporal comparison. In spite of the crisis, the youth unemployment rate in Italy was lower in 2010 than in 2000, and the same can be said of the NEET rate. These figures are consistent with the international statistics, and might either suggest that young people have been investing more time in human capital—and thus postponing their entry into the labour market—or that they have exited the labour force because of discouragement. Although double the OECD average, long-term unemployment in Italy has been reported to decrease considerably (-14%) because of Treu and Biagi reforms of 1997 and 2003, respectively, that have produced higher levels of flexibility.

The incidence of temporary jobs on youth employment has nearly doubled in Italy, bringing the country into line with—and to some respects exceeding—the OECD average. Finally, notwithstanding the increase in part-time jobs, its incidence remains lower than the European and OECD average.

[6] Perhaps this rate could be even higher since the status of "employed" and "student" often coincide.

Table A-1. Situation of 15-24 Year Olds in Italy, Europe and OECD Countries in the Period 2000 to 2010

Situation of 15-24 Year Olds in Italy, Europe and OECD Countries in the Period 2000 to 2010						
	2000			2010		
	Italy	EU[b]	OECD[b]	Italy	EU[b]	OECD[b]
Employment to population ratio (% population aged 15-24)	**27.8**	40.7	44.0	**20.5**	33.7	37.8
Unemployment rate (% of labour force)	**29.7**	16.9	14.6	**27.9**	22.2	18.9
Relative unemployment rate youth/adult (15-24)/(25-54)	**3.5**	2.3	2.5	**3.7**	2.7	2.6
Unemployment to population ratio (% of population aged 15-24)	**11.7**	7.6	6.9	**7.9**	8.9	8.2
Long-term unemployment incidence (% unemployment)	**58.2**	26.5	20.1	**44.4**	27.7	22.6
Temporary work incidence (% of employment)	**26.2**	32.0	31.0	**46.7**	40.1	38.0
Part-time work incidence (% of employment)	**10.6**	17.5	19.9	**21.5**	24.9	27.8
NEET rate (% of population aged 15-24)[c]	**23.4**	15.4	13.4	**15.9**	12.2	10.9
School dropouts (% of population aged 15-24)[d]	**30.9**	26.6	22.5	**21.4**	15.9	15.6
Relative unemployment low skills/high skills (ISCED < 3/ISCED > 3)[c]	**0.9**	2.3	2.2	**1.0**	2.4	2.3
NEET (neither in education nor in employment or training), ISCED 3: upper secondary level.						
a) Youth aged 16-24 for Iceland, Spain, Sweden, United Kingdom and United States; 15-24 for other countries. The school dropouts data refer to youth aged 20-24 years old.						
b) Simple average of 21 EU and 34 OECD						
c) 1998 and 2008.						
d) Share of youth not at school and without an ISCED 3; 1998 and 2008.						

Source: OECD.

3. School-to-work Transitions and the Role of Apprenticeship: An International Comparison

For several reasons, the transition from school to work for a number of young people is uncertain, as consisting of different work experiences, unemployment and inactivity spells. The transition to employment might vary, as it is regulated by different institutions and different labour markets that vary in efficiency, and so may employment outcomes.

On the basis of these considerations, it is important to become aware of the goals to be achieved at the time of shifting from school to work. Key factors of this analysis are the time needed to find the first job after completion of the studies and the quality of the transition. As argued by the OECD and the European Commission, the involvement in working activities while studying is positively correlated to career prospects and stimulates the acquisition—be it formal or informal—of knowledge that is useful to enter and remain in the working world. Comparatively, one might distinguish a faster transition in the United States than in Europe,[7] confirming the importance of a dynamic and flexible labour market for youth employability. However, the greater rigidity of the European labour markets might be dealt with by the recourse to apprenticeship. Whereas the market is characterised by high degrees of employment protection, and thus by lower flexibility, the implementation of apprenticeship produces more employability for young people.

Austria, Germany, Denmark, Ireland and the United Kingdom are the only countries in Europe where youth can find the first occupation after a year leaving education. In Austria and Germany, this is because of a well-established apprenticeship system; in Denmark, Ireland and the United Kingdom this happens as a result of a more flexible labour market. Significantly, in Italy, Spain and Greece the time needed to find the first job is nearly two years. Apprenticeship in Italy—a country marked by a rigid labour market, low economic growth and job creation rates, and late entry into the labour market on the part of youth—might be a reference model to offset such a rigidity and provide education. The apprenticeship system adopted in Germany represents an exception in the European scenario, as it allows 80% of the youth to spend (on average) 90% of time needed for such a transition on-the-job. Only 4.5% of the youth experience a transition to employment characterised by prolonged unemployment and

[7] Quintini, G., and T. Manfredi. 2009. "*Going Separate Ways? School-to-work Transitions in the United States and Europe*," OECD Social, Employment and Migration Working Papers. Paris: OECD Publishing.

discouragement. Therefore, this seems to be the most efficient instrument to provide a positive school-to-work transition for youth.[8] The transition from school to work is usually marked by the widespread use of temporary contracts, arguably because young people lack work experience. Fixed-term contracts are usually transformed into open-ended employment contracts once adult age is reached.

Fig. A-3. Incidence of Temporary Contracts on Employment in Different Ages (%). First Quarter of 2011.

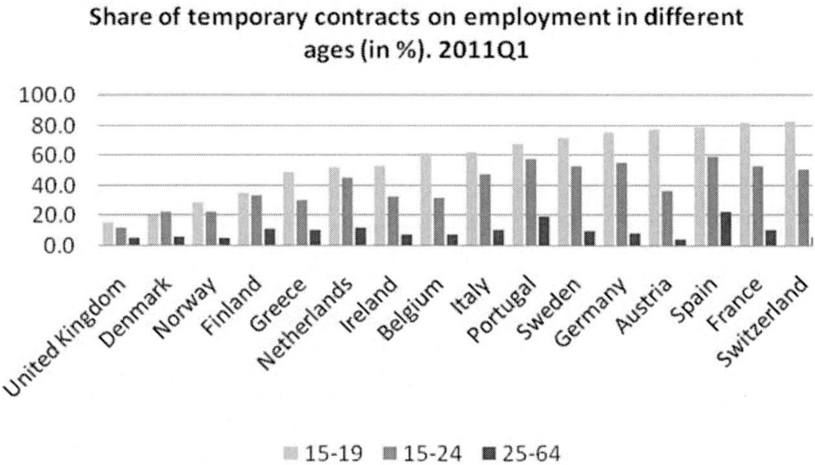

Source: Elaboration on OECD data.

Fig. A-3 shows the share of temporary workers for three bands of age: adolescents (15-19), young people (15-24) and adults (25-64). In Italy, the use of temporary contracts is in line with the European average, that is higher than the EU27 average but lower than the EU17 average. Sixty percent of adolescents enter into fixed term contracts, with this percentage that is equal to 47.6% for those aged 15-24, and only to 10% for adult workers. The share of temporary employment in Italy is lower than that of Portugal, Sweden, Germany, Austria, Spain, France and Switzerland.[9] The

[8] Blanchflower, D. G., and R. Freeman. 2000. *Youth Employment and Joblessness in Advanced Countries.* Chicago: University of Chicago Press and NBER.

[9] Although the apprenticeship contract in Italy is regarded as a permanent one, the Statistical Office of the European Union (Eurostat) includes it among temporary contracts. Temporary employment includes work under a fixed-term contract, as

status of temporary worker *per se* does not produce precariousness among young people. Rather, in many countries this is seen as the first step towards employment stability. What seems to be a determining factor is the combination of employment with education in terms of timing and contents. Considering the timing issue first, it is possible to group European countries into four categories, according to the way the shift from school to work takes place.

Young people in the Nordic Countries (Scandinavian countries, with the exception of Sweden and The Netherlands) stay longer in education and work while studying. The Anglo-Saxon countries (Australia, Canada, New Zealand, the United Kingdom and the United States) and Sweden are characterised by a length of study that is lower than the OECD average. As occurs in the Nordic Countries, young people living here work while in education. As for the traditional apprenticeship countries (Germany, Switzerland and Austria), work-study alternation programmes are implemented. Finally, there is a group of countries, which include Italy, where young people stay longer in education and do not work while studying.[10] Significantly, the best occupational performances have been reported among young people in countries belonging to the first three groups—as apprenticeship, training, internship, and temporary contracts are concluded—and this translates into effective school-to-work integration. Besides timing, the comparative analysis of the transition from school to work should also adopt a uniform way to measure the relationship between human capital investment and actual work, for the good match between skills acquired in education and on the job and those required in the labour market is essential to make the most of investments in human capital and promote strong and inclusive growth.[11]

---

opposed to permanent work that is open-ended. A job may be considered as temporary—and thus its holder a temporary employee—if both the employer and the employee agree that its end is decided upon by objective rules (usually written down in an employment contract). These rules should provide the exact date of beginning and completion of the assignment, or the date of return of the employee who has been replaced temporarily. According to Eurostat, special training contracts—e.g. apprenticeships—are a typical case of temporary employment.

[10] Quintini, G., J. P. Martin, and S. Martin. 2007. "*The Changing Nature of the School-to-work Transition Process in OECD Countries*," IZA Discussion Papers 2582. Bonn: Institute for the Study of Labour (IZA).

[11] Quintini, G. 2011. *"Right for the Job: Over-qualified or Under-skilled?"*, OECD Social, Employment and Migration Working Papers, No. 120. Paris: OECD Publishing.

Fig. A-4. Mismatch Index (%) in 2008.

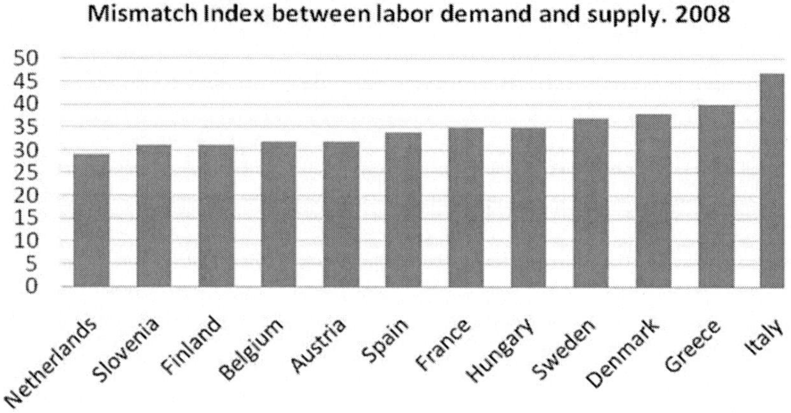

Source: Elaboration on OECD data.

Fig. A-4. shows that, in terms of content, Italy has the highest levels of education and job mismatch among all the European countries,[12] confirming the gap with other national realities also in this connection.[13]

The apprenticeship system can deal with this mismatch, acting as a *trait d'union* between educational and working experiences. In Italy, the combination of school and work might be workable—not only in the event of vocational training—but also in tertiary education and high-skilled positions, by resorting to a form of advanced-level apprenticeship (*alto apprendistato*).

Fig. A-5 offers the number of apprentices per 1,000 employees and their hourly labour cost, taking account of the purchasing power in the manufacturing, building and service sector for companies with at least 10 employees (Eurostat, *Labour Cost Survey*, 2008). In numerical terms, countries that adopt the dual system apprenticeship (Germany and Austria in Table No. 6) have a higher share of apprentices.

---

[12] Among the countries for which data from Eurostat are available for 2008.

[13] The job mismatch is measured by Eurostat as the discrepancy between the job and what has been studied at school. Those in an occupation which is different from their educational investment are considered as non-match. Since lower secondary school level provides education of a general nature, it is not included in the mismatch analysis, nor are upper secondary and tertiary education.

Fig. A-5. Incidence of Apprenticeship Contracts (No. per 1000 Occupied) and Hourly Cost of Apprenticeship (in PPPs) in 2008.

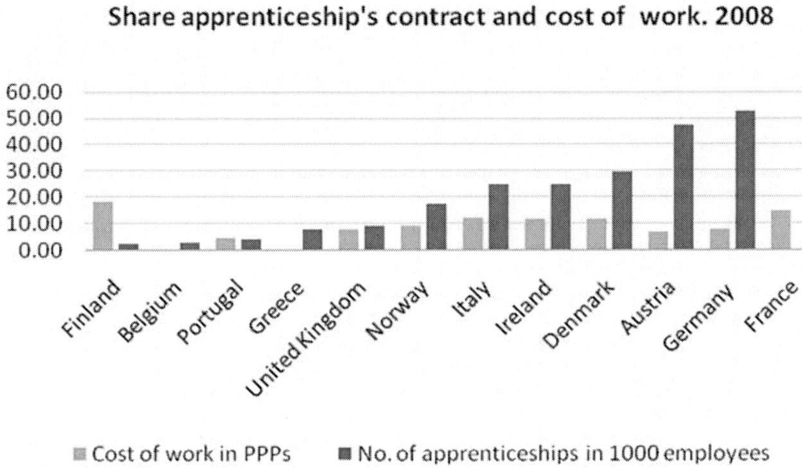

Source: Eurostat, *Labour Cost Survey*, 2008. Data refer to companies with at least 10 employees in the manufacturing, building and service sector.

In Germany, the apprentices are 52 per 1000 employees (1 out of 20), while in Italy they are only 24 (1 out of 40). The dual system countries are also marked by a lower hourly labour cost with regard to apprenticeship. In Italy, this cost—expressed in PPPs—is 12.27, that is double that of Germany, Austria and the United Kingdom (7.55, 6.95, 7.80, respectively), similar to that of Denmark and Ireland (11.65 and 11.76) and lower than the hourly labour cost in France (14.80) and Finland (18.10). Whereas apprentices in Germany are usually paid a wage that is equal to 33% to 50% of what is earned by more experienced workers in the same occupation, in Italy the wage for apprentices and skilled employees is almost the same.

The data also clarified that the wider use of apprenticeship and the increase in employment among young people are the results of lower labour costs, which in "genuine" apprenticeship can be explained by the effective exchange of work and training.

4. Apprenticeship in the Global Economy and ICT Sector: The Advanced-level Apprenticeship

The rapid evolution of economies and societies, the globalisation process and the presence of new competitors, higher educational attainments, the industrial restructuring resulting from advanced technologies and the shift from the manufacturing to service sector, as well as the increasing use of immaterial products may put the German dual system of apprenticeship in a crisis,[14] while encouraging the recourse to the advanced-level apprenticeship implemented in Italy. The fast-paced economic globalisation calls for adaptability and innovation as a way to keep up with more recent developments in the labour market. The economic base is moving further and further from manufacturing, which is the traditional base of the German apprenticeship system, towards traditional, highly technological and advanced services, fields in which apprentices are less prevalent in Germany.[15] The demand for craftsmen and apprentices in manufacturing is also undermined by the industrial reorganisation process, which is replacing manual labour with technological investments. With special reference to the advanced service sector—e.g. professional advising, the ICT sector and "creative" occupations—special skills are needed that ought to be acquired on the job, and while in tertiary education. In this sense, more and more young people opt for post-secondary education, somehow eroding talents to vocational education and therefore draining the talent pools of German apprenticeship (Soskice, 1992). This aspect is further emphasised by the fact that many apprentices who engage in dual apprenticeship training find it difficult to move to courses in tertiary education. In a few words, the German dual system attracts criticism for being rigid, thus widening the gap between low-skilled and high-skilled workers.

Notwithstanding the ever-changing economic and social context where traditional apprenticeship is used, the literature puts forward a number of arguments to highlight that this instrument is still important and valuable. The core of the apprenticeship approach—on-the-job learning—has a number of advantages in educational terms which are still relevant today. In a time of sluggish economic recovery and high youth unemployment

---

[14] Eichhorst, W., and P. Marx. 2009. "From the Dual Apprenticeship System to a Dual Labour Market? The German High-Skill Equilibrium and the Service Economy," IZA Discussion Papers 4220. Bonn: Institute for the Study of Labour (IZA).

[15] Thelen, K. 2007. *Contemporary Challenges to the German Vocational Training System*, Regulation and Governance, 1 No. 3:247–260.

rates, the German apprenticeship system still represents, as evidenced in this paper, one of the most effective forms of school-to-work transition. This point is further confirmed by the difficulty faced by employers, also in Italy, in recruiting skilled workers with technical knowledge and skills, reflecting a mismatch between labour demand and supply, that can be solved by a widespread implementation of apprenticeship. Further, apprenticeship can be seen as a recruitment screening device for job-applicants, and a form of employment that allows employers to invest in human capital, supplying them with both general and special education.

Following the reform of the Italian apprenticeship system, which took place by means of Legislative Decree of 28 July 2011—the Consolidated Text on Apprenticeship (*Testo Unico dell'apprendistato*)—this form of training has been provided with higher levels of flexibility than that implemented in Germany, as the apprenticeship scheme adopted in Italy can adapt to current economic changes and satisfy the new job opportunities arising from the new economy. Enhanced flexibility is also the result of the power actors of collective bargaining have been entrusted with at company and local level. Equally relevant is the fact that apprenticeship contracts can be also concluded in the public sector, by Doctoral students and professionals, a point which further confirms the innovative and strategic nature of this training scheme.

References

Bassanini, A., and R. Duval. 2006. "Employment Patterns in OECD Countries: Reassessing the Role of Policies and Institutions," OECD Economics Department Working Papers 486. Paris: OECD Publishing.

Blanchflower, D. G., and R. Freeman. 2000. *Youth Employment and Joblessness in Advanced Countries.* Chicago: University of Chicago Press and NBER.

Card, D., and T. Lemieux. 1997. "Adapting to Circumstances (The Evolution of Work, School, and Living Arrangements among North American Youth)," NBER Working Paper No. 6142.

Clark, D. 2000. *How Transferable is German Apprenticeship Training?* University of Oxford and CEP.

Clark, K. B., and L. H. Summers. 1982. *The Dynamics of Youth Unemployment*, NBER Chapter 0272.

Eichhorst, W., and P. Marx. 2009. "From the Dual Apprenticeship System to a Dual Labour Market? The German High-Skill Equilibrium and the Service Economy," IZA Discussion Papers 4220. Bonn: Institute for the Study of Labour (IZA).

Franz, W, and V. Zimmerman. 2002. "The Transition from Apprenticeship Training to Work," *International Journal of Manpower* 23, No. 5:411-425.

Gersbach, H., and A. Schmutzler. 2006. "The Effects of Globalization on Worker Training," IZA Discussion Paper No. 2403. Bonn: Institute for the Study of Labour (IZA).

Hollenstein, H., and T. Stucki. 2008. "The Impact of ICT Usage, Workplace Organisation and Human Capital on the Provision of Apprenticeship Training. A Firm-level Analysis Based on Swiss Panel Data," KOF Working Papers No. 205.

Quintini, G. 2011. "Right for the Job: Over-qualified or Under-skilled?" OECD Social, Employment and Migration Working Papers, No. 120. Paris: OECD Publishing.

Quintini, G., and T. Manfredi. 2009. "*Going Separate Ways? School-to-work Transitions in the United States and Europe*," OECD Social, Employment and Migration Working Papers. Paris: OECD Publishing.

Quintini, G., J. P. Martin, and S. Martin. 2007. "*The Changing Nature of the School-to-work Transition Process in OECD Countries*," IZA Discussion Papers 2582. Bonn: Institute for the Study of Labour (IZA).

Ryan, P. 2001. "The School-to-Work Transition: A Cross-National Perspective," *Journal of Economic Literature* 39, No. 1:34-92.

Scarpetta, S. 1996. "Assessing the Role of Labour Market Policies and Institutional Settings on Unemployment: A Cross Country Study," OECD Economic Studies 26:43–98.

Soskice, D. 1992. *Reconciling Markets and Institutions: The German Apprenticeship System*. Wissenschaftszentrum Berlin and Oxford University, Institute of Economics and Statistics.

Thelen, K. 2007. *Contemporary Challenges to the German Vocational Training System*, Regulation and Governance, 1 No. 3:247–260.

GENERATIONS, WORK AND SOCIAL COHESION

PATRICIA VENDRAMIN

1. Introduction[1]

For more than twenty years now, Western European countries have been facing long-term mass unemployment with substantial changes reported in both working and employment conditions—e.g. new organisational models, increasing diversification in employment status, the rise of both expertise and standardisation, and so forth. Individuals are more educated and women have definitively gained a large hold on the labour market. Meanwhile, the uncertain nature of working life has soared and inequalities in working conditions, security and income are spreading in almost all industries. Youth unemployment and the ageing of the workforce are major concerns of governments. In such a context, very roughly described indeed, work remains an important value, although not in the way it used to be. It is still seen as crucial in individual and collective lives, as involving a sense of belonging and social cohesion. This paper is based on different studies conducted in Europe. One of the main references is the European survey, the SPReW[2] project (Social

[1] This article is based on a book, Vendramin, P., ed. 2010. *Generations at Work and Social Cohesion in Europe*. Brussels: Peter Lang; and an article published in Spanish: Vendramin, P. 2011. "Trabajo, sentido de pertenencia y cohesión social," in *Sentido de pertenencia en sociedades fragmentadas: América Latina en una perspectiva global*, eds. Hopeynhayn, M., and A. Sojo, (Buenos Aires: Editorial Siglo XXI), 59-73.

[2] The main empirical material of this research consists of both a qualitative and a quantitative approach. The qualitative investigation was carried out by conducting 163 individual narrative interviews—around 25 in each country, involving three different age groups: those below 30 years old, those from 30 to 50 years old and those above 50 years old; a mix of women and men, most of whom in employment —and 18 group interviews, in six European countries. The quantitative approach was designed in order to map the existing relevant surveys at national, European or international level (European Value Survey, European Social Survey, International Social Survey Programme) that give additional information on the specific issues

Patterns of Relations to Work) carried out in the context of the 6th Framework Programme of the European Union. It brought together researchers from six countries (Belgium, France, Germany, Hungary, Italy, and Portugal) as well as different stakeholders (public bodies and trade unions). The objective of this research was to analyse the factors leading to solidarity or tension in inter-generational relations, in the specific area of employment and related fields. It addressed the challenge of cohesion in the area of work, its meaning for individuals and the nature of relationships among different generations. In Section I, the paper examines how the perception of work has changed over time. Section II points out some key developments of the workplace in terms of identity (distance, polycentricism and gender models). Subsequently, Section III concentrates on social cohesion from a generational standpoint. The literature referred to in this study concerns Western European countries. Nevertheless, the analyses carried forward might also be relevant for current developments in other geographical areas.

2. The Sense of Work

What work is and what relevance should be given to it in society and in individual life has been the subject of research and debate for many years. This section makes some points of reference considering an abundant and widely discussed body of literature. It starts with an overview of the meaning of work over a certain period, and then describes the contemporary perspective on work in post-industrial societies.

2.1. Long-term Changes in the Meaning of Work

In her widely discussed book—mainly because of its provocative title: "Work. A Disappearing Value" (*Le Travail. Une valeur en voie de disparition*), Méda distinguishes three periods in the construction of the concept of work. These three stages relate to the introduction of a new layer of interpretation or meaning, which had become more established over the previous centuries. The first stage is that of the economists of the 18th century. Work became a production factor that provided an income. This century has witnessed the success and formalisation of this initial meaning, particularly in the works of Smith, after several centuries of theoretical preparation in which work, until then scorned, was recognised

---

addressed in this research. See http://www.ftu-namur.org/sprew (accessed July 10, 2011).

as having a value. Work was then defined as "that which creates wealth". This is our current "production factor". Nonetheless, it continues to be considered as a punishment, a sacrifice, or, as economists would say, a "disutility". The second period—19th century—established work as the essence of man, a human activity that enables men to express themselves and transform the world (Hegel and Marx). This second meaning was significantly different from the first: work was considered as the creative freeing of men, the transformational and negative power of men, enabling them to both obliterate nature and to make the world in their image, thus expressing and transforming themselves.

Originally expressed in Hegel's philosophy, this concept was fully developed in Marx's analysis, where work appears as the key human activity that allows men to express themselves. Finally, the third layer of meaning is that of the 20th century. Work became a means for distributing income, rights and protection. It corresponds to the development of the wage-earning society; various rights were entitled to safeguard workers, e.g. the right to work, the right to social protection and so forth. Work also became employment[3] and it therefore came to be appreciated not only for the income or the expression of self-provided, but also for the rights to which it gives access. As Méda explains in her book, these three layers of meaning of work were regarded as a *continuum*, that is that they did not replace each other.

Over the last forty years, changes in the approach to work have occurred. In the sixties and seventies, the increased division of labour and the development of Taylorism generated a new literature on work, denouncing the damage done by progress to human work.[4] In the eighties and nineties, the upheaval of mass unemployment in the European countries produced a new thinking on the effects of enduring mass unemployment on the value of work. Specific international surveys[5] started to collect comparative data in order to understand changes in contemporary values. Inglehart[6] developed a theory of post-materialism in European countries and he later used comparative data at an international level to refine his hypothesis. According to him, economic evolution

---

[3] Habermas, J. 1987. *Théorie de l'agir communicationnel* [Theory of Communicative Action]. Paris: Fayard.
[4] Friedmann, G. 1956. *Le travail en miettes* [Fragmented Work]. Paris: Gallimard.
[5] Concerning the value of work, three international surveys are particularly relevant: the European Values Surveys (EVS), the International Social Survey Programme (ISSP) and the European Social Survey (ESS).
[6] Inglehart, R. 1971. "The Silent Revolution in Post-Industrial Societies," *American Political Science Review* 65: 991-1017.

would tend to modify the meaning attached to work. The wealthiest countries would be characterised by "post-materialistic" values. Whereas economic security is no longer a priority, the quality of life and individual well-being become major values. In this perspective, work should above all enable individuals to fulfil themselves. In European countries, the end of the 20th century could thus be marked by the rise of post-materialistic hopes: the individual no longer hides behind the group, and his fulfilment becomes a central value.[7] This tendency, which affects the most diverse fields of society, could also be found in the sphere of work. This interpretation, which highlights the role of the economic context, remains, of course, simplistic and mono-causal.[8] This point is made in a cogent manner by the author, who resorts to an image in his conclusion: "economic development pushes societies in the same direction but they follow parallel trajectories, marked by history, in the framework of a phenomenon of pathway dependence". Inglehart underlines in this way the persistence of religious and historical divisions. Furthermore, the path to modernisation is not linear, as proven by the trajectory of countries in the former Soviet bloc, which went back to traditional values. Factors other than economic evolution enter into account in the structuring of values.

2.2. The Contemporary Perspective: The Double or Triple Dimension of Work

Understanding the importance and role of work in the identity and lives of individuals is a complex process, with surveys that mirror this complexity. Indeed, if the figures demonstrate that work still has a central position in the life of Europeans, they also show that they would like to see it taking less space in their lives.[9] Many scholars have suggested theoretical frameworks for the understanding of the meaning of work, since the simple statement that work is important gives very little information on what its significance involves.

---

[7] Inglehart, R. 1993. *La transition culturelle dans les sociétés avancées* [Cultural Transition in Advanced Societies]. Paris: Economica.

[8] Davoine, L., and D. Méda. 2008. "Place et sens du travail en Europe: une singularité française? [Place and Meaning of Work in Europe: a French Singularity?]," Document de travail CEE, Paris, No. 96-1.

[9] Ibid.

Inglehart and Baker[10] distinguish the extrinsic or materialistic orientation (salary, job security, and so forth) and the intrinsic or post-materialistic orientation (personal development). Broadly speaking, surveys on values in Europe show a spread of post-materialistic values that relativise all aspects concerning material survival, giving more space to issues referring to personal development. For these authors, economic development tends to modify the value of work. This was also the hypothesis of Goldthorpe in his book "The Affluent Worker".[11] Sociologists also suggest similar approaches. For example, Paugam,[12] in "The Employee of Precariousness" (*Le salarié de la précarité*), distinguishes three paradigms: the *homo faber*—with reference to the task to be performed—the *homo œconomicus* —concerning the instrumental dimension of work—and the *homo sociologicus* — with reference to the social framework of work. Nicole-Drancourt and Roulleau-Berger[13] also distinguish a triple dimension in contemporary work: instrumental, social and symbolic. The instrumental dimension has to do with material expectations—e.g. salary and social security—the social dimension concerns the importance of human relations at work, while the symbolic dimension relates to opportunities for self-development, to the content of work, the feeling of success, autonomy, social usefulness, and so on. Some scholars gather the social and symbolic aspects of work in a single dimension called "expressive".[14]

Aside from their differences, all the theoretical approaches converge in showing that multiple expectations are attached to work, all non-exclusive. The foregoing SPReW research confirms the double—materialistic, instrumental, extrinsic and post-materialistic, expressive, intrinsic—or triple meanings of work—instrumental, social and symbolic. It clarifies what is suggested by quantitative studies, i.e. that the various dimensions of work do not replace each other, and that increased intrinsic expectations do not supplant extrinsic expectations. The qualitative approach to this research confirms the importance of the instrumental dimension of work,

---

[10] Inglehart, R., and W. E. Baker. 2000. "Modernization, Cultural Change, and the Persistence of Traditional Values?" *American Sociological Review* 65, No 1: 19-51.

[11] Goldthorpe, J. 1963. *The Affluent Worker: Political Attitudes and Behaviour*. Cambridge: Cambridge University Press.

[12] Paugam, S. 2000. *Le salarié de la précarité* [Precarious Workers]. Paris, PUF.

[13] Nicole-Drancourt, C., and L. Roulleau-Berger. 2001. *Les jeunes et le travail* [Youth and Work]. 1950-2000. Paris: PUF.

[14] Habermas, J. 1987. *Théorie de l'agir communicationnel* [Theory of Communicative Action]. Paris: Fayard. Zoll, R. 1992. *Nouvel individualisme et solidarité quotidienne* [New Individualism and Daily Solidarity]. Paris: Kimé.

but also underlines its complexity. For example, the meaning of "money/salary" is not only instrumental. Money also has symbolic value. The salary is also the measure of the value of a person, an objective sign of recognition and esteem, a sign of emancipation. Young people particularly illustrate this point, notably when access to independent living is delayed for all young people. The research also shows the complexity of the expressive expectations associated with work. Some people share individual expectations—e.g. autonomy and accountability—while others have more collective or altruistic expectations—e.g. being recognised or having socially useful work. The relational dimension of work is also fundamental, especially for the younger generations. However, this relationship to the collective takes different forms. What seems important is the need to be part of a small network of people who meet on a daily basis, or at least regularly, rather than belonging to a social group with some social purposes.

3. Work and Identities in Post-industrial Societies

Post-industrial societies are characterised by relative economic security, even if inequalities and exclusion are still part of the system. The democratisation of education leads to an increased number of qualified people, particularly among young people who hold higher degrees of education, especially young women. The current labour market is also characterised by widespread participation of women, even if they still face unfair treatment compared to their male colleagues in the areas of employment status, wages and careers.

There is abundant literature on the centrality of or distance from work. For some scholars, the distance from work is growing and threatens social cohesion. Other studies suggest that work remains central in the construction of identity, for all generations. However, they also add that if work is still important in life and identity, it is also increasingly relativised and other areas of life (family, leisure, social life and so on) also occupy an important place. It is among the younger generations that work is supposed to be more relativised.

3.1. A Certain Distance from Work among the Young Generation?

There are different hypotheses concerning the role of work in the life of young people.[15] The first concerns the progressive entry into adulthood. During this period, young people are tempted to invest in many areas of life available to them, not only in the field of work. Then, when confronted with increased responsibilities in their private and professional life, the young people will give more importance to work. That being said, the differences between generations remain significant, even in the case of young people whose living conditions are comparable to adult life (e.g. life with a partner, having children, having an occupation). A second hypothesis concerns structural changes in modern societies, including the development of education. Socialisation at school probably has an impact on how young people consider their lives. This increased education will produce both a greater distance from work but also more self-confidence as regards the labour market. The distance to work, particularly among young graduates, cannot be understood without highlighting the disenchantment caused by the decline of status that goes with the entry into the labour market and more generally, the frustration and dissatisfaction regarding a social model that no longer links higher degrees, work and social mobility. Chauvel[16] names this the failure of the social elevator (*la panne de l'ascenseur social*) for young people. Paradoxically, discussions about the distance from work are contemporary with debates on subjective involvement in work, which can culminate in over-investment in work and burnout.

At the European level, the European Value Surveys (EVS) have for 20 years now gathered comparative data on the relationship to work of European citizens. Research that analyses the EVS surveys is generally based on the analytical framework developed by Inglehart and Baker[17] and their distinction between the extrinsic or materialistic orientation (salary, job security, prestige, and so forth) and the intrinsic or post-materialistic orientation, which relates to personal development. Globally, the surveys

---

[15] Tchernia, J-F. 2005. "Les jeunes européens, leur rapport au travail [The Relationship to Work of Young Europeans]," in *Les valeurs des jeunes,* eds. Galland, O., and B. Roudet, (Paris: La Découverte): 205-228.

[16] Chauvel, L. 2002. *Le destin des generations* [The Destiny of Generations]. Paris: PUF.

[17] Inglehart, R., and W. E. Baker. 2000. "Modernization, Cultural Change, and the Persistence of Traditional Values?" *American Sociological Review* 65, No 1: 19-51.

show a growing affirmation in Europe of post-materialist values that relativise the importance of factors relating to survival and give more space to factors concerning personal development. Is there cohesion between generations in this regard? In Europe, the importance given to work is quite variable among countries but, in a majority of them, more than one out of two citizens considers work as "very important". Overall, the opinion of young people is in line with that of the older generation. When work is highly valued by the older generation, this is also the case for young people and conversely, when work is less valued, the youth share the same opinion. However, over a long period, data show that the value given to work by the older generation is declining. This is not only a matter for the young generation, but a long-term trend that was initiated by the previous generations. However, Tchernia[18] insists that this drop in value should be well understood. The issue is not to deny the importance of work but to reject the social norms associated with it. Work as a value in itself has lost its aura but it remains an area that can foster new values such as self-expression, independence, personal achievement and creativity. As such, it can be seen as a potential area for developing such values, but not the only one. This is basically what characterises the changing values towards post-materialism: the main areas where individual identity can express itself are no longer seen as values *per se* but as fields of action where other values can find their place. This development has been highlighted for several years and it reveals the shift from a hegemonic value of work to a polycentric conception of existence. This complicates and diversifies the sense of belonging of individuals, in keeping with the concept of plural identity developed by a number of scholars.[19]

3.2. From a Hegemonic Value of Work to a Polycentric Conception of Existence

A lot of research converges in demonstrating that, if work remains important, it is no longer the only most important dimension of identity-building and existential equilibrium. Family, friends, hobbies, social life, social involvement and civic life are also significant parts of identity-building. For example, all the European surveys have effectively shown over the last few years the strength of expectations, often unsatisfied,

---

[18] Tchernia, J-F. 2005. "Les jeunes européens, leur rapport au travail [The Relationship to Work of Young Europeans]," in *Les valeurs des jeunes,* eds. Galland, O., and B. Roudet, (Paris: La Découverte): 205-228.

[19] Lahire, B. 1998. *L'homme pluriel: les ressorts de l'action* [Plural Man. The Springs of Action]. Paris: Nathan.

placed in the family. Far from appearing only as a refuge or as a value or an activity all the more appreciated if work is disappointing, the family appears on the contrary to be an extremely attractive domain of emotional investment and self-fulfilment, likely not only to be affected by what happens within the sphere of work but also to affect life at work, and as a time-consuming activity which is in direct competition with work, especially for women. The challenge of the work/life balance has become an important topic for both women and men. The hegemony of the value of work appears in a polycentric conception of life. Polycentricism as opposed to work as the centre of life is a key contemporary issue confirmed by research. It means that life does not revolve around work, but that work is merely one of the ingredients –although not necessarily the main one—of identity. Work is an important dimension, but it is also important to put some checks on it in order to avoid it invading the rest of life.

3.3. A Gender Perspective

In the relationship to work and the place of work in the identity, the SPReW research demonstrates some blurring of boundaries between the gender models,[20] with young men sharing female expectations and young women sharing male models.

On the one side, there emerges a "feminisation" of the male model of the relationship to work. In fact, for men of the older generation, work was central to their life and was a key element on which to build their social identity. Indeed, masculinity in capitalist society was, and partially still is, strongly dependent upon success gained in the labour market through the occupation of more important positions in a work organisation, which permitted a man to gain money, power, a high level of social status and to assume his duty as principal breadwinner of the family. Therefore, men more often than women had a more instrumental work orientation, striving to achieve those jobs that permitted a high level of income and security, and sometimes sacrificing their passions and their more profound self-realisation. For the men of the younger generation, on the contrary, the SPReW research confirms that work has a less central role in their life. Work is important but other aspects of life are likewise important, such as their intimate relations, their hobbies and leisure time, and their own

[20] Lebano, A., M-T. Franco, and G. Greco. 2010. "So Far so Close. Generations and Work in Italy," in *Generations at Work and Social Cohesion in Europe,* ed. Vendramin, P., (Brussels: Peter Lang): 195-220.

family. In addition, the work orientation of young men seems to be driven by a more expressive dimension: they choose their jobs according to their interests and passions much more than the older generation. They also stress the importance of building satisfying human relations at their workplace. In addition, young men appear to be changing their attitudes towards paternity. Unlike the older generation of men, they are fathers who want to be, and also are, much more present in their own family and more committed to the care of their children. Although the burden of care and household activities is still higher for the female partner than for the male partner, this commitment increases with the rise in the level of education of the male partner and in those families in which both partners are employed.

On the other side, there is a "masculinisation" of the female relationship to work in the younger generation of women. Indeed, for women of the older generation, who had a lower level of education and employment, work often represented the major instrument for an emancipation process in order to gain autonomy and independence from their family and to escape from their traditional role of mother and wife. Women with a higher education level chose their job on the basis of their passions and interests and were concentrated in the tertiary public sector, which permitted them to build their own family and have children, thanks to the stronger protection and the maternity support in the public sector. For young women, work no longer represents an instrument of emancipation, which they often take for granted, although gender discrimination and segregation in the labour market persist. Work becomes more and more a key element on which they build their social identity, and for obtaining their self-realisation. Having acquired a high level of education, which may also be higher than that of the young men of their generation, they are strongly motivated to engage in their careers and advance more rapidly than women of the older generation.

4. Social Cohesion at Work

The value of work is evolving and individual identities are organised according to a polycentric conception of existence. Gender models regarding work are changing and male and female identities are partly taking new routes. The generations appear to be subjectively and objectively different. Are these changes threatening social cohesion? This section develops a generational standpoint. It looks at the differentiation of the generations and questions the hypothesis of a clash between them.

Lastly, it develops the specific vision of solidarity and social ties of the older and younger generations.

4.1. A Generational Standpoint

Generations at work are defined through objective characteristics and singular attitudes. A quick glance at labour market data confirms the differentiation of the generations. Data relating to levels of education show how, in the six countries investigated in the SPReW research (see introduction) educational capital has increased in the younger groups and, connected to this, how the incidence of low levels of education is steadily reducing over time. Women—especially younger ones—also have an advantage over men in their levels of education. They are, in all six countries, significantly more likely to graduate from higher education than men. However, higher levels of unemployment and atypical work also indicate the persistence of unfair conditions for women—in most countries. So, we are in a historical situation where the younger generation is significantly more educated than previous generations. However, this educational advantage does not lead to social or labour market progression—as was the case for previous generations. On the other hand, in all countries, unemployment rates are highest among young people. A cross-country comparison shows how often youth unemployment rates follow economic fluctuations.

A look at social protection expenditure also shows different levels of concern for different age groups. As an example, in 2000, Germany devoted 42% of its social protection expenditure to the older generation, 8% to the unemployed and 11% to families and children, while in Italy, the percentages were 63%, 2%, and 4%, respectively. The median age at which young people leave their parents is 23 years old in Germany and 28 years old in Italy. This confirms the relevance of an institutional approach for understanding the particularities of each country. They are all embedded in specific configurations of institutional arrangements and social structures that explain the differences between societies. In short, all the available data on the generations at work indicate that youth are increasingly more educated compared to previous generations, that women have an advantage as regards levels of education, that generations are unfairly used to adjust to economic fluctuations, and that states make unequal provision for social protection in their expenditure on different social groups. However, though there appear to be substantial differences between the generations in terms of their "subjective" attitudes—the value of work and their conception of existence—and expectations and their "objective" working conditions, the research has not uncovered—actual or potential—tensions at the workplace. There are few signs of an imminent social rebellion among younger workers, along the lines of "a clash between generations" predicted by some scholars some ten years ago.[21] Various factors might explain this state of affairs.[22] First of all, in some countries younger people do not even inhabit the same workplace as older ones: for example, in many large manufacturing companies, early retirement schemes have removed the older generation while, at the same time, young people are more likely to be found in qualified tertiary sector jobs or in call centres, fast-food undertakings and other low qualified service jobs. So, in some occupations, real face-to-face contact between the generations does not even take place. Our investigation also suggests that young people do not identify themselves with a specific generation; other factors, which shape other identities, appear to be more important determinants of group cultures at the workplace: to be a woman, to be in a qualified profession or hierarchical grade, to be an employee of a well-known organisation and so forth. Another explanation, or perhaps a consequence, of this unexpected lack of conflict between the generations might be the fact that both the younger and the older generations are collectively represented by the same unions: the identity of a worker, in this case, overrides inter-generational rivalry, although almost everywhere younger workers are much less likely to be union members than are their older counterparts. Moreover, particularly in those countries where the family retains a strong role as social organiser and agency of income redistribution, we can also point out with Cavalli[23] a "paradoxical complicity" between young people/children and older people/their parents. He emphasises the paradox and yet the reality of collusion between children and their parents: the children do not reject the help and support of their parents, while, at the same time, their parents compete with them in the labour market or defend their retirement benefits. These children are well aware that these privileges guarantee them a safety net. Indeed, divisions within age groups can be greater than those between age groups. The potential areas of tension between the generations are not related to work (sense) but rather to employment (security). In other words, the

[21] Chauvel, L. 2002. *Le destin des generations* [The Destiny of Generations]. Paris: PUF.

[22] Ponzellini, A-M., "Perspectives for a Good Management of Generations at Work and Pathways for more Social Cohesion," in *Generations at Work and Social Cohesion in Europe,* ed. Vendramin, P., (Peter Lang): 275-304.

[23] Cavalli, A. 2004. "Generations and Value Orientation," *Social Compass* 51, No. 2: 155-168.

discourse of one generation regarding another is more contentious when employment is at stake. Consequently, the age group with the most divisive discourse about the generations is the middle-aged group (30 to 50 years old), perhaps those who feel most threatened by competition at work. Indeed, they tend to feel threatened by the increasing deregulation of the labour market and their lack of new skills in comparison to younger workers. They also feel somewhat envious both of their older colleagues, who will still enjoy early retirement, and of younger ones, who are more at ease in the digital and flexible society. However, globally there is no awareness of conflicting interests between the generations and even a denial of the importance of age. Moreover, there is no awareness of belonging to a generation. The lack of awareness of belonging to a specific generation prevents them from being a true "generation unit", in Mannheim's sense[24] of being a "driver of social movements", an agent of change through a process of political self-consciousness. The hypothesis of a conflict between the generations presupposes on the one hand, the existence of awareness among the younger generation of a common social situation and on the other hand, that the divide between the generations is perceived as a structuring dimension of differentiated (and unfair) treatment. A conflict between the generations would assume that a cohort would be aware of a common social situation, and that the cleavage between the generations would be perceived as structuring inequities. At the moment, this does not appear to be the case however, recent youth rebellions in Europe (students in France and Italy, young workers in Greece and Spain) suggest that such awareness is emerging.

4.2. Perspectives on Solidarity and Social Ties at Work

In the SPReW research, all the interviewees were asked to talk about the generations at work through open questions, in a narrative way: what is their view of the other generations, what are their mutual relationships, what are their behaviours and values at work, etc. Analyses of all the discourses—narrative interviewees and group discussions—concerning the generations at work highlight some recurrent issues. One of these issues relates to the vision of solidarity and social ties at work. It was most often raised by older workers through an opposition between individualism and solidarity. This is supposed to threaten social cohesion. The impression is that the world of work is becoming more individualistic and that solidarity

---

[24] Mannheim, K. 2005. *Le problème des generations* [The Problem of the Generations]. Paris: Armand Colin (first published in 1928).

is declining, for different reasons linked to individuals but also to society as a whole. Generally, young workers are seen as the flagship of this increased individualism in society. However, such a statement is extremely ambiguous, because even while saying so, people also put forward stories demonstrating that social ties at work are not disappearing.

Complaints about solidarity appear as complaints about the meeting between two conceptions of the enterprise. Generations are associated with different conceptions of organisations. Most of the trajectories of older workers have been in communitarian enterprises, while young workers are entering the labour market with the image of an open organisation, a model promoted in public discourses, at school, in the media, and at the policy level. In the communitarian enterprises in which the older generation was socialised, solidarity was a mechanism of social regulation. It was managed by large unions in which the collective was more important than individuals. Typically, this is the profile of traditional activist bodies based on membership, organised around formal rules with a pyramidal structure and a collective voice expressing the common interest. It was the era of given belonging. This means that identities were given to individuals; they had not, or could not choose them. Entering into a collective—an enterprise, a professional group, and so forth—provided them with a strong identity, a sense of belonging and a reference group with specific norms and rules. Common life and experience was for the long term. The open enterprise belongs to another era: the era of mobility and the short term. This is the context in which young workers are socialised. For these new entrants into the labour market, who experience difficult and discontinuous trajectories, belonging is chosen, multiple and perhaps more fragile. It is no longer given and unique. These young people are at some distance from unions and generally from traditional activist bodies, and they appear as individualistic to the older generation. However, if they are not numerous in unions and political parties, they are more often engaged in new forms of activism: spontaneous actions, networks of individuals, short-lived mobilisation around concrete projects. Such new forms of solidarity and social involvement have few formal rules, few clear boundaries between internal (us) and external (them), and they value personal involvement more than voice delegation. Of course the reality is not so clearly split between a past and a present, between young and old, between communitarian and open. The purpose of this distinction is to show the coexistence of two ways of considering solidarity and social ties that goes beyond the simplistic opposition between individualism and solidarity. Our working hypothesis is that solidarity is no longer, or not only, linked to assigned belonging but it is a built value that has to be developed and reinforced through actions and common experience. The opposition between individualism and solidarity is not only discussed in the area of work; it is a long-term debate that concerns society as a whole and that raises questions as regards social cohesion. Different forms of solidarity and collectives are associated with different societal contexts and stages in the definition of the individual and the identity.[25]

5. Conclusions

Work has always been and still remains a powerful integrator in society. It gives place to duties and rights and distributes individuals on a scale of social prestige. Work is still a key element in the inclusion/exclusion process within societies. However, over a long period, the sense of work has changed for individuals. It has become more diversified and is now a matter for high expectations at different levels—instrumental, social, symbolic—that do not replace each other. In post-industrial societies, work and identities remain strongly intertwined despite a progressive distance *vis-à-vis* work (if work is considered as a value *per se*). Work remains a social integrator but no longer has a hegemonic value. It supports the building of identities, yet through a more polycentric conception of existence in which other values, such as the family, play similar roles. Moreover, the gender models of relationship to work appear less opposite in the new generation of workers. There is a generational component in all these changes, both in the subjective meaning of work and in its objective conditions (status, trajectories, security), unfairly distributed among age groups, and men and women. Moreover, there is also a significant generational differential as regards educational levels, although these generational differentiations do not unavoidably lead to divisions in social cohesion. Work is a concrete and symbolic place where different conceptions of work, existence and social ties meet but do not collide. However, in the future, we can suspect that a continuing discrepancy between work and life expectations and the nature of places available in society could become more threatening for social cohesion. Many indicators show that young people are facing unfavourable conditions for their entry into active life but at the same time they have great and varied expectations with regard to work. On the one hand, they are constrained to remain in an extended adolescence,

---

[25] Vendramin, P. 2004. *Le travail au singulier. Le lien social à l'épreuve de l'individualisation* [Work in the Singular. The Social Bond Facing Individualisation]. Louvain-la-Neuve: Académia Bruylant / Paris: L'Harmattan.

autonomous but not independent, with few resources for planning their future. On the other hand, they are immersed in a globalised, mobile and multicultural world. They suffer from staying on the periphery of the world of work for a long time. A constrained lengthy youth does not permit one to take hold of certain responsibilities. It does not allow young people to become actively involved in the building of society. This situation leads to indignation and revolt.

References

Cavalli, A. 2004. "Generations and Value Orientation," *Social Compass* 51, No. 2: 155-168.

Chauvel, L. 2002. *Le destin des generations* [The Destiny of Generations]. Paris: PUF.

European Commission. 2003. *Living Conditions in Europe, Statistical Pocketbook, Theme 3: Population and Social Conditions*. Brussels: European Commission.

Davoine, L., and D. Méda. 2008. "Place et sens du travail en Europe: une singularité française? [Place and Meaning of Work in Europe: a French Singularity?]," Document de travail CEE, Paris, No. 96-1.

—. 2010. "The Importance and Meaning of Work in Europe. Trends and Differences between Countries," in *Generations at Work and Social Cohesion in Europe*, ed. Vendramin, P., (Brussels: Peter Lang): 47-72.

Friedmann, G. 1956. *Le travail en miettes* [Fragmented Work]. Paris: Gallimard.

Goldthorpe, J. 1963. *The Affluent Worker: Political Attitudes and Behaviour*. Cambridge: Cambridge University Press.

Habermas, J. 1987. *Théorie de l'agir communicationnel* [Theory of Communicative Action]. Paris: Fayard.

Inglehart, R., and W. E. Baker. 2000. "Modernization, Cultural Change, and the Persistence of Traditional Values?" *American Sociological Review* 65, No 1: 19-51.

Inglehart, R. 1971. "The Silent Revolution in Post-industrial Societies," *American Political Science Review* 65: 991-1017.

—. 1993. *La transition culturelle dans les sociétés avancées* [Cultural Transition in Advanced Societies]. Paris: Economica.

Lahire, B. 1998. *L'homme pluriel: les ressorts de l'action* [Plural Man. The Springs of Action]. Paris: Nathan.

Lebano, A., M-T. Franco, and G. Greco. 2010. "So Far so Close. Generations and Work in Italy," in *Generations at Work and Social*

Cohesion in Europe, ed. Vendramin, P., (Brussels: Peter Lang): 195-220.

Mannheim, K. 2005. *Le problème des generations* [The Problem of the Generations]. Paris: Armand Colin (first published in 1928).

Méda, D., and P. Vendramin, "Les générations entretiennent-elles un rapport différent au travail? [Do the Generations Have Different Relationships to Work?]," *SociologieS*, Théories et recherches, online since December 27, 2010.
URL : http://sociologies.revues.org/index3349.html

Méda, D. 1995. *Le travail. Une valeur en voie de disparition* [Work. A Disappearing Value]. Paris: Alto-Aubier.

Nicole-Drancourt, C., and L. Roulleau-Berger. 2001. *Les jeunes et le travail* [Youth and Work]. *1950-2000.* Paris: PUF.

Paugam, S. 2000. *Le salarié de la précarité* [Precarious Workers]. Paris, PUF.

Ponzellini, A-M., "Perspectives for a Good Management of Generations at Work and Pathways for more Social Cohesion," in *Generations at Work and Social Cohesion in Europe,* ed. Vendramin, P., (Peter Lang): 275-304.

Tchernia, J-F. 2005. "Les jeunes européens, leur rapport au travail [The Relationship to Work of Young Europeans]," in *Les valeurs des jeunes,* eds. Galland, O., and B. Roudet, (Paris: La Découverte): 205-228.

Vendramin, P. 2004. *Le travail au singulier. Le lien social à l'épreuve de l'individualisation* [Work in the Singular. The Social Bond Facing Individualisation]. Louvain-la-Neuve: Académia Bruylant / Paris: L'Harmattan.

Vendramin, P. 2011. "Trabajo, sentido de pertenencia y cohesión social [Work, Sense of Belonging and Social Cohesion]," in *Sentido de pertenencia en sociedades fragmentadas: América Latina en una perspectiva global,* eds. Hopeynhayn, M., and A. Sojo, (Buenos Aires: Editorial Siglo XXI), 59-73.

—. ed. 2010. *Generations at Work and Social Cohesion in Europe.* Brussels: Peter Lang.

Zoll, R. 1992. *Nouvel individualisme et solidarité quotidienne* [New Individualism and Daily Solidarity]. Paris: Kimé.

CHAPTER ONE:

THE CONTRIBUTION OF EDUCATION AND TRAINING TO THE EMPLOYABILITY OF YOUTH

WHAT FORCES YOUTH OUT OF LABOUR MARKETS? THE CASE OF SOUTH KOREA

BYOUNG-HOON LEE AND JONG-SUNG KIM

1. Introduction

Both advanced and developing countries have faced a youth employment crisis, exemplified by the sustained deterioration of the youth labour market going beyond economic cycles.[1] In these countries, youth labour market problems have worsened, although youth cohorts are smaller in number and better educated than their older counterparts.[2] In OECD countries, youth unemployment has been more than twice the level of adult unemployment. Moreover, over the past decade many countries have reported an increase of youth who are idle or inactive, that is those not in education, employment, or training (the NEET). It is also common in industrialised economies that the youth's transition from school to work has become elongated and more disturbed than ever (Inui 2005).[3]

In a similar vein, and for a long time now, youth joblessness has become a matter of societal concern in South Korea (hereafter Korea). Until the late 1990s, Korea had a dynamic youth labour market, derived from its rigorous economic growth, with a virtuous cycle combining the

[1] Blanchflower, D., and R. Freeman. 2000. *Youth Employment and Joblessness in Advanced Countries*. Chicago: the University of Chicago Press. Matsumoto, M., and S. Elder. 2010. "Characterizing the School-to-work Transitions of Young Men and Women: Evidence from the ILO School-to-work Transition Survey," Employment Working Paper No. 51.

[2] Quintini, G., J. Martin, and S. Martin. 2007. "The Changing Nature of the School-to-Work Transition Process in OECD Countries," IZA Discussion Paper No. 2582. Bonn: IZA. Kim, A. 2003. "Analysis of Trends and Causes for Jobless Youths [in Korean]," *Korean Labour Economic Journal* 26, No. 1:23-52.

[3] Inui, A. 2005. "Why Freeter and NEET are Misunderstood: Recognizing the New Precarious Conditions of Japanese Youth," *Social Work and Society* 3, No. 2:244-251.

sustained increase of labour demand with the supply of highly educated youth labour.[4] During the 2000s, however, the country has been confronted with serious problems of a deteriorating youth labour market. As illustrated in Table 1-1, although the unemployment rate of youth aged 15 to 24 in Korea has been below the average of OECD countries during the 2000s, the country's youth employment rate has been much lower than those of other OECD countries in this period, with its sharp decline down to 23.0% in 2010.[5] This implies that the majority of Korean youth experience damaging difficulties in their school-to-work transition and are forced out of labour markets.[6] Thus, the central issue of the youth labour market in Korea is extensive inactiveness, associated with low employment, rather than high unemployment. Over the last decade and during the recent global economic crisis, the government has made strenuous policy efforts to tackle the problem of youth joblessness, producing a mixed result of further increased inactiveness as well as capped unemployment. The country's youth inactiveness might be attributed to macro-level changes in labour markets, such as youth over-education, firms' altered HRM practices, and labour market institutions.[7] At the same time, joblessness or inactivity varies among youth subgroups, reflecting their differing individual and household characteristics.

---

[4] OECD. 2007. *Jobs for Youth: Korea*. Paris: OECD.

[5] Similarly, OECD (2008) reports that Korea has a serious problem of inactive youth and that prolonged inactiveness of youths who stay out of labour markets for five years after leaving school is the highest among OECD countries.

[6] These days, jargon *Itaebaek*, denoting that the absolute majority of 20s are jobless, is a widespread term among the youth. It reflects their frustration and anger towards their status.

[7] Lee, B. 2010. *Problem Diagnosis and Policy Tasks of Youth Unemployment* [in Korean]. (Mimeo). Lee, B. 2003. *Analysis of Youth Labour Market* [in Korean]. Seoul: Korea Labour Institute. Chung, I., and G. Kim. 2005. *Policy Issues of Youth Unemployment* [in Korean]. Seoul: Korea Labour Institute. Kim, A. 2003. "Analysis of Trends and Causes for Jobless Youths [in Korean]," *Korean Labour Economic Journal* 26, No. 1:23-52.

Table 1-1. Cross-national Comparison of Youth Employment and Unemployment (Unit: %)

	Employment Rate			Unemployment Rate		
	2000	2005	2010	2000	2005	2010
OECD Average	45.5	42.7	39.5	12.1	13.4	16.7
Korea	29.4	29.9	23.0	10.8	10.2	9.8
Germany	47.2	42.6	46.8	8.4	15.2	9.7
Japan	42.7	40.9	39.2	9.2	8.6	9.2
United Kingdom	61.5	58.6	50.9	11.7	12.2	19.1
United States	59.7	53.9	45.0	9.3	11.3	18.4
France	28.3	30.5	30.8	20.6	20.3	22.5
Spain	36.3	41.9	27.4	25.3	19.7	41.6
Mexico	48.9	43.7	42.7	5.1	6.6	9.5

Source: OECD (http://stats.oecd.org/Index.aspx). The above statistics refer to youth aged 15-24.

Taking as a starting point the growing attention given to discouraged, jobless or inactive youth in problematic school-to-work transition, this study investigates the trends and determinants of youth inactiveness in Korea. Section 2 reviews the existing literature related with youth inactiveness, by focusing on its conception and causal mechanism. Section 3 sketches and discusses the changing trends of the youth labour market by mainly drawing upon the nationwide Economically Active Population Survey (EAPS) data. Section 4 delineates variables and analytical methods to examine the causal mechanism of youth inactiveness, using the Korea Labour and Income Panel Survey (KLIPS) data, and presents the results of the analysis. The determinants of youth inactiveness considered in this study are individual and household characteristics. Section 5 summarises the key findings of our analysis and addresses some research implications, which might be useful for other countries encountering inactive youth issues.

2. Literature Review Concerning Youth Joblessness and Inactiveness

The school-to-work transition presumes that youth leave school and parental care and get jobs in the labour market, thereby acquiring socio-economic independence and forming their own families as young adults.[8] While some youth succeed in making a fast-track transition, many others are disrupted in this process, whether falling into the state of unemployment, or getting away from labour markets. Today's highly volatile labour markets lead to more and more youths experiencing joblessness in the transition. As many studies indicate, jobless youth who do not obtain employment status are characterised as heterogeneous.[9] They are typically categorised into three groups:

(1) jobseekers who actively search for jobs in the labour markets;

---

[8] Hammer, T. 2007. "Labour Market Integration of Unemployed Youth from a Life Course Perspective: The Case of Norway," *International Journal of Social Welfare* 16:249–257.

[9] Cho, J. 2009. *Youth Unemployment, Causes and Policy Recommendations* [in Korean]. Seoul: FKI Research Report. Furlong, A. 2006. "Not a very NEET Solution: Representing Problematic Labour Market Transitions among Early School-leavers," *Work, Employment and Society* 20, No. 3:553-569. Rees, A. 1986. "An Essay on Youth Joblessness," *Journal of Economic Literature* 24, No. 2:613-628.

(2) involuntary job search dropouts who have a desire to work but do not search for jobs; and

(3) voluntary job search dropouts who have no desire to find jobs.[10]

Group (1) is traditionally termed 'the unemployed'. Although Group (2) and Group (3) are regarded as being part of the inactive population in the official labour market statistics, the reasons for becoming inactive vary between the two groups. Group (2) does not try to find jobs since they know that it is difficult to get desirable jobs in the given labour market conditions, so they are labelled "discouraged" or belonging to hidden unemployment. By way of contrast, Group (3) does not want to get jobs, because of their unpaid activities or responsibilities such as family care, schooling and human resource development, and disability.

Many studies admit that the categorisation of jobless youth into the three groups is fluid rather than fixed, since they tend to be on the borderline between seeking jobs and not seeking jobs, and show high mobility to switch from one group to the other.[11] Accordingly, youth labour markets are viewed as "chaotic", in that many youth jump in and out of labour markets, whether for job shopping or job floundering.[12] In light of the heterogeneity and fluidity of youth joblessness, it is worth noting that there is an ongoing debate as to whether or not the categories "unemployed" and "inactive or out of the labour force" are behaviourally distinct labour market states for jobless youths. Some scholars argue that the traditional distinction between being unemployed and being out of the labour force for the youth is so ambiguous and arbitrary that it is of little analytical value.[13] Some others present the contrasting argument that

---

[10] Genda, Y. 2007. "Jobless Youths and the NEET Problem in Japan," *Social Science Japan Journal* 10, No. 1:23-40.

[11] Freeman, R., and D. Wise. 1982. *The Youth Labour Market Problem: Its Nature, Causes, and Consequences*. Chicago: the University of Chicago Press.

[12] Ryan (2001) depicts early working life of youths as a "moratorium period" containing "churning, milling, and floundering", and summarizes that there are two differing interpretations of high youth mobility in the transition period: the informational approach which sees high youths' turnover as efficient, given information costs, and the segmentationist one, as inefficient, wasting their human capital potential. Neumark, D. 1998. "Youth Labour Markets in the U.S.: Shopping around vs. Staying out," National Bureau of Economic Research Working Paper 6581.

[13] Freeman, R., and D. Wise. 1982. *The Youth Labour Market Problem: Its Nature, Causes, and Consequences*. Chicago: the University of Chicago Press. Rees, A. 1986. "An Essay on Youth Joblessness," *Journal of Economic Literature* 24, No.

"unemployment" and "out of the labour force" are meaningfully distinct classifications, since there are significant differences between the two states in terms of the quantity and intensity of job search.[14] Given the considerable controversy over the distinction of unemployed and inactive youth, we have seen growing research attention paid to a group of jobless youth, the NEET, who are literally not in education, employment, or training.[15] The proliferation of literature on those NEET reflects a noticeable rise in inactive jobless youth commonly observed in many advanced countries and contributes to shedding light on and capturing a more accurate picture of the precarious condition of their school-to-work transition.[16] The NEET concept, however, has often been challenged as a universal labour statistics measurement, because of the different conception and value-laden perception on the part of scholars, largely linked to country-specific labour market conditions, as well as the heterogeneity of the NEET youth.[17] Despite the lack of common understanding and

---

2:613-628. Singell, L., and J. Lillydahl. 1989. "Some Alternative Definitions of Youth Unemployment: A Means for Improved Understanding and Policy Formulation," *American Journal of Economics and Sociology* 48, No. 4:457-473. Quintini, G., J. Martin, and S. Martin. 2007. "The Changing Nature of the School-to-Work Transition Process in OECD Countries," IZA Discussion Paper No. 2582. Bonn: IZA.

[14] Burdett, K., and D. Mortensen. 1980. "Search, Layoffs, and Labour Market Equilibrium," *Journal of Political Economy,* 88:652-672. Flinn, C., and J. Heckman. 1983. "Are Unemployment and Out of the Labour Force Behaviourally Distinct Labour Force States?" *Journal of Labour Economics* 1, No. 1:28-42. Baum, S., and W. Mitchell. 2010. "Labour Underutilisation and Gender: Unemployment Versus Hidden-Unemployment," *Population Research and Policy Review* 29, No. 2:233-248. In a similar vein, Gönül addresses that while the two states are distinct for young women, they are not for young men (Gönül, F. 1992. "New Evidence on Whether Unemployment and out of the Labour Force are Distinct States," *The Journal of Human Resources* 27, No. 2:329-361.)

[15] The NEET was coined by the Social Exclusion Unit (1999) of the British Government as a measurement concept to diagnose the idleness of teenagers aged 16 to18 years old.

[16] Furlong, A. 2006. "Not a very NEET Solution: Representing Problematic Labour Market Transitions among Early School-leavers," *Work, Employment and Society* 20, No. 3:553-569. Kolev, A., and C. Saget. 2005. "Understanding Youth Labour Market Disadvantage: Evidence from South-east Europe," *International Labour Review* 144, No. 2:161-188.

[17] Furlong, A. 2006. "Not a very NEET Solution: Representing Problematic Labour Market Transitions among Early School-leavers," *Work, Employment and Society* 20, No. 3:553-569. Finlay, I., M. Sheridan, J. McKay, and H. Nudorl. 2010. "Young People on the Margins: In Need of More Choices and More Chances

measurement of jobless youth, including the NEET, it is generally acknowledged that youth joblessness, including inactiveness as well as unemployment, have a harmful effect on both individuals and the society, particularly in cases where it is prolonged. On an individual level, joblessness causes youth to fall into the vulnerable conditions of economic marginalisation and disengagement, social exclusion, and psychological stigmatisation at the early stage of adulthood and the long-term job career, and even in the inter-generational life-course.[18] On a social level, youth joblessness is likely to increase the costs of labour market policies and social welfare supporting those vulnerable youth, worsen national competitiveness caused by the constraints on the supply of new skilled labour, and deepen social disintegration, associated with the growth of youth crime and/or disruptive behaviour as well as their structured poverty and family formation failure.[19]

A number of youth labour market studies have investigated what causes youth joblessness, including unemployment and the NEET phenomenon. According to the existing literature, the causal factors influencing youth joblessness can be classified as having two levels: the macro level of national economy and labour markets, and the micro level of individual and household attributes. At the macro level, youth joblessness is mainly explained by economic and labour market factors conditioning the demand and supply of youth labour as well as their transition to work in labour economics literature. Among macro factors influencing the demand of youth labour are aggregate economic conditions, economic growth's job creation effect, the overall unemployment rate, industrial composition and sectoral development, skill-biased technological changes, corporate HRM, particularly staffing levels, practices and restructuring, wage determination schemes and minimum

---

in Twenty-first Century Scotland," *British Educational Research Journal* 36, No. 5:851-867. Yates, S., and M. Payne. 2006. "Not so NEET? A Critique of the Use of 'NEET' in Setting Targets for Interventions with Young People," *Journal of Youth Studies* 9, No. 3:329-344.

[18] Finlay, I., M. Sheridan, J. McKay, and H. Nudorl. 2010. "Young People on the Margins: In Need of More Choices and More Chances in Twenty-first Century Scotland," *British Educational Research Journal* 36, No. 5:851-867. Lee, B. 2003. *Analysis of Youth Labour Market* [in Korean]. Seoul: Korea Labour Institute.

[19] Singell, L., and J. Lillydahl. 1989. "Some Alternative Definitions of Youth Unemployment: A Means for Improved Understanding and Policy Formulation," *American Journal of Economics and Sociology* 48, No. 4:457-473. Cho, J. 2009. *Youth Unemployment, Causes and Policy Recommendations* [in Korean]. Seoul: FKI Research Report. Federation of Korean Industries. 2009. "Analysis of Youth NEET: Trends and Policy Issues [in Korean]," Issue Paper No. 139.

wages, and employment protection legislation.[20] For instance, the labour demand for youth is more sensitive to economic downturns than for adults, since companies are likely to stop hiring and lay off young employees with lower seniority under sluggish economic conditions.[21] The demographic composition, particularly the size of youth cohorts, increases in substitute labour such as women, the elders, and immigrants, and the education and vocational training system tends to affect the supply of youth labour into labour markets.[22] In addition, asymmetric labour market information, insufficient employment service infrastructure, and poor school-business networking are said to constrain smooth school-to-work transitions of youth.[23] Interestingly, Kang[24] points out that socio-cultural norms influence youths' active or inactive transition to work.

---

[20] Freeman, R., and D. Wise. 1982. *The Youth Labour Market Problem: Its Nature, Causes, and Consequences*. Chicago: the University of Chicago Press. Ryan, R. 2001. "The School-to-Work Transition: A Cross-National Perspective," *Journal of Economic Literature* 39:34-92. Raffe, D. 2003. *Young People Not in Education, Employment or Training.* (Mimeo). Blanchflower, D., and R. Freeman. 2000. *Youth Employment and Joblessness in Advanced Countries*. Chicago: the University of Chicago Press. Kolev, A., and C. Saget. 2005. "Understanding Youth Labour Market Disadvantage: Evidence from South-east Europe," *International Labour Review* 144, No. 2:161-188.

[21] O'Higgins, N. 2001. *Youth Unemployment and Employment Policy: a Global Perspective*. Geneva: ILO. Blanchflower, D., and R. Freeman. 2000. *Youth Employment and Joblessness in Advanced Countries*. Chicago: the University of Chicago Press.

[22] Blanchflower, D., and R. Freeman. 2000. *Youth Employment and Joblessness in Advanced Countries*. Chicago: the University of Chicago Press. Kolev, A., and C. Saget. 2005. "Understanding Youth Labour Market Disadvantage: Evidence from South-east Europe," *International Labour Review* 144, No. 2:161-188. Freeman, R., and D. Wise. 1982. *The Youth Labour Market Problem: Its Nature, Causes, and Consequences*. Chicago: the University of Chicago Press. Ryan, R. 2001. "The School-to-Work Transition: A Cross-National Perspective," *Journal of Economic Literature* 39:34-92.

[23] Cho, J. 2009. *Youth Unemployment, Causes and Policy Recommendations* [in Korean]. Seoul: FKI Research Report. Nam, J., C. Lee, Y. Jeon, and S. Woo. 2011. *Policy Study on the Entry and Settlement into Youth Labour Markets* [in Korean]. Seoul: Korea Labour Institute. Ryan, R. 2001. "The School-to-Work Transition: A Cross-National Perspective," *Journal of Economic Literature* 39:34-92. Chung, I., and G. Kim. 2005. *Policy Issues of Youth Unemployment* [in Korean]. Seoul: Korea Labour Institute.

[24] Kang, Y. 2001. "A Phenomenological Study on Japanese Youths' Transition to Labour Markets [in Korean]," *Japan Studies* 9:1-28.

At the micro level, many studies indicate that individual and household attributes of youths influence their joblessness or failed integration to labour markets. Individual factors affecting youth joblessness range from key demographic attributes, particularly linked to the disadvantaged groups, such as gender, age, race or minority ethnic membership, and disability, to educational attainment and school performance, job or unemployment experiences, occupational skills and qualifications, attitudinal inclinations (i.e. consumerism, self-confidence, and perception of work value or work ethics), and behavioural problems (i.e. crime and drug use).[25] The studies, focusing on the micro-level causal factors of youth joblessness, also examine the effect of household characteristics over its disruptive transition. The household attributes, considered by these studies, are household's income and financial-cultural resources, parents' education and occupation, family cohabitation forms, parental interest in and support for children's education, and residential area.

As discussed above, the literature abounds with the causal factors of youth joblessness, reflecting the gravity of its problematic side effects. However, it is noteworthy that research has hardly always shown consistent findings concerning the causal factors of youth joblessness. This reflects not only the complexity of the youth joblessness problems, but it might also be related to varying timeframes and country-specific contexts for those studies, in addition to differing data and analysis methods adopted. Moreover, the causal factors for youth inactiveness have been relatively unexplored until the NEET literature attempted to capture

---

[25] Kang, Y. 2001. "A Phenomenological Study on Japanese Youths' Transition to Labour Markets [in Korean]," *Japan Studies* 9:1-28. Genda, Y. 2007. "Jobless Youths and the NEET Problem in Japan," *Social Science Japan Journal* 10, No. 1:23-40. Hammer, T. 2007. "Labour Market Integration of Unemployed Youth from a Life Course Perspective: The Case of Norway," *International Journal of Social Welfare* 16:249–257. Chen, Y. 2011. "Once a NEET Always a NEET? Experiences of Employment and Unemployment among Youth in a Job Training Programme in Taiwan," *International Journal of Social Welfare* 20, No. 1:33-42. Coles, B., S. Huttons, J. Bradshaw, G. Craig, C. Godfrey, and J. Johnson. 2002. "Literature Review of the Costs of being 'Not in Education, Employment or Training' at Age 16-18," Department for Education and Skills Research Report 347. Bynner, J., and S. Parsons. 2002. "Social Exclusion and the Transition from School to Work: The Case of Young People Not in Education, Employment, or Training (NEET)," *Journal of Vocational Behavior* 60, No. 2:289-309. Kim, A. 2003. "Analysis of Trends and Causes for Jobless Youths [in Korean]," *Korean Labour Economic Journal* 26, No. 1:23-52. Raffe, D. 2003. *Young People Not in Education, Employment or Training.* (Mimeo). Hill, J. 2003. "Young People not in Education, Training or Employment: Key Indicators," Youth Transitions Report.

their problematic characteristics over the past decade, since the inactive population tends to fall out of the traditional labour market analysis because of its inactivity. On the basis of these considerations on who are inactive jobless youth and the reasons that lead them to be inactive, our study tries to capture a clearer picture of inactive youth in the Korean context.

3. Trends and Problems of the Youth Labour Market in Korea

In Korea, the youth labour market has shown substantial changes over the past decade. As demonstrated in Table 1-2, the size of youth cohorts, that is those aged 15 to 29 years old,[26] has shrunk from over 11 million in 2000 to 9,705 thousand in 2010. As a consequence, the share of youth cohorts among the total population has declined from 29.7% in 1992 to 20.2% in 2009. Meanwhile, the Korean youth have been highly educated over the two decades, as evidenced by the fact that the advancement of high school graduates to tertiary education has risen from 33.2% in 1990 through 68.0% in 2000 to 79.0% in 2010. Given the decrease and high education of the youth cohorts, their labour market integration has not improved, as much as it has in many advanced countries. As illustrated in Table 1-2, both the active participation and employment rates of youth cohorts continue to decrease by more than 3% between 2000 and 2010, although their unemployment rate has stayed at around 8%. Fig. 1-2, comparing the rates of employment and unemployment between youth and adults (aged 30 to 54), shows that the gap between the two labour market indicators has widened over the past decade: the employment gap between youth and the primary labour force has increased from 30.3% in 2000 to 34.5% in 2010, while the relative ratio of youth unemployment, compared to that of adults, has soared from 2.31 times in 2000 to 2.76 times in 2010. In particular, the idleness of youth cohorts, used in the government's policy statistics, has also risen from 9.7% in 1997 to 15.7% in 2010.[27]

---

[26] In Korea, the youth usually include those aged 15-29. This definition is intended to reflect the factors of mandatory military service of 24 months on average for men and high enrollment rates in tertiary education, which together result in a prolonged transition for young people (OECD 2007).

[27] The idleness rate is calculated as follows: (unemployed youth + inactive youth – youth in education) / the youth population * 100.

Table 1-2. Trends in Employment and Unemployment of Youth, 2000~2010 (Unit: Thousands, %)

	2000	2001	2002	2003	2004	2005	2006	2007	2008	2009	2010
Youth population	11,243	10,952	10,651	10,368	10,141	9,920	9,843	9,855	9,822	9,780	9,705
Active youth	5,308	5,227	5,160	5,007	4,990	4,836	4,634	4,530	4,398	4,304	4,254
Employed youth	4,879	4,815	4,799	4,606	4,578	4,450	4,270	4,202	4,084	3,957	3,914
Unemployed youth	430	413	361	401	412	387	364	328	315	347	340
Inactive youth	5,934	5,725	5,491	5,361	5,151	5,084	5,209	5,325	5,423	5,477	5,452
Active youth rate	47.2	47.7	48.4	48.3	49.2	48.8	47.1	46.0	44.8	44.0	43.8
Unemployment rate	8.1	7.9	7.0	8.0	8.3	8.0	7.9	7.2	7.2	8.1	8.0
Employment rate	43.4	44.0	45.1	44.4	45.1	44.9	43.4	42.6	41.6	40.5	40.3

Source: Statistics Korea (http://www.kosis.kr/index/index.jsp).

Fig. 1-1. Trends of Employment and Unemployment Rates for Youths and Adults.

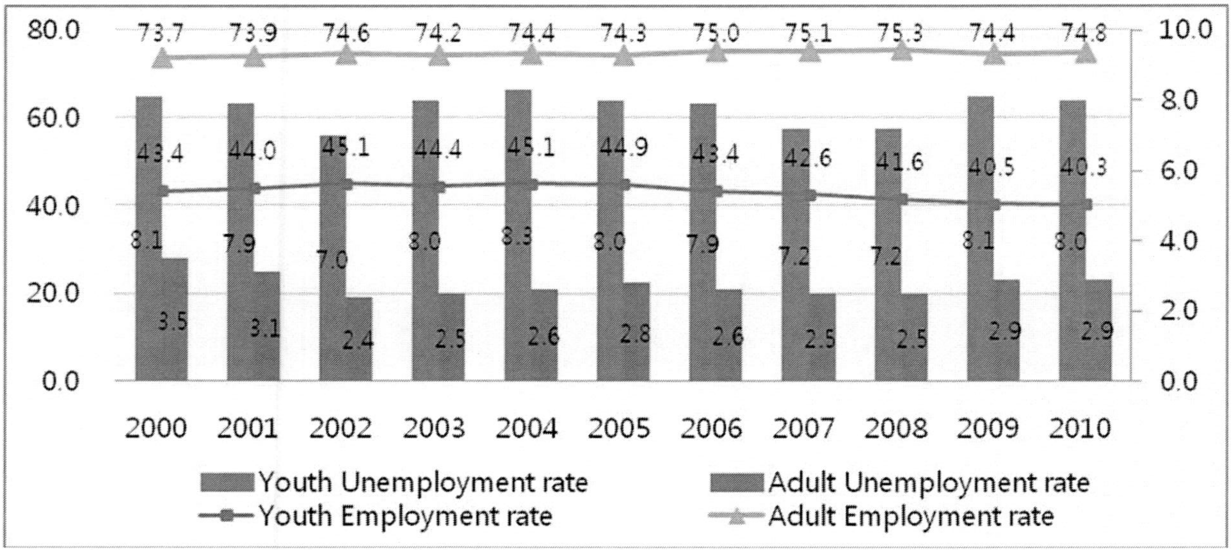

Source: Statistics Korea (http://www.kosis.kr/index/index.jsp).

Fig. 1-2 and 1-3 demonstrate the relative share of labour market activities for male and female youth along their ages, as of 2010. A notable point is that male youth cohorts between the ages of 19 and 22 are less in education and more inactive than other age cohort groups, which might be largely explained by waiting or preparatory periods for their mandatory military service and disrupted advancement to tertiary education. Another significant point is that the share of inactive female youth continues to increase from the age of 19, and particularly during their late 20s, and that the share of employed female youth declines from the age of 23 and is overtaken by that of employed male youth at the age of 27. From the mid-2000s, however, the labour market activity of female youth exceeds that of male youth in terms of employment, while the unemployment of the latter group has been consistently higher—by 35% to 68%—than that of the former group, as displayed by Fig. 1-4.

Fig. 1-2. Share of Male Youths by Activity Status in 2010.

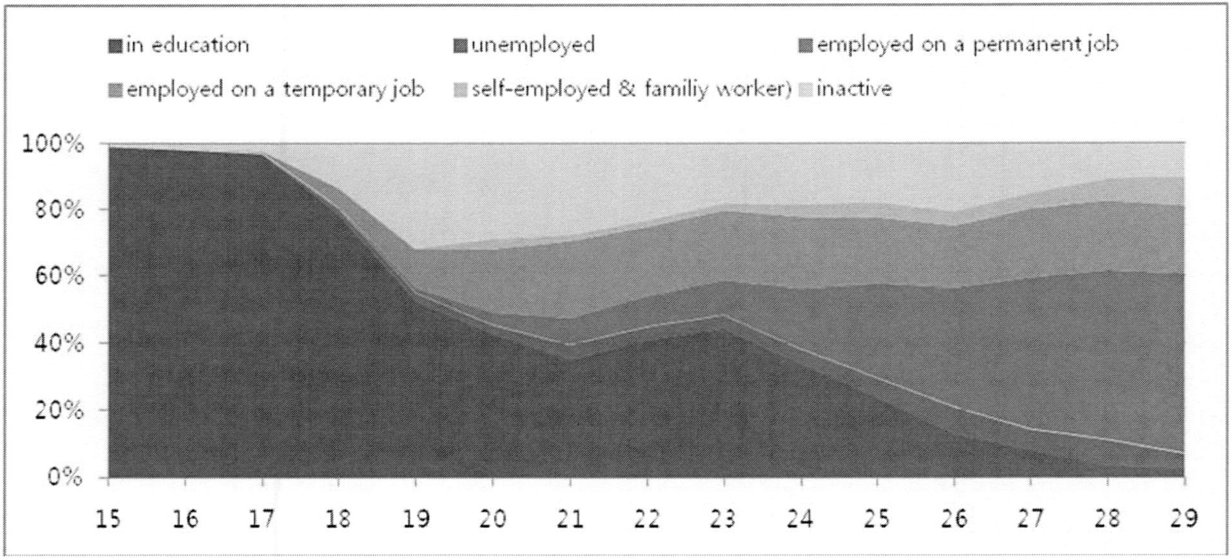

Source: Economically Active Population Survey Data in 2010.

Fig. 1-3. Share of Female Youths by Activity Status in 2010.

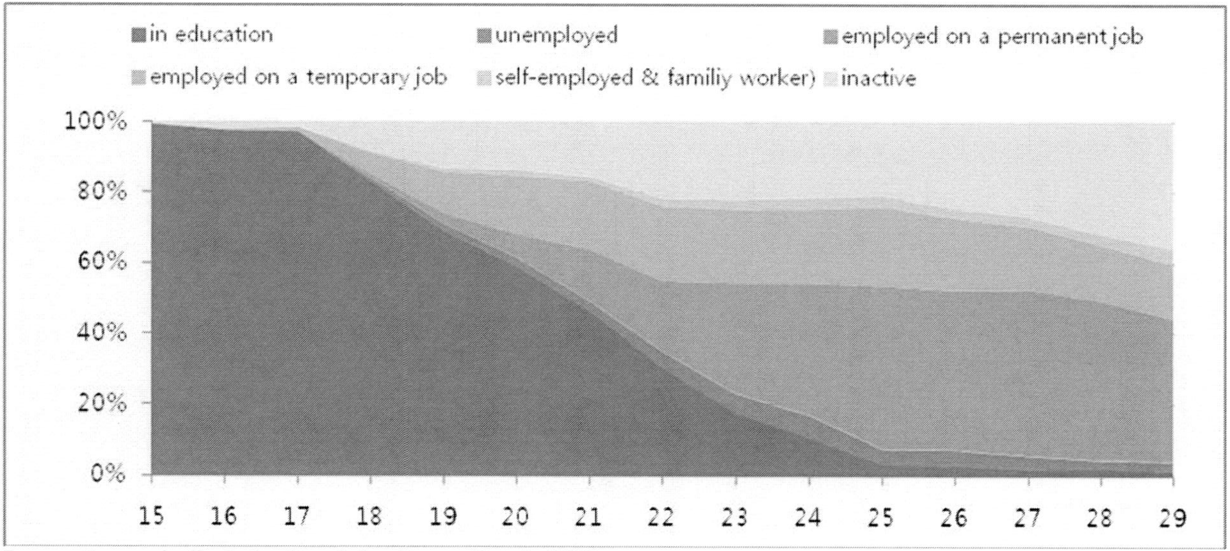

Source: Economically Active Population Survey Data in 2010.

Fig. 1-4. Trends in the Status of Youth Labour Market Activity by Gender.

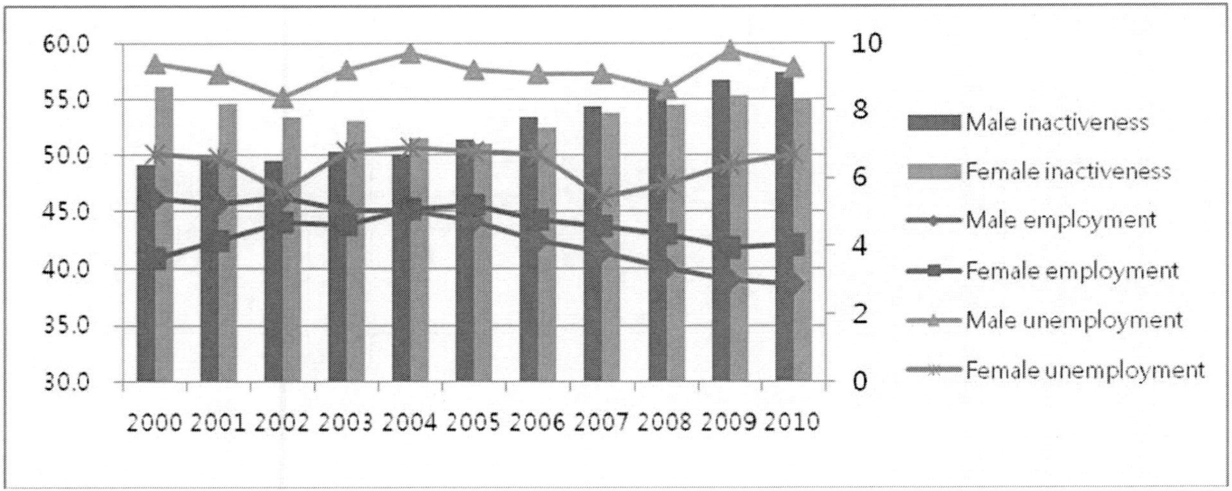

Source: Statistics Korea (http://www.kosis.kr/index/index.jsp).

Table 1-3 shows the detailed state of youth activity, as of 2010. While over 80% of the youth population is working or in education, 7.7% is looking for jobs or attending job training programmes, including the preparation for the civil service examination. Interestingly, 29.9 thousand (3.1% of total youth population) are reported as doing nothing, according to the Economically Active Population (EAP) Survey. This group is purely composed of inactive youth, who are not working or attending any school and job training programmes, nor looking for jobs. Male and female youth have a similar composition of most detailed activities, except that males outnumber females in education by 5.1%, whereas the share of females is much higher in housework. The absolute majority of the 15-19 age cohorts are reported to be in schooling, while over two thirds of the 25-29 age group is in employment. The 20-24 age cohort consists of young people between the transition from school to work. When comparing the composition of detailed activities by education status, a notable finding is that 12.6% of university graduates are taking part in job training programmes. This might be attributed to the fact that a number of highly educated youth are attending private institutes in order to prepare for examinations leading to work in the civil service or as teachers which are believed to guarantee employment security under the condition of precarious adult labour markets. According to Oh H.[28], around 300 thousand youths are estimated to enter those private institutes for the civil service and teacher examination in the process of tertiary education or thereafter.

---

[28] Oh, H. 2006. "Civil Service Examination and University Education [in Korean]," *Human Resource Development Studies* 9, No. 1: 49-79.

Table 1-3. The State of Youth Activities by Individual Attributes (Unit: thousands, %)

		Working[1]	Schooling	Job Seeking	Housework[2]	Job Training	Rest	Others[3]
Youth Population		37.7	42.8	2.8	4.6	4.9	3.1	4.1
Gender	Male	36.7	45.6	3.3	0.1	5.1	3.7	3.7
	Female	38.7	40.1	2.4	9.1	4.8	2.4	2.4
Age	15-19	3.6	89.6	0.5	0.2	0.4	0.8	0.8
	20-24	39.4	35.6	3.6	2.9	7.5	5.2	5.2
	25-29	67.1	6.0	4.3	9.8	7.1	3.6	3.6
Education Status	High school & below	21.1	63.2	1.7	5.2	1.3	2.7	2.7
	2-year college graduate	75.2	0.0	4.9	9.1	5.8	3.7	3.7
	University graduate	69.4	3.6	4.7	5.3	12.6	2.6	2.6
	College/university attending or dropout	25.0	57.1	2.4	1.2	5.4	3.6	3.6

Source: Economically Active Population Survey Data in 2010
1) Working includes temporary leave and waiting for a job.
2) Housework includes childcare.
3) It also includes preparation for school entrance examination and weddings, disabilities, and waiting for military enlistment.

Table 1-4 delineates the trends in the labour market status of youth, particularly including the estimation of the real unemployed. In light of the fact that youth in job training and those resting are treated as part of the inactive population in the official labour statistics, the formal unemployment data is underestimated by excluding these inactive youths. Thus, we can offer an estimate of real unemployment, covering inactive youth in job training, those resting and youth working under 18 hours per week, as well as the officially unemployed youth, as illustrated in Table 1-4. The scope and degree of formal unemployment has improved between 2003 and 2010. However, the estimation of real unemployment reveals quite a different picture. Over the same period, the size of real unemployment increased by 169.7 thousands, and its rate soared by 5.3%, in contrast to formal unemployment. When comparing the degree of real unemployment by education attainment, the youth group (24.7%) of high school graduates and below, including college and university dropouts, is 5.3% higher in 2010 than those (19.4%) of college graduates and above. However, the composition of real unemployment differs between the two groups. The youth group with low education concentrates in the status of those working under 18 hours a week and those resting, whereas the highly educated youth group is included in the category of job training for civil service examination, as discussed above. Moreover, it is worth mentioning that the precariousness of youth in the labour market is observed in the high share of non-regular employment.

As the youth labour survey provided by the government offers the information regarding the duration of youth joblessness from 2007 onwards, we can check the length of the jobless period for the youth cohorts, as shown in Table 1-5 and 1-6. The share of jobless youth within 12 months has increased from 51.6% in 2007 to 56.3% in 2010. At the same time, the share of jobless youth in the category of 24 months and above is considerable, although it has declined from 30.5% to 25.4% in this period. Table 1-6 delineates the composition of the jobless duration, broken down by individual attributes. Female youth account for the majority in the share of joblessness and have a longer jobless period than their male counterparts. The 25-29 age cohorts are more vulnerable than the other two age groups, in terms of both the share of joblessness and the jobless duration. The youth group having low education status (i.e. high school and below) spend a relatively longer time jobless than the highly-educated groups.

Table 1-4. Trends in Labour Market Status of Youth (Unit: Thousands, %)

	2003			2010		
	Total	High school & below	College & above	Total	High school & below	College & above
No. of Formal Unemployed	370.2	232.2	138.0	294.9	146.8	148.1
Formal Unemployment Rate	7.4	8.1	6.5	7.0	7.6	6.5
Employed Working below 18 hours	30.3	28.9	1.4	30.1	26.1	4.0
Job Training	274.7	120.6	154.1	439.8	182.6	257.2
Rest	241.7	191.0	50.7	321.7	220.6	101.1
No. of Real Unemployed[1]	916.9	572.7	344.1	1,086.6	576.2	510.3
Real Unemployment Rate[2]	16.6	18.0	14.8	21.9	24.7	19.4
Non-regular Employment Rate	31.7	36.7	25.7	33.5	41.3	27.4

Source: Economically Active Population, Additional Youth Survey Data, each year
1) Real Unemployed = (Formal Unemployed + Employed working below 18 hours per week + Job Training + Rest).
2) Real Unemployment Rate = Real Unemployed ÷ (Active Population + Job Training + Rest) * 100.

Table 1-5. Trends in the Duration of Youth Joblessness (Unit: Thousands, %)

	2007	2008	2009	2010
Within 6 months	40.7	41.4	38.3	44.0
6 to 12 months	10.9	8.9	10.3	12.3
12 to 24 months	17.9	22.0	21.3	18.3
24 to 36 months	11.4	10.5	12.0	7.5
Above 36 months	19.1	17.2	18.2	17.9
Total No. of Jobless Youths	1,498	1,504	1,470	1,401

Source: Economically Active Population, Additional Youth Survey Data each year. The duration is estimated by the length of the jobless period after leaving school or after quitting the previous job.

Table 1-6. Duration of Youth Joblessness by Individual Attributes (Unit: Thousands, %)

		Within 6 months	6 to 12 Months	12 to 24 months	24 to 36 months	Above 36 months
No. of Jobless Youths		616	173	256	105	251
Gender	Male (37.6)	52.9	12.5	17.8	5.1	11.6
	Female (62.4)	38.6	12.1	18.5	9.0	21.7
Age	15-19 (11.1)	72.4	7.1	17.3	2.6	0.6
	20-24 (27.8)	52.8	12.3	17.7	5.9	11.3
	25-29 (61.0)	34.6	13.3	18.7	9.2	24.1
Education Attainment	High school & below (40.2)	43.3	10.3	17.2	6.0	23.2
	2-year college (26.2)	42.5	15.0	16.3	8.4	17.7
	University & above (33.6)	45.9	13.0	21.0	8.5	11.7

Source: Economically Active Population, Additional Youth Survey Data in 2010. Each education status covers graduation and dropouts.

The reasons for joblessness and/or inactiveness of youth in Korea have been actively discussed in the research and policy arenas. At the macro level, a number of studies commonly indicate that the demand-supply mismatch of the youth labour market is the key factor explaining the problem of jobless or inactive youth. On the supply side, the share of youth advancing to tertiary education continued to rise up to around 80% over the past two decades (as discussed above). Meanwhile, the decent jobs of the public sector and large firms, to which the highly educated youth aspire, have decreased sharply in the same period. In fact, the number of youth aged 15-29 years old employed in the public sector or large firms with 300 employees or more has declined from 876 thousand in 1993 down to 466 thousand in 2010.[29] This is because those organisations reduced the hiring of new school graduates and expanded their recruitment of experienced and skilled older workers from external labour markets.[30] The vulnerable and precarious quality of jobs at small firms and in non-regular employment contributes to the worsening of the mismatch in the youth labour market, causing highly educated youth to prolong their job search or preparation for obtaining decent jobs, or to become discouraged and stay inactive living in a parental home. Youth with low education—i.e. high school graduates and dropouts—show high mobility to move in and out of the labour force, mainly due to their poor job skills and disadvantaged labour market status. Moreover, one might note that public expenditure for active labour market policy is so low that the serious problem of youth jobless and inactiveness cannot be tackled properly by the government.[31]

We now turn to the analysis of micro factors which might lead to Korean youth to become inactive.

4. Analysis of Causal Factors Influencing Youth Inactiveness

4.1. Data and Methodology

In investigating the micro factors influencing youth inactiveness, our analysis uses the KLIPS data, which have been collected by the Korean Labour Institute since 1998 in the manner of longitudinal surveys regarding the labour market and income activities of households and individual constituents residing in urban areas. The original sample of the 1st KLIPS wave during 1998 was 5,000 households, selected by a stratified sampling method, and 13,321 members aged 15 and above. As this study intends to examine the micro-level factors, such as individual and

[29] Lee, B. 2010. *Problem Diagnosis and Policy Tasks of Youth Unemployment* [in Korean]. (Mimeo).

[30] Lee, B. 2003. *Analysis of Youth Labour Market* [in Korean]. Seoul: Korea Labour Institute.

[31] The government expenditure for the active labour market policy is only 0.13% of GDP, which is the second lowest among OECD countries, next to Mexico, as of 2006 (Park & Hong 2009).

household characteristics, causing youth to become inactive, our analysis focuses on jobless youth, who are seeking a job, taking part in job training programmes/institutes, or resting. Since the questionnaire on the detailed labour market activities was included from the 4th wave onwards, we construct a pooled dataset, comprised of the relevant cases of 4th to 11th waves. Our analysis sample of the pooled data totals 2,557 youth, and Table 1-7 displays the composition of youth activities (dependent variable) in our analysis sample.

Table 1-7. Composition of Youth Activities in the Analysis Sample

		Job Seeking	Job Training	Resting	Total
Gender	Male	313 (21.2)	393 (26.7)	768 (52.1)	1,474 (57.6)
	Female	201 (18.6)	384 (35.5)	498 (46.0)	1,083 (42.4)
Age	15 to 19	28 (8.9)	133 (42.5)	152 (48.6)	313 (12.2)
	20 to 24	214 (19.3)	268 (24.2)	624 (56.4)	1,106 (43.3)
	25 to 29	272 (23.9)	376 (33.0)	490 (43.1)	1,138 (44.5)
Education	High School & below	254 (20.1)	291 (23.0)	719 (56.9)	1,264 (49.8)
	2 year College	160 (21.1)	197 (26.0)	401 (52.9)	758 (29.9)
	University & above	100 (19.7)	288 (55.5)	127 (24.7)	515 (20.3)
Residence area	Seoul Metropolitan region	218 (20.1)	324 (29.9)	541 (50.0)	42.4 (1,083)
	Other regions	296 (20.1)	453 (30.7)	725 (49.2)	1,474 (57.6)
Total		514 (20.1)	777 (30.4)	1,266 (49.5)	2,557 (100)

The dependent variable is measured by three categories of jobless youth activities during the survey time: seeking a job, attending a job training programme or institute, and resting.[32] These categories of the dependent variable reflect the degree of inactiveness: the first category of jobseekers, who might be classified as the unemployed in the official labour statistics, are active youth intending to gain employment status; the second category are relatively semi-active youth, who are not looking for a job, but invest time in developing their employability; the third category of resting consists purely of inactive youth, who are not integrated in the labour market, thereby giving up job search as well as job training.

Individual and household characteristics considered as independent variables in our analysis are gender (male=1), age, educational attainments (reference category= high school and below), the number of attended job training, father's education (reference category= high school and below) and occupational prestige, averaged household income per members (transformed to the value of natural logarithm), and residential area (Seoul Metropolitan region=1). In order to check the convex pattern of the effect of age over youth inactiveness, age squared is included in the analysis model. Father's occupational prestige is measured by the International Socio-economic Index of Occupational Status (ISEI) score devised by Ganzeboom et al.[33] The residential area is also included, considering that there exists a substantial gap of economic development and labour market opportunities between the Seoul Metropolitan region and other regions. Moreover, our analysis model includes six dummies during the year 2002~2007 (reference category=2008), for controlling and testing the effect of economic and labour conditions of each year over youth inactiveness. Table 1-8 summarises the statistics of analysis variables. In light of the categorical characteristic of the dependent variable, multi-nominal logistic regression analysis is applied.

---

[32] The questionnaire, asking the states of youth activities, also includes the categories of working, schooling, and voluntary inactiveness for such reasons as childcare, housework, disabilities, waiting for military service and marriage. Those voluntary inactive youth are excluded from our analysis sample.

[33] Ganzeboom, H., P. De Graaf, and D. Treiman. 1992. "An International Scale of Occupational Status," Social Science Research 21:1-56.

Table 1-8. Description of Analysis Variables

Variables	No. of Cases	Mean	S.D.	Remarks
Independent Variables				
Gender	2,557	0.58	0.49	Male =1, Female=0
Age	2,557	23.77	3.29	
Married	2,557	0.04	0.19	Married=1, Unmarried=0
Education: 2 year college graduate University & above	2,537 2,537	0.30 0.20	0.46 0.40	Reference Category: High School & below
Job training attendance	2,557	0.05	0.23	No. of attended programmes
Father's education	2,418	0.88	0.33	High school & below=1, Others=0
Father's occupational prestige	2,009	37.72	11.88	Ganzeboom's ISEI Index
Household income per member(Log)	2,521	6.41	0.94	Transformed value of natural logarithm
Residing Area	2,557	0.42	0.49	Seoul Metropolitan area=1, Other areas=0
Dependent Variables				
Jobless Youth Activities: - Job seeking - Attending to training programmes - Resting	2557 2557 2557	0.20 0.30 0.50	0.40 0.46 0.50	Reference category: Job seeking

4.2. Analysis of Results

Table 1-9 displays the results of multi-nominal logistic regression analysis concerning the determinants of youth inactiveness in the Korean context. Male youth are less likely to take part in job training than their female counterparts. This means that the former group tends to be more active in seeking a job or integrating themselves into the labour force than the latter group. At the same time, it may imply that female youth, who are disadvantaged in the traditionally male-favouring labour market condition of the country, make more effort to obtain job qualifications or prepare for passing the examination of civil service and teacher positions, enabling them to achieve successful labour market integration. The effect of age over both job training attendance and resting is observed significantly following a U-typed pattern. More concretely, the possibility that youth attend job training rather than seeking a job declines until the age 25 and then increases from the age 26 onwards. 26 years old is the bottom of the similar convex pattern for resting youth. Accordingly, the age 25-26 tends to be a borderline where jobless youth begin to become more inactive, whether by attending job training, or resting. This finding implies that jobless youth who fail to make straight transitions to work after completing military service or tertiary education have a higher possibility of becoming inactive after the age 25-26 in Korea. Married youth in comparison to unmarried youth are more likely to seek a job than attend job training, although the former group does not show meaningful differences between the states of job seeking and resting, compared to the latter one. This might be associated with the fact that married youth, who are accountable to family, and have family support are required to get a job and are less likely to spend their time and money on job training.

Jobless youth with a university degree and above are more likely to take part in job training rather than seeking a job, compared with their counterparts with low education. This result might be explained by the fact that many highly educated youth having difficulty in finding decent jobs tend to postpone their transition into the labour market and spend more time for obtaining further job qualifications or preparing for civil service examinations by attending job training institutes, rather than directly looking for a job under the worsening condition of the youth labour market (as noted above). This reflects the unique situation of the Korean youth labour market that encounters the problem of over-education, in marked contrast to the advanced countries where youth less educated are more likely to run into the NEET status.[34] The prior experience of job training also leads jobless youth to participation in further job training programmes. This finding might be hypothetically interpreted as the state-dependence of job training. Like highly educated youth, youth who developed their job skills by attending job training tend to have a high expectation of obtaining a good job and return to the state of job training, rather than searching for a job of any quality, during the jobless period.

In the Korean context, the household income is observed to significantly lead to jobless youth staying out of labour force and attending job training, rather than seeking a job. Given the controversy on the economic effect of household conditions on youth NEETs, our finding supports the "silver

---

[34] The existing literature commonly indicates that low education attainment is related with higher possibility of the NEET status in the Western countries and some Asian countries, such as Japan and Taiwan (Chen 2011; Raffe 2003; Genda 2007; Hill 2003; Freeman & Wise 1982), which differs from our analysis result concerning Korean jobless youths.

spoon syndrome" hypothesis, assuming that jobless youth in a high income household are less pressured to seek a job and more likely to stay out of the labour market since they can gain economic support from their family.[35] According to our results, jobless youth from low income families are more active in seeking jobs, which is at odds with some literature[36] insisting that jobless youths from a poor family background are more likely to become inactive. An interesting finding is that the father's education and occupational standing in society has a significantly positive correlation with jobless youth becoming inactive. Presumably, fathers with a higher education background and particularly a better job—in terms of occupational status—have strong expectations of their children having a good job as well as sufficient economic resources to support them. As a consequence, youth, whose fathers have high socio-economic status, are more likely to continue attending job training or take a break and rest, rather than to seek any jobs falling short of their father's expectations. Moreover, the period 2004 to 2006 are negatively correlated with the possibility of resting, meaning that under better economic conditions of this period,[37] compared to year 2008, jobless youth were encouraged to get away from the state of resting and become more active in finding a job. This appears to be consistent with what the existing literature proves in the Western countries. The residing area has little effect on youth inactiveness. This is not only contrary to our expectation, in light of considerable economic imbalance between Seoul Metropolitan region and other regions, but also inconsistent with the Western literature highlighting regional differentiation of youth inactiveness.[38]

---

[35] Oh, M. 2007. "Analyzing Determinants of the NEET [in Korean]," Paper presented to the 6th Korean Youth Panel Symposium. Genda, Y. 2007. "Jobless Youths and the NEET Problem in Japan," *Social Science Japan Journal* 10, No. 1:23-40.

[36] Hill, J. 2003. "Young People not in Education, Training or Employment: Key Indicators," Youth Transitions Report. Kim, A. 2003. "Analysis of Trends and Causes for Jobless Youths [in Korean]," *Korean Labour Economic Journal* 26, No. 1:23-52.

[37] The economic growth and employment rates of 2004~2006 are respectively 4.6% and 59.8% on average, meaningfully better than those of 2008 (economic growth of 2.3% and employment of 59.5%).

[38] Isengard, B. 2003. "Youth Unemployment: Individual Risk Factors and Institutional Determinants. A Case Study of Germany and the United Kingdom," *Journal of Youth Studies* 6:357–376.

Bynner, J., and S. Parsons. 2002. "Social Exclusion and the Transition from School to Work: The Case of Young People Not in Education, Employment, or Training (NEET)," *Journal of Vocational Behavior* 60, No. 2:289-309.

Table 1-9. Results of Multi-nominal Logistic Regression Analysis

	Job Training (vs. Job Seeking)		Resting (vs. Job Seeking)	
	B	Odds Ratio	B	Odds Ratio
Intercept	26.657***		16.292***	
Male	-0.060***	0.942	0.122	1.130
Age	-2.271***	0.103	-1.310***	0.270
Age²	0.045***	1.046	0.025***	1.025
Married	-1.490***	0.225	-0.394	0.674
Education: 2 year college	0.169	1.184	-0.108	0.898
University & above	1.488***	4.430	-0.283	0.754
Job training attendance	1.410***	4.098	-0.186	0.831
Household income (Ln)	0.205**	1.228	0.079	1.082
Father's education (High school & below)	-0.643*	0.526	-0.422	0.656
Father's occupation prestige	0.021**	1.021	0.018**	1.018
Residing in Seoul Metropolitan Region	0.275	1.316	0.220	1.246
Year 2002	-0.322	0.724	-0.319	0.727
2003	-0.336	0.714	-0.406	0.666
2004	-0.512	0.600	-0.682**	0.506
2005	-0.217	0.805	-0.736**	0.479
2006	-0.329	0.720	-0.755**	0.470
2007	-0.018	0.982	-0.233	0.792
Pseudo. R^2(Nagelkerke)	0.205			
χ^2	381.195***			
No. of Cases	1,929			

Notes: * p<.05, ** p<.01, *** p<.001.

5. Conclusion

Over the past decades, Korea has exposed a new pattern of youth joblessness, which is not captured by the traditional unemployment indicators. The so-called youth inactiveness indicator becomes a focal issue of considerable public concern in the country, where the share of inactive youth has risen to around 56% in recent years, even though the youth unemployment rate remains relatively low, compared to other OECD countries. Likewise, the issue of youth inactiveness has gained attention in many advanced countries, along with the growing presence of inactive youth. As a consequence, we have seen the proliferation of research attempting to conceptualise and characterise this vulnerable youth group, whether it is called the NEET or not. As noted above, however, the lack of the universal conception and measurement concerning the inactive youth makes it difficult to theorise their behavioural pattern and figure out the commonalities and differences of this group across countries. Thus, it is necessary to devise the universal notion and measurement of youth inactiveness like unemployment and employment rates, in light of its growing significance observed in many countries.

Given the worsening trends in youth inactiveness and actual unemployment over the past decade in Korea, the reasons for these problematic trends are discussed at the macro and micro levels. At the macro level, the problem of youth joblessness is influenced by a complex combination of various socio-economic factors (i.e. economic growth, population structure, industrial composition, regional development, education system, corporate HRM practices, and labour market institutions) and can be theoretically explained on the three dimensions of labour supply, labour demand, and labour-job matching.[39] In the case of the Korean youth labour market, the dimension of labour demand is the most crucial in creating the problem of youth inactiveness, although the problem is also derived from the supply of over-educated youth and insufficient active labour market policy and infrastructure. The key reason leading to youth inactivity is that the quantity and quality of jobs for those new entrants to labour market are more attenuated, owing to structural changes in the country's political economy—i.e. the jobless growth, neo-liberal restructuring, the polarising economy, and proliferation of non-regular jobs—taking place during the past decade. Therefore, job creation

[39] Chung, I., and G. Kim. 2005. *Policy Issues of Youth Unemployment* [in Korean]. Seoul: Korea Labour Institute. Lee, B. 2010. *Problem Diagnosis and Policy Tasks of Youth Unemployment* [in Korean]. (Mimeo).

for jobless youth has become a top priority among policy-makers, researchers, and public media. As the government's neo-liberal policy to forge the business-friendly economic system and promote corporate investments failed to create enough jobs for jobless youths over the last decade, the new corporatist approach to job creation by adopting inter-generational work-sharing, working hours reduction and the expansion of public sector jobs, quality improvement of non-regular and small firm jobs, are gaining momentum in place of the market-driven policy approaches. As such, the tackling of youth joblessness, including inactiveness, involves intense power politics between socio-economic actors on how to reconfigure the country's political economy conditioning the youth labour market.

At the micro level, our analysis addresses three remarkable points. First, under the gendered context of the Korean youth labour market, female youth who are disadvantaged in the job opportunity structure are found to attend job training programmes for enhancing the condition of their labour market transition and quality of their future jobs, rather than directly moving into the labour market by actively looking for a job. This makes clear that whether one becomes active or inactive is not unilaterally determined by macro-level conditions, but mediated by an individual youth's strategic choice under those structural conditions. Secondly, high education leads jobless youth to become less active in order to further develop their employability, rather than becoming an active jobseeker. This finding, which is contrary to the existing literature, reveals that young people's low education tends to increase their inactiveness, and might be associated with the over-educated and precarious characteristics of the Korean youth labour market. Therefore, the effect of education on youth inactiveness might vary, depending on the overall state of the youth labour market in a particular country. Thirdly, such household characteristics as household incomes and father's socio-economic status are reaffirmed to be significant factors influencing youth inactiveness in a positive direction. This result appears to support the "silver spoon syndrome" argument that youth coming from high-income families are more likely to become inactive, since they have enough financial resources to stay out of the labour force. At the same time, the finding that a father's education and occupational prestige are likely to induce jobless youth to become less active (attending to job training) and sometimes purely inactive could be interpreted as parents' expectations, linked to their high socio-economic status, resulting in the increasing possibility of youth inactiveness by pressuring those jobless youths to get a good job. Accordingly, in examining the impact of household characteristics over youth joblessness, we should consider not only the economic effect of financial resources that those households have, but also the effect of socio-psychological interaction between the jobless youth and their parents (and other family members).

References

Baum, S., and W. Mitchell. 2010. "Labour Underutilisation and Gender: Unemployment Versus Hidden-Unemployment," *Population Research and Policy Review* 29, No. 2:233-248.

Blanchflower, D., and R. Freeman. 2000. *Youth Employment and Joblessness in Advanced Countries*. Chicago: the University of Chicago Press.

Burdett, K., and D. Mortensen. 1980. "Search, Layoffs, and Labour Market Equilibrium," *Journal of Political Economy,* 88:652-672.

Bynner, J., and S. Parsons. 2002. "Social Exclusion and the Transition from School to Work: The Case of Young People Not in Education, Employment, or Training (NEET)," *Journal of Vocational Behavior* 60, No. 2:289-309.

Chen, Y. 2011. "Once a NEET Always a NEET? Experiences of Employment and Unemployment among Youth in a Job Training Programme in Taiwan," *International Journal of Social Welfare* 20, No. 1:33-42.

Cho, J. 2009. *Youth Unemployment, Causes and Policy Recommendations* [in Korean]. Seoul: FKI Research Report.

Chung, I., and G. Kim. 2005. *Policy Issues of Youth Unemployment* [in Korean]. Seoul: Korea Labour Institute.

Coles, B., S. Huttons, J. Bradshaw, G. Craig, C. Godfrey, and J. Johnson. 2002. "Literature Review of the Costs of being 'Not in Education, Employment or Training' at Age 16-18," Department for Education and Skills Research Report 347.

Federation of Korean Industries. 2009. "Analysis of Youth NEET: Trends and Policy Issues [in Korean]," Issue Paper No. 139.

Finlay, I., M. Sheridan, J. McKay, and H. Nudorl. 2010. "Young People on the Margins: In Need of More Choices and More Chances in Twenty-first Century Scotland," *British Educational Research Journal* 36, No. 5:851-867.

Flinn, C., and J. Heckman. 1983. "Are Unemployment and Out of the Labour Force Behaviourally Distinct Labour Force States?" *Journal of Labour Economics* 1, No. 1:28-42.

Freeman, R., and D. Wise. 1982. *The Youth Labour Market Problem: Its*

Nature, Causes, and Consequences. Chicago: the University of Chicago Press.

Furlong, A. 2006. "Not a very NEET Solution: Representing Problematic Labour Market Transitions among Early School-leavers," *Work, Employment and Society* 20, No. 3:553-569.

Genda, Y. 2007. "Jobless Youths and the NEET Problem in Japan," *Social Science Japan Journal* 10, No. 1:23-40.

Gönül, F. 1992. "New Evidence on Whether Unemployment and out of the Labour Force are Distinct States," *The Journal of Human Resources* 27, No. 2:329-361.

Hammer, T. 2007. "Labour Market Integration of Unemployed Youth from a Life Course Perspective: The Case of Norway," *International Journal of Social Welfare* 16:249–257.

Hill, J. 2003. "Young People not in Education, Training or Employment: Key Indicators," Youth Transitions Report.

Ganzeboom, H., P. De Graaf, and D. Treiman. 1992. "An International Scale of Occupational Status," Social Science Research 21:1-56.

Inui, A. 2005. "Why Freeter and NEET are Misunderstood: Recognizing the New Precarious Conditions of Japanese Youth," *Social Work and Society* 3, No. 2:244-251.

Isengard, B. 2003. "Youth Unemployment: Individual Risk Factors and Institutional Determinants. A Case Study of Germany and the United Kingdom," *Journal of Youth Studies* 6:357–376.

Kang, Y. 2001. "A Phenomenological Study on Japanese Youths' Transition to Labour Markets [in Korean]," *Japan Studies* 9:1-28.

Kim, A. 2003. "Analysis of Trends and Causes for Jobless Youths [in Korean]," *Korean Labour Economic Journal* 26, No. 1:23-52.

Kolev, A., and C. Saget. 2005. "Understanding Youth Labour Market Disadvantage: Evidence from South-east Europe," *International Labour Review* 144, No. 2:161-188.

Lee, B. 2010. *Problem Diagnosis and Policy Tasks of Youth Unemployment* [in Korean]. (Mimeo).

—. 2003. *Analysis of Youth Labour Market* [in Korean]. Seoul: Korea Labour Institute.

Matsumoto, M., and S. Elder. 2010. "Characterizing the School-to-work Transitions of Young Men and Women: Evidence from the ILO School-to-work Transition Survey," Employment Working Paper No. 51.

Mitchell, D., A. Betts, and M. Epling. 2002. "Youth Employment, Mental Health and Substance Misuse: A Challenge to Mental Health Services," *Journal of Psychiatric and Mental Health Nursing* 9:191–

198.

Nam, J., C. Lee, Y. Jeon, and S. Woo. 2011. *Policy Study on the Entry and Settlement into Youth Labour Markets* [in Korean]. Seoul: Korea Labour Institute.

Neumark, D. 1998. "Youth Labour Markets in the U.S.: Shopping around vs. Staying out," National Bureau of Economic Research Working Paper 6581.

OECD. 2007. *Jobs for Youth: Korea*. Paris: OECD.

—. 2008. *Employment Outlook*. Paris: OECD.

Oh, H. 2006. "Civil Service Examination and University Education [in Korean]," *Human Resource Development Studies* 9, No. 1: 49-79.

Oh, M. 2007. "Analyzing Determinants of the NEET [in Korean]," Paper presented to the 6th Korean Youth Panel Symposium.

O'Higgins, N. 2001. *Youth Unemployment and Employment Policy: A Global Perspective*. Geneva: ILO.

Quintini, G., J. Martin, and S. Martin. 2007. "The Changing Nature of the School-to-Work Transition Process in OECD Countries," IZA Discussion Paper No. 2582. Bonn: IZA.

Park, K., and S. Hong. 2009. "Recent Changes in Employment Conditions and Policy Solution of Youth Unemployment [in Korean]," Studies of Financial Economy, Working Paper No. 364.

Raffe, D. 2003. *Young People Not in Education, Employment or Training.* (Mimeo).

Rees, A. 1986. "An Essay on Youth Joblessness," *Journal of Economic Literature* 24, No. 2:613-628.

Ryan, R. 2001. "The School-to-Work Transition: A Cross-National Perspective," *Journal of Economic Literature* 39:34-92.

Singell, L., and J. Lillydahl. 1989. "Some Alternative Definitions of Youth Unemployment: A Means for Improved Understanding and Policy Formulation," *American Journal of Economics and Sociology* 48, No. 4:457-473.

Social Exclusion Unit. 1999. *Bridging the Gap: New Opportunities for 16-18 Years Olds Not in Education, Employment, or Training.*

Yates, S., and M. Payne. 2006. "Not so NEET? A Critique of the Use of 'NEET' in Setting Targets for Interventions with Young People," *Journal of Youth Studies* 9, No. 3:329-344.

THE ROLE OF EDUCATION IN REDUCING POVERTY AND UNEMPLOYMENT

ELDAH ONSOMU AND BOAZ MUNGA

1. Introduction

Unemployment and poverty are major socio-economic challenges facing many countries. In Sub-Saharan Africa (SSA), unemployment and poverty continue to be major obstacles to full utilisation of human resources.[1] High levels of unemployment and poverty are associated with substantial social costs, and reducing both unemployment and the incidence of poverty are main goals for development policy.

In Kenya, the government identified illiteracy, ignorance, and poverty as major socio-economic challenges facing the nation at independence.[2] A key policy response by the government to tackle both unemployment and poverty was the dissemination of education and training. The Kenyan education system expanded rapidly through the years—and, accordingly, so did the educated labour force. Because of this, school-leavers unemployment was identified as a visible problem of Kenya's education system as far back as the mid-1980s.[3]

The policy focus on education and training is anchored in the expectation that higher levels of education are expected to confer benefits to households, communities, and countries. One of the recognised benefits of this state of affairs is the reduced risk of the incidence and duration of unemployment at higher levels of education,[4] as unemployment and poverty are interconnected. Individuals and households are usually poor

---

[1] ILO. 2008. *Global Employment Trends 2008*. Geneva: International Labour Office.

[2] Government of Kenya. 1965. *Sessional Paper No. 1 on African Socialism and its Application to Planning in Kenya*. Nairobi: Government Printer.

[3] Godia, G. 1987. "Education and the Unemployment Problem in Kenya," *The Journal of Negro Education*, 56, No. 3:356-367.

[4] Mincer, J. 1991. "Education and Unemployment," National Bureau of Economic Research (NBER) Working Paper No. 3838. Cambridge.

because they are unemployed or are employed in low productivity jobs. It is therefore assumed that more educated an individual the more likely they won't be poor. Poverty, on the other hand, affects educational achievement and is usually associated with low quality education, hence low income and perpetuation of poverty. Even so, education and training do not guarantee that individuals would escape unemployment and poverty. Indeed, evidence indicates that individuals with higher educational attainment may have higher unemployment rates due to:

(i) deficiency of labour demand resulting from poor economic performance, which may dampen the creation of employment opportunities for school graduates;
(ii) employers who prefer experienced workers over new market entrants, hence locking out for fresh graduates;[5]
(iii) employment practices; lack of employability, educational systems and skills mismatch, which can result from structural changes in the economy, thereby leading university and other graduates to not possessing the skills that employers are demanding and;[6] lack of information in the labour market;
(vi) reluctance by school graduates, especially university graduates, to work in the informal sector[7] or queuing for better jobs[8]; and government policies, as in the case of Israel.

The main objective of this study is to explore the role of education and training in reducing unemployment and poverty in Kenya. The study will examine the effects of education and training on unemployment and

---

[5] Bae, H. S., and H. J. Song. 2006. "Youth Unemployment and the Role of Career and Technical Education: A Study of the Korean Labour Market, " *Career and Technical Education Research* 31, No 1.

[6] Dias R., and D. Posel. 2006. "Unemployment, Education and Skills Constraints in Post-Apartheid South Africa," Paper presented at the Conference Accelerated and Shared Growth in South Africa: Determinants, Constraints and Opportunities, Johannesburg, South Africa, October 2006. United Republic of Tanzania. 1997. *The National Employment Policy.* Dar es Salaam: Ministry of Labour, Youth Development and Sports. Bae, H. S., and H. J. Song.2006. "Youth Unemployment and the Role of Career and Technical Education: A Study of the Korean Labour Market, " *Career and Technical Education Research* 31, No 1.

[7] Bae, H. S., and H. J. Song. 2006. "Youth Unemployment and the Role of Career and Technical Education: A Study of the Korean Labour Market," *Career and Technical Education Research* 31, No 1.

[8] Serneels, P. 2007. "The Nature of Unemployment among Young Men in Urban Ethiopia," *Review of Development Economics* 11, No. 1:170-186.

underemployment and the effects of education and training on the incidence of poverty in Kenya. The remainder of this paper is organised as follows. The next section presents the Kenyan context by analysing the trends of open unemployment, educational attainment and income poverty in the country. Section 3 provides a review of the relevant literature on the relationship between education and unemployment and poverty. Section 4 presents the model, while Section 5 discusses the empirical results. Section 6 concludes the paper and provides some policy implications.

2. The Kenyan Context

2.1. Trends in Unemployment and Educational Attainment

The rates of open unemployment estimated in various surveys in Kenya are presented in Table 1-10. The figures suggest that open unemployment has generally been rising since 1978, but declined slightly in 2006 relative to its 1999 level. High unemployment levels in the late 1990s can be explained in part by poor economic growth during the period. The Structural Adjustment Programmes (SAPs) which were largely implemented in the early 1990s were also a contributing factor. Cuts in government spending, privatisation, the collapse of some private firms and retrenchment in others, and public sector downsizing led to increased unemployment.[9] As observed by Pollin, Githinji and Heintz,[10] the period also experienced a shift in labour demand in favour of highly skilled labour, and an increase in part-time workers and casual workers at the expense of full-time jobs.

Since independence in 1963, there has been a rapid expansion of education in Kenya. The country recorded improvements in primary school enrolment in the first two decades after independence with the Gross Enrolment Rate (GER) increasing from 47 percent in 1963 to 62 percent in 1970 and 115 percent in 1980. The increased enrolment was

[9] Central Bureau of Statistics (CBS). 2002. *Kenya 1999 Population and Housing Census: The Labour Force Monograph, Analytical Report Volume IX.* Nairobi: Central Bureau of Statistics, Ministry of Planning and National Development, Government of Kenya. Manda, D. K. 2004. "*Globalisation and the Labour Market in Kenya,*" KIPPRA Discussion Paper No. 31. Nairobi: Kenya Institute for Public Policy Research and Analysis. Oiro, M. W., G. Mwabu, and D. K. Manda. 2003. "Poverty and Employment in Kenya," Discussion Paper, Kenya Institute for Public Policy Research and Analysis, Nairobi KIPPRA.

[10] Pollin, R., M. Githinji, and J. Heintz. 2007. *An Employment-Targeted Economic Programme for Kenya*. Amherst: Political Economy Research Institute (PERI).

among other factors attributed to rapid development of facilities and subsidised education.[11]

Table 1-10. Unemployment Rates in Kenya by Age Group in Percentage (1978-2005/06)

Age	1978*	1986*	1998/99*	1998/99**	2005/06**
15—19	26.6	36.2	47.0	24.3	25.0
20—24	18.5	29.2	47.3	27.1	24.2
25—29	4.8	8.6	25.1	15.5	15.7
30—34	2.0	2.7	14.3	10.8	7.5
35—39	1.8	2.1	12.0	8.4	7.6
40—44	0.7	0.7	11.2	9.1	6.4
45—49	1.1	2.0	14.7	8.2	5.7
50—54	1.4	0.9	18.9	8.7	4.7
55—59	1.5	4.1	40.6	13.5	4.0
60—64	3.2	---	45.2	11.7	2.5
Urban	**7.0**	**16.0**	**25.1**	**25.1**	**19.9**
Total (rural & urban)	**6.7**	**9.7**	**14.6**	**14.6**	**12.7**

Source: Wambugu, Munga and Onsomu (2010).
* - Urban unemployment rate.
** - Total unemployment rates (urban + rural)

The country experienced its first negative enrolment shock between 1984 and 1985 when primary enrolment rates fell from 107 percent to 99 percent and again in 1989 when the GER declined from 98 percent to 92 percent.[12] Bedi *et al.*[13] report that the GER was stable between 1985 and

[11] Government of Kenya. 1965. *Sessional Paper No. 1 on African Socialism and its Application to Planning in Kenya*. Nairobi: Government Printer. Government of Kenya. (various issues). *Economic Survey*. Nairobi: Central Bureau of Statistics: Government Printer.

[12] GERs greater than 100 percent are not expected to be sustained over a long time. This is because over-aged children are expected to reduce with time (UNESCO, 1984). Therefore, the fall of the GER from 107 percent to 99 percent in 1984/85 may simply imply that over-aged children were no longer being enrolled in large numbers and may not be an adverse occurrence. The decline in primary school enrolment between 1984 and 1985 can be attributed to severe drought conditions and the introduction of a costly curriculum (Government of Kenya. 1988. *Economic Survey*. Nairobi: Central Bureau of Statistics: Government Printer.). The 1989 shock is likely to be a reaction to the introduction of the formal cost sharing system of education in 1988 (Bedi, A., P. K. Kimalu, D.K. Manda, and N. N.

1989 but declined after 1989 until a GER of 88 percent was reached in 1993. The rest of the 1990s, i.e. the period after 1993, recorded a stable but relatively lower GER of about 88 percent. Enrolment rates did not change much until after 2003 when the government reintroduced free primary education among other policies. The NER also increased gradually from 82.2 percent in 2003 to 91.6 percent in 2007 and further to 91.4% in 2010.

There were consistent gains in secondary school enrolment prior to and including the early 1990s, partly as a result of the establishment of community-based *harambee* schools. Gross enrolment in secondary schools grew from 2 percent in 1960 to a peak of 28 percent of secondary-school-age children in 1991. The drop in enrolment since 1991 has been substantial and can be attributed to many factors including:

(i) rising costs of education in the wake of an introduction of user fees;
(ii) HIV & AIDS and increasing urban poverty which lowered living standards and left many school-going children orphans and vulnerable; and
(iii) poor growth and a lowering of employment opportunities amidst rising poverty levels.[14] After 2003, there was a deliberate government policy of expansion of secondary schools to respond to the declining enrolment rates.[15] Subsequently, the GER improved to 22.2 percent and 29.3 percent in 2004 and 2005, respectively, and further to 36.8 percent in 2007 before declining to 32 percent in 2010. The total enrolment in 2005 represented a 19.2 percent increase from its 2002 total enrolment figure of 778,601 students.[16] The number of tertiary institutions has increased tremendously since the mid-1990s and continues to grow.

Nafula. 2002. "The Decline in Primary School Enrolment in Kenya," KIPPRA DP No. 14. Nairobi: KIPPRA.).

[13] Bedi, A., P. K. Kimalu, D. K. Manda, and N. N. Nafula. 2002. "The Decline in Primary School Enrolment in Kenya," KIPPRA DP No. 14. Nairobi: KIPPRA.

[14] Bedi, A., P. K. Kimalu, D. K. Manda, and N. N. Nafula. 2002. "The Decline in Primary School Enrolment in Kenya," KIPPRA DP No. 14. Nairobi: KIPPRA. Oiro, M. W., G. Mwabu, and D. K. Manda. 2003. "Poverty and Employment in Kenya," Discussion Paper, Kenya Institute for Public Policy Research and Analysis, Nairobi KIPPRA, Nairobi.

[15] Partly achieved through relaxing the regulatory requirements for the establishment of schools.

[16] Government of Kenya. 2006. *Economic Survey*. Nairobi: Central Bureau of Statistics: Government Printer.

2.2. Poverty Trends

Unemployment is closely associated to poverty which has been a major social and economic concern in the country since independence.[17] It is likely that Kenya achieved a reduction in the incidence of poverty between 1963 and 1990 given the relatively high economic growth rate—averaging about 6 percent from 1966-1980 and 4.3 percent in the period 1981-1990[18]—which was higher than the inter-censual population growth rate of 3.41 percent between 1969-1979 and 3.34 percent in 1979-1989.

Several surveys and studies offer indicative poverty trends for Kenya for the period after 1990. Table 1-11 indicates that the incidence of poverty is high in Kenya. The 2005/06 measure of 45.9 percent appears to suggest that there was a decline in the incidence of poverty especially after the year 2000 when more than half of Kenya's population (57%) was estimated to be poor.[19] However, this decline came in the wake of a possible steady rise in poverty levels throughout the 1990s as suggested by various measures using the Welfare Monitoring Survey (WMS) data for 1992, 1994, and 1997.

---

[17] Geda, A., N. De Jong, G. Mwabu, and M. Kimenyi. 2001. "Determinants of Poverty in Kenya: Household-Level Analysis," Kenya Institute for Public Policy Research and Analysis (KIPPRA) DP. 9/2001.

[18] Government of Kenya. (various issues). Economic Survey. Nairobi: Central Bureau of Statistics: Government Printer.

[19] Mwabu G., M. W. Kimenyi, P. K. Kimalu, , N. N. Nafula, and D. K. Manda. 2002. "Predicting Household Poverty: A Methodological Note," *African Development Review* 15, No. 1.

Table 1-11. Summary of Poverty Estimates for Kenya, 1990 to 2006

Author	Reference Year	Data Source	Poverty Incidence
Mukui (1993)	1992	1992 WMSI	Rural: 46% for 1992 Urban: 29.3 % for 1992
Republic of Kenya (1998)	1994	1994 WMS I	46.8% rural population 29% urban population 40% national estimates
Mwabu *et al.* (2000)	1994	1994 WMS II	39.7% rural population 28.9% urban population 38.8% national population
Republic of Kenya (2000) results for WMS III	1997	1997 WMS III	52.9% rural population 49.2% urban population 52.3% national population
Mwabu *et al.* (2002)	2000	Predictions based on GDP and Gini coefficients and poverty estimates for 1997 using WMS III	59.6% rural population 51.5% urban population 56.8% national population
KNBS (2007)	2005/2006	KIHBS	49.1% rural population 33.7% urban population 45.9% national population

Sources: Government of Kenya. (various issues). *Economic Survey*. Nairobi: Central Bureau of Statistics: Government Printer; Mwabu, G. 2000. *Poverty in Kenya: Profiles and Determinants, Department of Economics*. University of Nairobi and Ministry of Finance and Planning, unpublished. Kimalu, P., N. Nafula, D. K. Manda, G. Mwabu, and M.S. Kimenyi. 2002. *A Situational Analysis of Poverty in Kenya*. KIPPRA Working Paper No. 6, Nairobi: KIPPRA.

3. Related Literature

3.1. Poverty versus Education and Training

The human capital approach regards education as an important instrument for the reduction of poverty. According to the model, investment in education leads to formation of human capital, which is an important factor in economic growth and development. The human capital framework implies that education and training imparts skills and knowledge which are positively associated with employment, productivity and earnings.[20]

Empirically, both micro and macro level analysis seem to suggest that education is important for poverty reduction. At the micro level, literature reaffirms the negative relationship between education and poverty. Income poverty is found to decline consistently with increasing levels of education in developing countries.[21] Analyses of Kenyan household-level data indicate that education reduces the incidence of poverty. Poverty decreases as the level of education increases.[22] Geda, *et al.*[23] and Bigsten and Shimeles[24] using a logit model and the 1994 Welfare Monitoring Survey data for Kenya concluded that educational attainment of the head of the household was the most important factor associated with less poverty.

---

[20] Blaug, M. 1972. "Correlation between Education and Earnings," *Higher Education* 1, No. 1:53-76. Mincer, J. 1972. "Schooling, Experience and Earnings," New York: National Bureau of Economic research (NBER). World Bank. 2006. *Development and the Next Generation, World Development Report 2007*. Washington, DC: The World Bank. Fields, G. S. 2008. "Segmented Labour Market Models in Developing Countries," in *The Oxford Handbook of Philosophy of Economic Science*, eds. Kincaid, H., and D. Ross, (USA: Oxford University Press).

[21] Appleton, S., J. Knight, L. Song, and Q. Xia. 2001. "Labour Retrenchment in China: Determinants and Consequences," unpublished paper. Tilag, J. B. G. 1994. *Education for Development in Asia*. New Delhi: Sage Publications.

[22] Geda, A., N. De Jong, G. Mwabu, and M. Kimenyi. 2001. "Determinants of Poverty in Kenya: Household-level Analysis," Kenya Institute for Public Policy Research and Analysis (KIPPRA) DP. 9/2001. Kenya National Bureau of Statistics. 2007b. *Basic Report on Well-being in Kenya: Based on Kenya Integrated Household Budget Survey (KIHBS) 2005/06*. Nairobi: KNBS. Oiro, M. W., G. Mwabu, and D. K. Manda. 2003. "Poverty and Employment in Kenya," Discussion Paper, Kenya Institute for Public Policy Research and Analysis, Nairobi KIPPRA.KNBS (2007b) finds that in rural areas, the incidence of poverty drops from 65.5, to 51.5 and to 27.2 percent for household heads with no education, those with primary education and those with secondary education, respectively. The corresponding incidence of poverty for urban areas is 68.7, 47.9 and 22.0 respectively.

[23] Geda, A., N. De Jong, G. Mwabu, and M. Kimenyi. 2001. "Determinants of Poverty in Kenya: Household-level Analysis," Kenya Institute for Public Policy Research and Analysis (KIPPRA) DP. 9/2001.

[24] Bigsten, A, and A. Shimeles. 2003, "Growth and Poverty Reduction in Ethiopia: Evidence from Household Panel Surveys," *World Development* 31:81-106.

3.2. Unemployment versus Education and Training

Economic theory suggests that there is a relationship between education and earnings. The central idea is that education is an investment in the acquisition of skills and knowledge which can increase earnings. The human capital theory therefore suggests that the level of education should be inversely related to the rate of unemployment.[25] The human capital theory is commonly contrasted with signalling models and screening models. In these latter models, education is assumed to act as a filter with successful completion of education or possession of educational credentials signalling high levels of ability. According to signalling models, workers get educated in order to signal to employers that they are inherently more productive than other workers. Such workers are therefore expected to be hired preferentially.[26]

It is not always the case that more education and training, or acquisition of skills by individuals, will translate into lower unemployment rates as suggested by the human capital model and the screening models. One explanation as to why individuals may fail to have lower unemployment rates at higher levels of education and training is the presence of labour market segmentation. Segmented labour market models recognise that labour markets are differentiated and jobs differ in quality.[27] There are "good jobs" and "bad jobs" with access to "good jobs" not available to all who want better jobs. Those who fail to secure good jobs (also referred to as formal) must either take up an informal job, be engaged in agricultural activity or remain unemployed. Education and training may thus fail to protect one against unemployment. Empirical studies using household level data for developed countries find the expected inverse relationship between unemployment and education as observed by Weisberg and Meltz[28] and Isengard.[29] On the other hand, most developing country studies

---

[25] Mincer, J. 1972. *Schooling, Experience and Earnings*. New York: National Bureau of Economic research (NBER).

[26] Stiglitz, J. E. 1975. "The Theory of Screening, Education and the Distribution of Income," *American Economic Review* 65, No. 3:283-300. Fields, G. S. 2008. "Segmented Labour Market Models in Developing Countries," in *The Oxford Handbook of Philosophy of Economic Science*, eds. Kincaid, H., and D. Ross, (USA: Oxford University Press).

[27] Fields, G. S. 2008. "Segmented Labour Market Models in Developing Countries," in *The Oxford Handbook of Philosophy of Economic Science*, eds. Kincaid, H., and D. Ross, (USA: Oxford University Press).

[28] Weisberg, Y. J., and N. M. Meltz. 1999. "Education and Unemployment in Israel, 1976-1994: Reducing the Anomaly," University of Toronto, Department of Economics Working Paper.

do not find the expected inverse relationship between unemployment and education. As examples, Kuepie, Norman and Roubaud[30] study the effects of education on urban labour market participation and earnings in the West African Economic and Monetary Union (WAEMU) countries and find that unemployment levels generally increase with the level of education, at least until the end of the secondary level of education. Rama[31] considers unemployment in Tunisia and finds that it is concentrated among the young and relatively well educated. This is reaffirmed by the World Bank[32] study which reports that the Tunisian unemployment rate for youth with higher education was 1.6 times higher than those with primary education. Related findings are also reported for Côte d'Ivoire, Ethiopia, Rwanda, Senegal, Tanzania and other low-income countries.[33] Similar conclusions, i.e. of unemployment rising with educational attainment, have been arrived at by studies in other regions and include: Rama[34] for Sri Lanka and Tenjo[35] for Colombia. Rama[36] notes that unemployment is largely voluntary and the underlying problem is that there is a large gap between good jobs and bad jobs. Even among the more developed countries, there are cases where the expected negative relationship

---

[29] Isengard, B. 2003. "Youth Unemployment: Individual Risk Factors and Institutional determinants. A Case Study of Germany and the United Kingdom," *Journal of Youth Studies* 6, No. 4.

[30] Kuepie, M., C. J. Nordman, and F. Roubaud,. 2006. "Education and Labour Market Outcomes in Sub-Saharan West Africa," DIAL Working Paper, 2006/16. Paris: DIAL.

[31] Rama, M. 1998. "How Bad is Unemployment in Tunisia? Assessing Labour Market Efficiency in a Developing Country," *The World Bank Observer* 13, No. 1:59-77.

[32] World Bank. 2003. "Republic of Tunisia: Employment Strategy," Report No. 25456-TUN. Washington, DC: The World Bank.

[33] Cling J-P., F. Gubert, C. J. Nordman, and A. S. Robilliard. 2007. "Youth and Labour Markets in Africa. A Critical Review of Literature," Working Paper No. 49, Département de la Recherche, Agence Française de Développement. World Bank. 2006. *Development and the Next Generation*, *World Development Report 2007*. Washington, DC: The World Bank. Serneels, P. 2004. "The Nature of Unemployment in Urban Ethiopia," CSAE Working Paper, 2004-18, Oxford: Centre for the Study of African Economies.

[34] Rama, M. 1999. *The Sri Lanka Unemployment Problem Revisited.* Washington DC: The World Bank, Development Research Group.

[35] Tenjo, J. 1990. "Opportunities, Aspirations, and Urban Unemployment of Youth: The Case of Colombia," *Economic Development and Cultural Change* 38, No. 4:733-761.

[36] Rama, M. 1999. *The Sri Lanka Unemployment Problem Revisited.* Washington DC: The World Bank, Development Research Group.

between education and unemployment is violated. A well-known case is the relationship between unemployment and education in Israel, which has long been observed to be exhibiting an inverted u-shaped relationship.[37] The review suggests that education, under certain circumstances, may not have a protective effect against unemployment.

4. Models, Data and Variables

The methodological approach utilised in this paper involves estimating different models to evaluate the impact of education in its different forms (years of education, education type, that is, general versus vocational training, level reached) on: (i) the participation in the labour market (employment participation and sectors); and (ii) poverty reduction. The labour force constitutes the population aged 15-64 years and unemployment consists of the working age population who are not working, are available for work, and were actively seeking work during the last one week prior to the survey.[38]

Two models are estimated in establishing: (i) the link between poverty and education; and (ii) the link between unemployment and education. First an ordered logit model is used to establish the probability of being poor given one's educational attainment, controlling for other factors such as age, household head's education (proxy for family background), household head's employment status, and location; among other socio-economic factors. Next, a multinomial logit model is used to establish the probability of being underemployed, fully employed or openly unemployed given individuals' education and training attainment and controlling for other variables such as age, household head's education, gender, location (rural or urban) and other socio economic factors. Individuals who did not indicate their employment status were excluded.

---

[37] Weisberg, Y. J., and N. M. Meltz. 1999. "Education and Unemployment in Israel, 1976-1994: Reducing the Anomaly," University of Toronto, Department of Economics Working Paper.

[38] Generally, this is the definition used in the KNBS labour force surveys. The 2005/06 survey included in the definition of the unemployed: (i) persons who did not work in the reference period due to temporary layoff or who are seasonally unemployed; and (ii) persons who had made arrangements to take up paid or self-employment at a date subsequent to the reference period. The reference period used was 1 week.

4.1. Modelling Effects of Education on Poverty

An ordered logit model is used as in Bigsten and Shimeles[39] and Geda *et al.*[40] to estimate the effects of education on poverty. The dependent variable represents the poverty status of the individuals in a household. The poverty index of the household indicates whether a household is extremely poor, poor or non-poor during the survey period in 2005/6. The index takes a value of zero if the individual lives in a household that is not poor; 1 if (moderately) poor and 2 if extremely poor. An individual is categorised as being in a non-poor household if the household consumption expenditure per adult equivalent is more than the absolute poverty line; moderately poor if the household consumption per adult equivalent is above the food poverty line but below the absolute poverty line and extremely poor if the household consumption per adult equivalent is below the food poverty line. Since these categories have a natural ordering, ordered logit is the appropriate model to employ to compute the associated poverty probabilities.[41]
It is assumed that the probability of being in a particular poverty category is determined by an underlying response variable of individual characteristics (including education and training) whose disturbance term is normally distributed with mean zero and constant variance 1. The logit model has several advantages over the ordinary least squares (OLS) model, the most important of these being a specification that makes predicted probabilities well defined. The model we estimate takes the following form:

$$y^* = \beta' x + \varepsilon \quad \text{.........................(1)}$$

y^* is the dependent dummy variable taking value 0 if non poor; 1 if moderately poor and 2 if extremely poor. β' is a vector of unknown parameters; x is a vector of observed explanatory variables. The explanatory variables used in the application of this model include:

---

[39] Bigsten, A, and A. Shimeles. 2003, "Growth and Poverty Reduction in Ethiopia: Evidence from Household Panel Surveys," *World Development* 31:81-106.

[40] Geda, A., N. De Jong, G. Mwabu, and M. Kimenyi. 2001. "Determinants of Poverty in Kenya: Household-Level Analysis," Kenya Institute for Public Policy Research and Analysis (KIPPRA) DP. 9/2001.

[41] Greene, W. H. 1993. *Econometric Analysis.* New York: MacMillian Publishing Company.

education, training, household characteristics, access to assets and occupational status of household head, among others. The objective is to capture the effects of education and training on poverty and by extension their role in poverty reduction.

An individual's poverty status can be grouped into any of the three poverty categories depending on observable factors (x_s) and unobserved (ε) factors that determine the poverty status. Assuming three categories (0, 1 and 2); and associated probabilities (P_0, P_1 and P_2), an individual would fall in category 0, 1 or 2 where these relationships may be formally presented in the following specification:

$$\begin{aligned} \Pr ob(y=0) &= \phi(-\beta' x) \\ prob(y=1) &= \phi(\mu_1-\beta' x)-\phi(-\beta' x) \quad \text{.........................} (2) \\ prob(y=2) &= 1-\phi(\beta' x+\alpha) \end{aligned}$$

A logistic distribution is assumed (ϕ). Given equation (2) the associated log-likelihood function and its derivatives can be obtained. To obtain the marginal effects of the regressors, x, on the probabilities, the derivative of the function (of each category) is calculated. For the probabilities stated above, the marginal effects of changes in the regressors are given by:

$$\frac{\partial \Pr ob(y=0)}{\partial x} = -\phi(-\beta' x)\beta,$$

$$\frac{\partial \Pr ob(y=1)}{\partial x} = (\phi(-\beta' x)-\phi(\mu-\beta' x)\beta, \text{ and}$$

$$\frac{\partial \Pr ob(y=2)}{\partial x} = \phi(\mu-\beta' x)\beta. \quad \text{.....................} (3)$$

Where, ϕ(.) is the standard normal density function. Equation 2 can be intuitively estimated to obtain the marginal effects of various variables on poverty status, and by extension their roles in poverty reduction.

4.2. Model for Unemployment and Education and Training

A probability model is used to establish effects of education and training on the probability of persons aged 15-64 years employment status while controlling for other socio-economic factors. The general model is given as:

$$y^{*}i = \beta_1' X_{i1} + \varepsilon_{i1} \text{ where, } \varepsilon_i \approx N(0,1) \qquad (4)$$

Where y_i^{*} is a dummy variable that takes the value of 1 if the individual aged 15-64 years is underemployed, 2 if fully employed and 3 if openly unemployed. β_1 is a vector of parameters for the various explanatory variables including education and training; X_{i1} is a vector of exogenous factors; and ε_{i1} is the error term which is normally distributed with the mean of zero and constant variance. The probability response model is defined by transforming βx in equation 1 into a response probability function using a probit model of the form:

$$prob(y_i = 1 \mid x) = P(y = 1 \mid x_1, x_2 \ldots\ldots, x_k) \qquad (5)$$

where x denotes the full set of explanatory variables and y denotes the discrete dependant variables, with outcomes 1, 2 and 3 as described above. The response probability model is defined by transforming βx into a probability (Johnston and Dinardo, 1997) such that:

$$prob(y_i = 1) = F(X_i \beta) \qquad (6)$$

By choosing F to be the standard normal function, we get the probit model given by the cumulative density function of the standard normal distribution

$$prob(y_i = 1) = \Phi(X_i \beta) = \int_{-\infty}^{X_i \beta} \frac{1}{\sqrt{2\pi}} \exp\left(\frac{-z^2}{2}\right) dz \qquad (7)$$

The standard normal transformation $\Phi(\bullet)$ constrains the probability to lie between zero and one. To estimate the above model we use the likelihood function given as:

$$L = \prod_{i=1}^{m} \Phi(X_i \beta)^{y_i} [1 - \Phi(X_i \beta)]^{1-y_i} \quad \ldots\ldots\ldots\ldots\ldots\ldots\ldots\ldots\ldots\ldots\ldots(8)$$

and a log likelihood function given as

$$Ln = \sum_i \{y_i . \ln[\Phi(X_i \beta) + (1 - y_i) \ln[1 - \Phi(X_i \beta)]\} \quad \ldots\ldots\ldots (9)$$

The aim is to obtain the $\hat{\beta}$ that maximises the above log likelihood function. In order to interpret both the sign and the magnitude, we estimate the marginal effects. From equation 3 above, the marginal effects for the probit model for continuous variables can be derived by differentiating equation 3 with respect to the independent variables which yields the probability density function given as:

$$\partial P(Y = 1 / X) / \partial X_k = \beta_k f(X\beta) \quad \ldots\ldots\ldots\ldots\ldots\ldots\ldots\ldots\ldots\ldots(10)$$

Where $f(\bullet) = \dfrac{\partial F(\bullet)}{\partial F(X\beta)}$

The marginal effects for discrete variables are computed using the specification:

$$P(Y = 1) / X_k = 1) - P(Y = 1 / X_k = 0)$$
$$= F(X\beta / X_k = 1) - F(XB / X_k = 0) \quad \ldots\ldots\ldots\ldots\ldots\ldots (11)$$

Thus the probability that an individual was unemployed equals the probability that this alternative occurs. The functional form of the probability function depends on that of the event (unemployment) occurring and on the distribution of stochastic variables. The logistic distribution yields a logit model of the form:

$$prob(y_i = 1) = \wedge(X_i \beta) = \tfrac{\exp X_i \beta}{1 + \exp X_i \beta} \quad \ldots\ldots\ldots\ldots\ldots\ldots (12)$$

Where X_i denotes a set of predictors. To test for the significance of the effect of X_i on the response probability, the null hypothesis is set as $H_0 = 0$, that is, the probability of success is independent of *x*. A Likelihood Ratio (LR) test is carried out, which compares well with the Maximum Likelihood function since the latter is normally distributed in a large sample size. From equation 9 above, we can derive the marginal effects for the model for continuous variables. The marginal effects for discrete variables are computed using the specification:

$$P(Y=1)/X_k=1)-P(Y=1/X_k=0)$$
$$=F(X\beta/X_k=1)-F(XB/X_k=0) \qquad \ldots\ldots\ldots\ldots (13)$$

The parameters of the estimates therefore represent the effect of a given characteristic on the chances of being underemployed, fully employed or openly unemployed. Thus the multinomial logit model was based on the assumption of three exclusive choices (fully employed, underemployed and openly unemployed).

4.3. Data and Variables

The main data source for this investigation was the Kenya Integrated Household Budget (KIHBS) 2005/06 survey data collected by the Kenya National Bureau of Statistics (KNBS). It contains information covering a variety of dimensions including incomes and expenditures, education of all household members, labour supply, employment status, asset ownership, and land holdings. The study sample mainly constituted the labour force that is individuals aged 15-64 years and their characteristics. Following this classification, sample size consisted of 22,792 observations (18.4 percent unemployed, 63.6 percent fully employed and 17.9 percent openly unemployed).

The variables used in the analysis include: educational attainment or level of education and training completed - primary education (1 = primary education), secondary education (1 = secondary education), university education (1 = university education), technical training (1 = technical training) household characteristics (household size, age of household head, sex of household head); type of employment (wage, non-wage, sector of employment); highest level of education attained by household member; physical capital (area of cultivated land owned, number of livestock; occupation (main income source e.g. manufacturing, agriculture, etc); and region of residence (urban = 0 or rural = 1). Sex (1 =

male), marital status (1 = married), employment sectors (public, private, informal), are dummy variables taking the value of one, otherwise zero.

5. Empirical Results

5.1. Descriptive Statistics

The summary statistics are presented in Table 1-12. The mean household size is 6 members, and the means for consumption per adult equivalent and wage was Ksh. 3,289 and Ksh. 4,269 respectively. The average number of years of schooling in Kenya is 8.5 years indicating that the majority of Kenyans have only attained primary education.

Table 1-12. Summary Statistics

Variable	Observation	Mean	Std. Deviation	Min.	Max.
Secondary Education	22499	0.218	0.413	0	1
University Education	22499	0.012	0.109	0	1
Technical Training	22488	0.223	0.416	0	1
Consumption per Adult Equivalent (Ksh)	28411	3,289	5632	16	191,734
Years of Education	22499	8.451	3.313	1	19
Age	28533	33.285	12.440	15	64
Gender	28533	0.526	0.499	0	1
Experience	21577	9.600	3.486	0	12
Experience Squared	21577	104.308	52.153	0	144
Location	28411	0.667	0.471	0	1
Household Size	28411	6	3	1	29
Monthly Wages (Ksh)	21577	4,269	20,439	0	775,000
Monthly Public Wages (Ksh)	1,283	20,024	32,095	0	775,000
Monthly Private Wages (Ksh)	1,094	24,021	62,432	0	640,000
Monthly Informal Wages	10,653	1,882	7,274	0	350,000

5.2. Effects of Education and Training on Poverty

The results on the effects of education and technical training on poverty status while controlling for other factors such as individual and household characteristics such as age, gender and physical capabilities are presented in Table 1-13. Educational status, especially technical training, secondary education and university education, significantly reduces the probability of household members being poor compared to the attainment of only primary education. This suggests the critical role played by education in poverty reduction. Increasing the aggregate number of years of schooling, especially by promoting post primary education would decrease poverty probably because secondary education and tertiary education (university and technical education) are associated with acquisition of skills and hence higher earnings. This finding is consistent with Manda *et al.*[42] who established that earnings for employed workers increase with level of education.

Households with a head who was fully employed had a low risk of being extremely poor. Consequently, tackling underemployment would contribute towards further reduction in poverty levels. The fact that household members who were engaged in the informal sector were earning low incomes relative to their counterparts in the formal public and private sector implies that besides targeting the informal sector for employment creation, issues of productivity need to be addressed concurrently.

The effects on residential area are captured through the location variables which highlight not only whether an individual resides in a rural or urban area but also which province they live in. The marginal effects results show that residing in rural areas significantly increases the probability of being extremely poor and poverty rates are relatively higher in rural areas than in urban areas. Households in rural areas have limited access to better paying economic opportunities resulting in a lower welfare status.

Demographic factors, as captured through marital status and household size, play a role on either increasing or reducing the risk of being extremely poor. Perhaps, this is due to the associated increase in dependency ratios, especially if the number of children and the elderly in a given household is higher than the number of the working age population. Households headed by a married person depict low probabilities of being poor relative to their counterparts. Gender also plays a role in poverty

[42] Manda D. K., G. Mwabu, and M. S. Kimenyi. 2002. "Human capital Externalities and Returns to Education in Kenya," KIPPRA Discussion Paper No 13. Nairobi: Kenya Institute for Public Policy Research and Analysis.

status. Female headed households have a higher probability of being extremely poor relative to male headed household and married couples staying together. These demographic characteristics show a need to encourage strong social systems as one way of tackling poverty in an environment where the strength of social networks is threatened.

Table 1-13. Marginal Effects after Ordered Logit of Education and Training on Poverty Status

Marginal effects after ordered logit (z values in parentheses)			
Variables	**Poverty outcome for extremely poor (2)**	**Poverty outcome for moderately poor (1)**	**Poverty outcome for non-poor (0)**
Individual Characteristics			
Secondary Education	-0.078* (-10.48)	0.019* (12.25)	0.0597* (9.70)
University Education	-0.282* (-20.81)	-0.079* (-4.34)	0.361* (11.47)
Technical Training	-0.134 * (-17.99)	0.027 * (18.81)	0.108 * (15.71)
Age in years	0.0012* (3.60)	-0.0004* (-3.58)	-0.0085* (-3.60)
Gender of household head	-0.030* (-4.66)	0.009* (4.62)	0.021* (4.65)
Marital Status	0.052* (6.33)	-0.016* (-6.20)	-0.036* (-6.33)
Location	-0.174* (-21.13)	0.595* (17.30)	-0.114* (22.02)
Household Characteristics			
Household Size	0.069* (51.38)	-0.0208* (-26.70)	0.048* (-51.92)
Employment in agriculture	0.024* (2.99)	-0.007* (-2.93)	-0.016* (-3.01)
Trade/business	-0.030* (-3.24)	0.0083* (3.58)	-0.022* (3.12)*
Wage Employment	-0.040* (-5.29)	0.011* (5.69)*	0.029* (5.11)*

dy/dx is for discrete change of dummy variable from 0 to 1.

Dependent variable is poverty status taking value 0= non poor; 2=moderately poor, 2=extremely poor. z values in parenthesis; significant at 1 percent (*), 5 percent (**) and ten percent (***).

5.3. Effects of Education on Unemployment

The estimation results on the effects of education (controlling for other observable variables) on reducing unemployment are presented in Table 1-14. The results show that higher education plays a critical role in reducing the risk of being unemployed. Lower levels of education increase the risk of being openly unemployed and or under-employed. The attainment of university education and technical training reduces the probability of being underemployed and openly unemployed while the attainment of only primary education increases the risk of being either underemployed and or openly unemployed.

There appears to be an advantage for male workers relative to potential for female workers in the labour market. The finding reflects the general observation that in many developing countries, women tend to have a lower chance at obtaining employment owing to their lower educational attainment levels as compared to their male counterparts. Women also face challenges of balancing between their reproductive and productive roles which decreases their probability of receiving job offers in the formal labour market.

The findings indicate that persons with physical handicaps are more likely to be openly unemployed. Having no physical handicap reduces the probability of being openly unemployed and underemployed. This finding is consistent with Serneels (2007) who posits that employers use physical appearance as a screening device in offering jobs to their first-time potential employees. This calls for targeted interventions for the physically handicapped population to attain some capabilities so that they are able to earn a living and to ensure that they are not trapped in poverty.

The effects of economic status are captured through the average monthly total household consumption expenditure per capita. Persons from medium- and high-income groups are less likely to be unemployed compared to the persons from low-income groups. Perhaps this is because of the strong social networks that the high- and middle-income groups have in job seeking behaviour relative to the low-income groups. The potential labour force from high-income groups have also attained higher levels of education and hence less risk of unemployment and increased possibility of their placement into the labour market. This shows the importance of social capital and human capital in determining employment outcomes and the contribution of the ineffective labour market in Kenya.

Table 1-14. Marginal Effects of Education and Training on Unemployment (open and under-employment)

Variables Individual Characteristics	Underemployed (1) Marginal effects - *dy/dx* (Standard errors in parentheses)	Open Unemployment (3) Marginal effects - *dy/dx* (Standard errors in parentheses)
Secondary Education	-0.0071 (0.007)	0.036* (0.0065)
University Education	-0.0343* (0.008)	-0.0076 (0.352)
Technical Training	0.0303 (0.0355)	-0.0433 ** (0.0199)
Age in years	-0.0109 (0.0017)*	-0.190 (0.0017)*
Age in years squared	0.00016 (0.00002)*	0.00013* (0.00002)
Gender	0.0539 (0.006)*	0.085* (0.0052)
Marital Status	-0.0125 (0.0085)	0.0139** (0.0065)
Physical handicap	-0.028 (0.31)	0.105* (0.037)
Location	0.0915 (0.007)*	-0.1074* (0.00696)
Household Characteristics		
Middle Economic Status	-0.0086 (0.0072)	-0.029* (0.00598)
High Economic Status	-0.051 (0.0085)*	-0.063 (0.007)*
Household Size	0.0017 (0.0012)	0.0049* (0.00084)
Provincial Dummies (Province=1)		
Central Province	0.0026 (0.0209)	-0.0468* (0.0089)
Coast Province	-0.009 (0.0215)	0.029** (0.0136)
Eastern Province	0.321 (0.0219)	-0.0386* (0.126)
North Eastern Province	-0.0119 (0.044)	0.254* (0.044)
Nyanza Province	0.136* (0.027)	-0.0.0611* (0.008)
Rift Valley Province	0.0222 (0.0209)	-0.035* (0.0093)
Western Province	0.183* (0.029)	-0.0384* (0.0093)
No of Observation	18,020	18,020

dy/dx is for discrete change of dummy variable from 0 to 1

Dependent variable is Employ taking value 1= Underemployed; 2=Fully employed, Openly Unemployed =3; Standard errors in parenthesis; significant at 1 percent (*) and 5 percent (**).

6. Conclusions and Policy Implications

This study analyzes the effects of education and technical training on unemployment and poverty using the most recent micro data for Kenya i.e. the KIHBS, 2005/6. A key finding is that relative to higher levels of educational attainment, realisation of only primary education is associated with an increased likelihood of being poor. Specifically; secondary education, technical training, and university education reduce the probability of a household member being extremely poor relative to attaining only primary education; and individuals with only primary education are more likely to be moderately poor than those with university education. Consequently; while increasing access to primary education is critical in laying the foundations for entry into higher education, post primary education is crucial in reducing the incidence of poverty.

In other findings, relative to the attainment of only primary education, individuals with secondary education exhibit a higher chance of being openly unemployed (underemployment rates are not significantly different). It is possible that secondary school graduates are queuing for better jobs – since they are more likely to come from relatively better off households than primary graduates, and are thus more likely to afford to be unemployed. It is also possible that the secondary school graduates still lack the requisite skills needed in the labour market—given that both technical training and university education reduce the risk of being openly unemployed.

The association of technical training and university education with a lower likelihood of open unemployment and the role of a university education in reducing the risk of being underemployed suggests that making post primary education, especially technical training and university education, more accessible would be an important step for developing an employable and skilled labour force.

Investments in human capital may have greater impacts if jobs perceived to be of good quality (and that are sufficiently productive) are created. This could address the problem of poverty and also assist job seekers queuing for better jobs as could be possible with secondary graduates. Kuepie *et al.*, (2006) found that even when education fails to have a protective effect against unemployment it may still offer substantial growth in earnings in the informal sector (Kuepie *et al.,* 2006). This observation implies that investments made in education are worthwhile (considering the unavailability of demanded jobs in the formal sector) particularly if the government can support the growth of the informal sector through policies that make these jobs more attractive even to those individuals who can afford unemployment.

References

Appleton, S., J. Knight, L. Song, and Q. Xia.2001. "Labour Retrenchment in China: Determinants and Consequences," unpublished paper.

Bae, H. S., and H. J. Song. 2006. "Youth Unemployment and the Role of Career and Technical Education: A Study of the Korean Labour Market, " *Career and Technical Education Research, Volume 31, No 1.*

Barro, R., J. 1991. "Economic Growth in a Cross-section of Countries," *Quarterly Journal of Economics* 106 (2): 407-43.

Bedi, A., P. K. Kimalu, D. K. Manda, and N. N. Nafula. 2002. "The Decline in Primary School Enrolment in Kenya," KIPPRA DP No. 14. Nairobi: KIPPRA.

Bigsten, A, and A. Shimeles. 2003, "Growth and Poverty Reduction in Ethiopia: Evidence from Household Panel Surveys," *World Development* 31:81-106.

Blaug, M. 1972. "Correlation between Education and Earnings," *Higher Education* 1, No. 1: 53-76.

Central Bureau of Statistics (CBS). 2002. *Kenya 1999 Population and Housing Census: The Labour Force Monograph, Analytical Report Volume IX.* Nairobi: Central Bureau of Statistics, Ministry of Planning and National Development. Government of Kenya.

—. 2003. Report of the 1998/99 Labour Force Survey, Nairobi: CBS.

Cling J-P., F. Gubert, C. J. Nordman, and A. S. Robilliard. 2007. "Youth and Labour Markets in Africa. A Critical Review of Literature," Working Paper No. 49, Département de la Recherche, Agence Française de Développement.

Dias R., and D. Posel. 2006. "Unemployment, Education and Skills Constraints in Post-Apartheid South Africa." Paper presented at the Conference Accelerated and Shared Growth in South Africa: Determinants, Constraints and Opportunities" Johannesburg, South Africa, October 2006.

Dickens W. T., and K. Lang. 1996. "An Analysis of the Nature of Unemployment in Sri Lanka," *Journal of Development Studies* 31(4): 620-636.

Fields, G. S. 1980. *Poverty Inequality and Development.* Cambridge: Cambridge University Press.

—. "A Guide to Multisector Labour Market Models," Paper prepared for the World Bank Labour Market Conference, Washington D.C., USA, November 2004.

—. 2008. "Segmented Labour Market Models in Developing Countries," in *The Oxford Handbook of Philosophy of Economic Science*, eds. Kincaid, H., and D. Ross, (USA: Oxford University Press).

Geda, A., N. De Jong, G. Mwabu, and M. Kimenyi. 2001. "Determinants of Poverty in Kenya: Household-Level Analysis," Kenya Institute for Public Policy Research and Analysis (KIPPRA) DP. 9/2001.

Glewwe, P. 1989. "Unemployment in Developing Countries: Economist's Models in Light of Evidence from Sri Lanka," *International Economic Journal* 1, No.4:1-17.

Godia, G. 1987. "Education and the Unemployment Problem in Kenya," *The Journal of Negro Education*56, No.3 :356-367.

Government of Kenya. 1965. *Sessional Paper No. 1 on African Socialism and its Application to Planning in Kenya*. Nairobi: Government Printer.

—. (various issues). *Economic Survey*. Nairobi: Central Bureau of Statistics: Government Printer.

Greene, W. H. 1993. *Econometric Analysis.* New York: MacMillian Publishing Company.

Ikiara G. K, and N. S. Ndung'u. 1997. *Employment and Labour Market During Adjustment: The Case of Kenya.* Geneva: ILO.

International Labour Organization (ILO). 1976. *Employment, Growth and Basic Needs: A One World Problem*. Geneva: International Labour Office.

—. (ILO). 2008. *Global Employment Trends 2008*. Geneva: International Labour Office.

Isengard, B. 2003. "Youth Unemployment: Individual Risk Factors and Institutional determinants. A Case Study of Germany and the United Kingdom," *Journal of Youth Studies* 6, No. 4.

Johnston, J., and J. Dinardo. 1997. *Econometric Methods*. The McGraw-Hill Companies.

Kenya National Bureau of Statistics. 2007a. *Kenya Integrated Household Budget Survey (2005/2006)*. Nairobi: Government Printer.

—. 2007b. *Basic Report on Well-being in Kenya: Based on Kenya Integrated Household Budget Survey (KIHBS) 2005/06*. Nairobi: KNBS.

Kiiru J., E. Onsomu, and F. Wamalwa. 2009. "Education, Training and Youth Unemployment in Kenya," Working Paper, Global Development

Network (GDN) and African Economic Research Consortium (AERC) Institutional Capacity Strengthening Project.

Kimalu, P., N. Nafula, D. K. Manda, G. Mwabu, and M. S. Kimenyi. 2002. "A Situational Analysis of Poverty in Kenya," KIPPRA Working Paper No. 6. Nairobi: KIPPRA.

Kingdon, G., and J. Knight. 1999. "Unemployment in South Africa: A Spatial Approach, Centre for the Study of African Economies," CSAE Working Paper 1999-12. Oxford: Centre for the Study of African Economies.

—. 2001. "Unemployment in South Africa: The Nature of the Beast." CSAE Working Paper, Centre for the Study of African Economies.

Kuepie, M., C. J. Nordman, and F. Roubaud,. 2006. "Education and Labour Market Outcomes in Sub-Saharan West Africa," DIAL Working Paper, 2006/16. Paris: DIAL.

Manda, D. K. 2004. "*Globalisation and the Labour Market in Kenya,*" KIPPRA Discussion Paper No. 31. Nairobi: Kenya Institute for Public Policy Research and Analysis.

Manda D. K., G. Mwabu, and M. S. Kimenyi. 2002. "Human Capital Externalities and Returns to Education in Kenya," KIPPRA Discussion Paper No. 13. Nairobi: Kenya Institute for Public Policy Research and Analysis.

Mincer, J. 1972. *Schooling, Experience and Earnings*. New York: National Bureau of Economic research (NBER).

—. 1991. Education and Unemployment. National Bureau of Economic research (NBER) Working Paper No. 3838. Cambridge.

Mwabu, G. 2000. *Poverty in Kenya: Profiles and Determinants, Department of Economics*. University of Nairobi and Ministry of Finance and Planning, unpublished paper.

Mwabu G., M. W. Kimenyi, P. K. Kimalu, N. N. Nafula, and D. K. Manda. 2002. "Predicting Household Poverty; A Methodological Note," *African Development Review* 15, No. 1.

Noor, A. 1980. "Education and Basic Needs," Staff Working Paper No. 450. Washington D.C.

Oiro, M. W., G. Mwabu, and D. K. Manda. 2003. "Poverty and Employment in Kenya," Discussion Paper, Kenya Institute for Public Policy Research and Analysis, Nairobi KIPPRA, Nairobi.

Onsomu, E. N., D. Muthaka, and D. K. Manda. 2006. Determinants and Strategies for Expanding Secondary Education in Kenya. KIPPRA, Discussion Paper.

Pollin, R., M. Githinji, and J. Heintz. 2007. *An Employment-Targeted Economic Programme for Kenya*. Amherst: Political Economy Research Institute (PERI).

Rama, M. 1998. "How Bad is Unemployment in Tunisia? Assessing Labour Market Efficiency in a Developing Country," *The World Bank Observer* 13, No. 1:59-77.

—. 1999. *The Sri Lanka Unemployment Problem Revisited.* Washington DC: The World Bank, Development Research Group.

Government of Kenya. 1965. *Sessional Paper No. 10 of 1965 African Socialism and its Application to Planning in Kenya.* Nairobi: Government Printer.

—. 2007. *Economic Survey.* Government Printer, Nairobi.

Sen, A. 1984. *Resources, Values and Development*. New Delhi: Oxford University Press.

—. 1999. *Development as Freedom*. New Delhi: Oxford University Press.

Serneels, P. 2004. "The Nature of Unemployment in Urban Ethiopia," CSAE Working Paper, 2004-18, Oxford: Centre for the Study of African Economies.

—. 2007. "The Nature of Unemployment among Young Men in Urban Ethiopia. *Review of Development Economics*," 11, No. 1:170-186.

Stiglitz, J. E. 1975. "The Theory of Screening, Education and the Distribution of Income," *American Economic Review* 65, No. 3:283-300.

Streeten, P. 1977. "The Distinctive Features of a Basic Needs Approach to Development," *International Development Review* 3:8-16.

Tenjo, J. 1990. "Opportunities, Aspirations, and Urban Unemployment of Youth: The Case of Colombia," *Economic Development and Cultural Change* 38, No. 4:733-761.

Tilak, J. B. G. 1986. "Education in an Unequal World," in *Educational Planning: A Long Term Perspective,* ed. Raza, M., (New Delhi: Concept Publishing Company).

—. 1994. *Education for Development in Asia.* New Delhi: Sage Publications.

—. "Education and Poverty," Keynote address delivered at the Poverty Conference on "Education—A Road Out of Poverty?" Sweden, 2001.

UNECA. 2005. "African Agricultural Performance in Perspective: Constraints, Achievements and the Impact of Multilateral Trade Reforms" in *Mutual Review of Development Effectiveness in the Context of NEPAD,* (Addis Ababa).

UNESCO. 1997. *Adult Education in a Polarizing World*, Paris: UNESCO.

United Republic of Tanzania, (URT) (1997). *The National Employment Policy,* Ministry of Labour, Youth Development and Sports, Dar es Salaam.

Verner, D. 2004. "Education and its Poverty-Reducing Effects: The Case of Paraiba, Brazil," World Bank Policy Research Working Paper No. 3321 The World Bank.

Wambugu A., B. Munga, and E. Onsomu. 2010. "Unemployment in Kenya: A Situational Analysis," NESC Discussion Paper No. 1/2010.

Weisberg, Y. J., and N. M. Meltz. 1999. "Education and Unemployment in Israel, 1976-1994: Reducing the Anomaly," University of Toronto, Department of Economics Working Paper.

World Bank. 2003. "Republic of Tunisia: Employment Strategy," Report No. 25456-TUN. Washington, DC: The World Bank.

—. 2006. *Development and the Next Generation, World Development Report 2007*. Washington, DC: The World Bank.

LABOUR MARKET COMPETITIVENESS OF YOUNG PEOPLE IN RUSSIA: DOES EDUCATION PROTECT THEM FROM UNEMPLOYMENT?

IRINA SOBOLEVA

1. Introduction

In today's world, the rise of youth unemployment constitutes a major challenge for development. As described in economic literature, unemployment in the beginning of one's labour market career leads to negative consequences such as scarring.[1] On the one hand, failure to integrate in the world of work may have a dangerous psychological impact on young jobseekers, gradually forming a culture of unemployment. On the other hand, employers may be reluctant to hire applicants with a past history of unemployment.

The recent economic crisis led to an exacerbation of the youth unemployment problem all over the world.[2] Russia was no exception: as compared to older workers, the younger generation proved to be more vulnerable. One possible explanation may lie in the quality and type of

---

[1] Belzil, C. 1995. "Unemployment Duration Stigma and Reemployment Earnings," *Canadian Journal of Economics* 28, No. 3: 568-585; Blanchflower, D.G., and R. Freeman. 2000. *Youth Employment and Joblessness*. Chicago: University of Chicago Press; Scarpetta, S., Sonnet A., and T. Manfredi. 2010. "Rising Youth Unemployment During the Crisis: How to Prevent Negative Long-term Consequences on a Generation?" OECD Social, Employment and Migration Working Papers. No. 6, Paris: OECD. Skans, O. N. 2011. "Scarring Effects of the First Labour Market Experience," IFAU, HECER, UCLS and IZA. IZA Discussion Paper No. 5565. Bonn: IZA.

[2] International Labour Organization. 2010. *Global Employment Trends for Youth: August 2010: Special Issue on the Impact of the Global Economic Crisis on Youth*. Geneva: ILO.

education received by young people. This paper discusses the impact of post-Soviet educational reform on the employability of youth.

2. Youth Labour Market Trends

2.1. Unemployment Trends

In post-Soviet Russia, young people graduating from educational institutions are no longer guaranteed a smooth transfer to the world of work and many of them experience unemployment. The scale and dynamics of unemployment have been different according to the age group of young people (Fig. 1-5).

Through both decades of market transformation the largest scale of unemployment is characteristic for the age group 15-19 years old. A significant rise in adolescent unemployment during the 1990s was accompanied by an even more pronounced drop in the overall labour force participation rate (Fig. 1-6). The first signs of the strengthening of the adolescent labour market only appeared in 2006-2007 just to be overturned by the crisis in 2008.

In the age group 20-24 years encompassing the largest share of college and university graduates, the rise of unemployment during the recession of the 1990s was not so sharp and the recovery from the unemployment decline was more pronounced. But with the recent crisis, the unemployment rate has peaked, followed by a very slight fall during 2010. In contrast to the crisis of 1998, this time the middle youth group demonstrated a pattern of rising economic activity, and preferred job search to economic inactivity.

On their part, the senior youth group demonstrates another story. In many respects, this category of workers resembles the adult working population. Until the recent crisis, its unemployment dynamics closely followed fluctuations of the average unemployment rate. However, the negative impact of the crisis for this group was relatively more severe than average and its unemployment rate did not follow the downward turn of the average rate in 2010.

Fig. 1-5. Unemployment Rate Dynamics by Age Group.

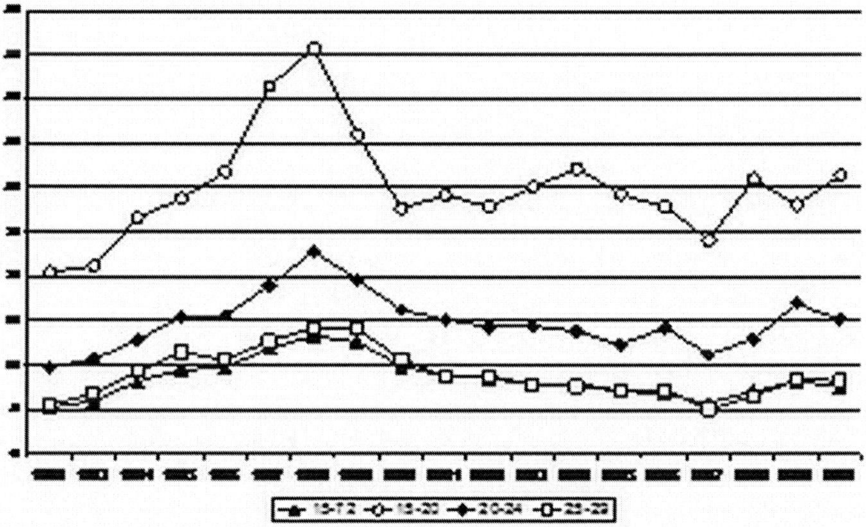

Fig. 1-6. Economic Activity Rate Dynamics by Age Group.

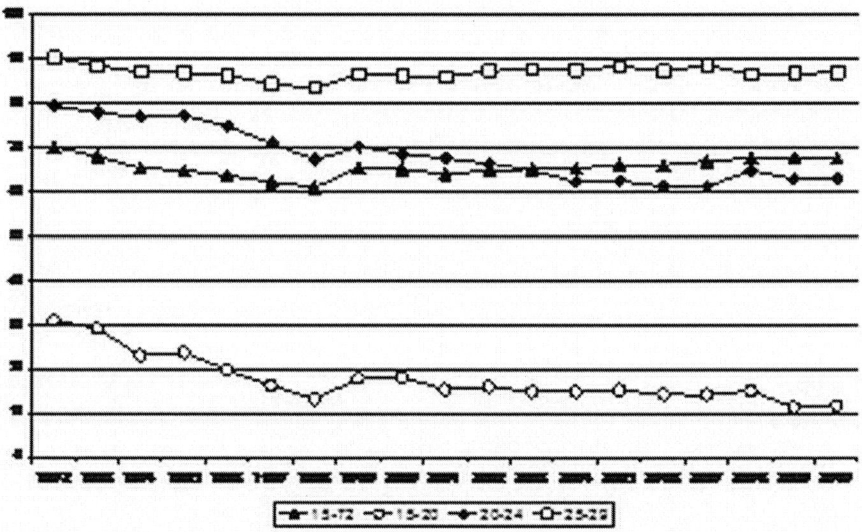

2.2. Patterns of Labour Market Behaviour

The main formal competitive labour market advantage of the younger generation is higher educational attainment while the main informal advantage is their quick adaptability to labour market demands. Researchers have noted that this leads to a "dualistic" career strategy. On the one hand, they "nurse" an ideal goal of self-realization in a profession, while on the other hand, they are pushed by pragmatic interests to the less rewarding sphere of work content, although rendering better salary options.[3] A higher and growing propensity of the young to migrate to more rewarding jobs irrespective of their educational profile is documented in the two rounds of the People's Security Survey (PSS) conducted by our research team in 2002 and 2007 (Table 1-15).

As a result, young people tend to be concentrated in labour market sectors with relatively higher wages and better working conditions such as public administration, financial activity and trade (the share of youth in total employment was 33.2%, 33.7% and 31.7% respectively) and least willingly opt for health (17.4%), education (17.8%), or manufacturing (22.3%). The share of those employed in jobs not matching the specialty acquired during university increased from 36% for graduates of 1993-1996 to 56% for those of 2001-2004 and reached the limit of 74% in 2008.[4]

One of the most pressing problems mentioned in our interviews with employers[5] in manufacturing enterprises was the unwillingness of the young to opt for "real sector" jobs. At the same time, the results of the two PSS rounds demonstrated an improvement in subjective perceptions of the younger generation concerning their labour market chances during the recovery decade.

---

[3] Avraamova, E., Kulagina E., and E. Vurpahovskaya. 2007. "Behaviour of Graduates on the Labour Market: New Trends [In Russian]," *Chelovek i Trud* No. 9: 48-55; Skutneva, S.V. 2006. "Youth Strategies for Self-Realisation in the World of Work" *Sociologic Research* No. 3: 89-92.

[4] Shishkin, S.V. 2005. "*Funktsionalnaya i socialnaya differentsiazia rossiiskoi sistemi visshego obrazovania* [Functional and Social Differentiation of University Education] in *Problemi doctupnosti visshego obrazovaniya,* ed. Shishkin, S.V., (Moscow: IISP), 13; Nikolaeva, E. 2011. "Development of the System of Training of Engineers and Skilled Workers for the Russian Economy [In Russian]," Paper presented at the Expert Group "Labour Market, Professional Education and Migration" in the NRU HSE, Moscow, Russia. April 2.

[5] We have conducted 15 interviews with employers: 10 in manufacturing enterprises and 5 in finance and trade.

Table 1-15. Distribution of Answers to the Question "How Important is it for You to Pursue the Received Profession when Choosing a Job?"

Category of Respondents	Share by answer			
	Very important	Rather important	Not very important	Not important at all
2002				
All respondents	23.2	34.7	32.5	9.6
Aged 15-29	20.3	32.5	36.4	10.8
2007				
All respondents	19.1	32.4	33.6	15.0
Aged 15-29	14.3	29.7	34.8	21.1

Source: Russian People's Security Survey 2002 and 2007.

Regretfully, we did not manage to conduct a third PSS round reflecting the change in perceptions with the beginning of the crisis. However, there is evidence of growing pessimism especially among the young. A survey conducted by the Fund "Public Opinion" (FPO) in February-March 2009 revealed that at least 45% of young people expected to encounter serious difficulties in their job search. Statistical data also points to a shrinking labour market for the young. According to the regular Labour Force Survey (LFS) conducted by Rosstat, the share of university educated youth (15-29) in total unemployment increased from 14.6% in February 2008 to 24.6% in February 2009. According to expert assessments of more than 1.5 million graduates of 2009, only about 700 thousand succeeded in finding a job during the next 6 months.[6] The result of a rise in youth unemployment during the crisis may be to a large extent rooted in the characteristics of vocational education.

[6] Trud. 2010. "Useless Education". 16 August: http://www.trud.ru/article/16-08-2010/248401 (accessed May 31, 2011).

Table 1-16. Distribution of Answers to the Question "Is it Probable that You will Lose Your Job in the Next 12 Months?"

Category of Respondents	Share by answer				
	Yes	Most possibly yes	Most possibly no	No	Hard to say
2002					
All respondents	6.1	8.9	24.6	44,0	16.3
Aged 15-29	6.7	8.0	31.7	37,5	16.0
2007					
All respondents	5.2	9.1	23.1	48.7	13.9
Aged 15-29	4.0	10.2	26.5	46.9	12.3

Source: Russian People's Security Survey 2002 and 2007.

Table 1-17. Distribution of Answers to the Question "In Case You Lose Your Job, Do You Think You will Find a New Decent One?"

Category of Respondents	Share by answer				
	Yes easily	Yes, but not easily	Most possibly no	No	Hard to say
2002					
All respondents	25.2	38.6	12.7	11.2	12.3
Aged 15-29	32.1	43.3	9.9	3.5	11.2
2007					
All respondents	33.3	35.9	11.9	8.1	10.7
Aged 15-29	51.9	30.9	4.6	1.9	10.8

Source: Russian People's Security Survey 2002 and 2007.

3. Flows of Vocational Education

Previously, and to this day, Russia has had a well-developed education system and in international comparisons, the educational attainment of the population ranks high.[7] But, recent trends are controversial.

The architects of the post-Soviet educational reform expected that reliance on market forces would eventually lead to better performance of educational institutions and produce gains in efficiency and quality. The practical implementation of reform started with the reduction of the

[7] Barro, R., and J. Lee. 2001. "International Data on Educational Attainment: Updates and Implications," *Oxford Economic Papers* 53, No. 3: 541-563.

governmental expenditure on education[8]. Centralized state control over the activities of the higher education institutions loosened. As a result, the steady cuts in financing were accompanied by the rapid growth of the number of universities and of enrolment rates[9]. The declining resources allocated to the sphere of education were being spread among a growing number of institutions and students. With the meagre resources in their possession, many colleges and universities had no other choice but to extend their commercial admission to replenish their budget with tuition fees.

3.1. Quality Erosion

Commercialisation of vocational education has set in motion mechanisms reproducing human capital mismatches and quality erosion.

The overwhelming majority of families (from 60% to 85% according to different surveys[10]) intend to give children nothing less than university education. According to expert assessments, the share of school-leavers admitted to universities the same year amounts to 70%, and of those who have participated in entrance exams to 90%.[11]

An abundance of recent university graduates makes employers raise their formal requirements. According to surveys carried out in the mid-2000s, 90% of employers demanded a university diploma when hiring any kind of managerial and professional staff, with this percentage that is equal to 50% at the time of hiring clerks and skilled workers. Thus, university education begins to act as a formal pass to decent work. In this situation many families make a forced choice for cheap low-quality education schemes to obtain a university diploma poorly backed up with real knowledge and skills.

---

[8] During the 1990s, its GDP share fell from 4.2% to 3.1%. Taking into account the crisis GDP decline, the overall reduction in educational expenditure was very substantial: in real terms it reduced to about a half of the pre-reform amount.

[9] Between 1990 and 2010, the number of public universities increased from 514 to 662 and another 452 private universities were established. The enrolment in tertiary education increased of almost 3 times.

[10] Fund “Public Opinion”. 2010. *Investment in Education and Social Mobility* [In Russian]. http://bd.fom.ru/pdf/edmom10.pdf (accessed May 31, 2011); Roschina, Y. M. 2006. “Social Differentiation of Youth in Professional Education [In Russian],” *Otechestvennie Zapiski*, 3, No. 30: http://www.strana-oz.ru/?numid=30&article=1266 (accessed May 31, 2011).

[11] Roschina Y. M., and M. A. Drugov. 2003. “Sotsialnie determinanti neravenstava doctupa [Social Determinants of Unequal Access],” in *Problemi doctupnosti visshego obrazovaniya,* ed. Shishkin, S.V., (Moscow: IISP).

Besides insufficient financial resources, there are other triggers of quality erosion. The process of human capital accumulation is interactive: it requires input of motivation and effort from students involved.[12] Thus if consumers of education services are seeking formal certificates it is a rational strategy to opt for cheaper educational schemes reducing their total costs[13]. This stimulates mild forms of corruption associated with deliberate lowering of the quality of standards by mutual agreement of producer and consumer (opportunistic behaviour on both sides). The result is grim: only about 15% of universities and academies currently operating in Russia meet the requirements of the European quality standards.[14]

Another factor negatively impacting education outcomes is extending the practice of combining work and studying[15]. Lowering education standards trigger off the mechanisms pushing students into the labour market. On the one hand, opportunistic behaviour of the 'sellers of educational services' allows students enough time for regular work. While on the other hand, employers regard recent graduates as a pig in a poke and pose an additional demand to jobseekers' work experience. The students' reaction is well predictable—they are keen to acquire an employment history before graduation usually at the cost of regular absenteeism at lectures.

3.2. Human Capital Mismatch

With over-reliance on market forces the structure of the education system has been increasingly shaped by demand of families possessing little information on labour market trends.[16] The result is the gradual destruction of VET (Table 1-18).

---

[12] Schultz, T. W. 1970. *Investment in Human Capital: the Role of Education and of Research.* New York: Free Pr, 82-83.

[13] According to university teachers' assessments, 50% to 90% (depending on the institution) of students seek first of all a diploma and only from 10% to 40% are interested in acquiring knowledge and skills.

[14] Verbitskaya, L. 2006. "Interview of the Day," *Moscow news,* No. 22. July 16.

[15] According to different surveys before the crisis, shrinkage of youth labour market from 50% to 75% of students in big cities had a regular full-time job. Today many of them form a pool of unregistered unemployed.

[16] Bolotov, V. 2003. *Malogo EGE ne budet* [The Uniform State Exam Postponed]. Izvestia; Nikolaeva, E. 2011. "Development of the System of Training of Engineers and Skilled Workers for the Russian Economy [In Russian]," Paper presented at the Meeting of Expert Group "Labour Market, Professional Education and Migration" in the NRU HSE, Moscow, Russia. April, 2.

Table 1-18. Dynamics of the Number of Graduates from Different Levels of Vocational Education (index, 1990=100)

Education level	Index							
	1995	1998	2000	2002	2004	2006	2008	2009
Vocational	66.1	61.7	60.0	58.6	55.7	53.4	47.5	42.3
Lower level tertiary	74.5	86.2	91.1	105.0	110.1	109.9	105.4	108.5
University	100.4	124.9	158.4	209.5	268.4	312.5	338.7	325.5

Calculated upon Rosstat data.

The destruction of the 'working class culture' leads to a growing unwillingness of young people—usually supported by parents—to enter manual occupations. According to the FPO survey conducted in June 2007, about ¾ of large city dwellers and about the same share of respondents aged 18-35 years consider going to vocational schools "degrading". Reluctance to send their children to vocational schools on the part of their parents is explained by a wide range of reasons like "very low educational standards", "bad company", "drinking, debauchery and narcotics", and "no chances to find a decent job".[17]

According to the FPO survey, among specialties associated with career and life success, economics and management (45% of respondents) and legal studies (32%) take the lead. The IT ranking 3rd , was mentioned only by 8% of respondents while the other technical specialties together barely made up 4%. Medical and teaching professions kept at the end of ratings with a negligible 2-3%.[18] As a result, discrepancies between occupational profile of the new labour market entrants and the *de facto* demand of the employers have been gradually widening.

Until the recent crisis, much of the national human capital mismatch remained hidden by the artificial bias in the labour demand engendered by the rapidly-spreading Dutch disease. A rise in oil prices made extractive industries and the new sectors of informational and financial infrastructure the key beneficiaries of growth. Other services and trade also gained from the oil money spill-over. These sectors provided abundant mid-level office jobs which offered decent wages and work conditions and were well-suited for the younger cohorts with 'general' university education.

---

[17] http://www.rambler.ru/news/science/education/534785011.html (accessed May 31, 2011).

[18] Fund "Public Opinion". 2005. *Survey on Educational Research* [In Russian]. http://bd.fom.ru/report/map/education/educat_mom/obzres1/edmom5 (accessed May 31, 2011).

With the break of the crisis, the artificially booming labour market for "quasi-professionals" shrank quickly. According to expert assessments, large ICT companies reduced their white-collar office personnel by at least 10-15%, and in oil-and-gas companies the reduction was even greater—up to 20%[19]. At the same time, the employers were reluctant to part with skilled workers and experienced engineers and technicians.

4. Barriers to Employability

It is generally agreed that the economic crisis has substantially weakened the employability of youth. However employers, employment service officers and young jobseekers themselves have different opinions as regards to barriers to employability.

According to the Rosstat survey of graduates of 2005-2009, only 9.3% of respondents mentioned insufficient skill level as a barrier to employment, while the irrelevance of received specialty to the labour market demand was mentioned by 9.7%. The main barrier mentioned was the lack of previous work experience (51.4%). In the crisis year 2009, the lack of vacancies became the main barrier. Still the vast majority of graduates did not perceive lack of skills as their weakness. However, the percentage of those perceiving their specialty as a wrong choice went up to 17.4%.

The perceptions of employers are very different. Their main belly ache is the poor skill level of the new labour market entrants and the lack of job applicants with needed qualification profiles. 14 out of 15 employers interviewed during this project especially complained that the system of vocational education does not prepare cadres with the qualifications needed. According to education monitoring, more than half of the employers state that the graduates of early 2000s have worse education and skills in comparison with the graduates of the early 1990s. The finding conforms to the evidence of our interviews with employers in 2009.

> The quality of instruction in today's universities is far worse than it used to be. We are utterly dissatisfied with the skills of newcomers–both engineers and workers. It takes at least three years to obtain an employee who meets our demands.

---

[19] Alekseeva, O., and I. Gahova. 2010. *Making Money on Redundancies* [In Russian]. http://wap.gazeta.ru/financial/2010/05/31/3377696.shtml (accessed May 31, 2011) and our evidence from interviews with employers.

> We have to go through 15-20 candidates to fill very simple vacancies. The quality of applicants each year gets worse while their self-apprehension goes up.

The employers are dissatisfied not only with professional skills of the new labour market entrants but also with their attitude to work and non-cognitive skills. Among the qualities mentioned most often are poor discipline, a lack of communicative skills, graduates who are ill-prepared for teamwork, and have an irresponsible attitude towards work.

> Today, educational institutions pay little attention to developing very important skills of professional socialization. When a university graduate enters a firm he is not familiar with the behaviour norms in a real working organization. He has to communicate with people, to make decisions and take responsibilities, and to participate in teamwork. And he has never been taught anything like this.

On the whole, the officers from employment centres[20] are of the same opinion as employers, placing more emphasis on high demands than on insufficient skills. However they point out that after some period of unproductive job searching many young employment office clients modify their initial demands.

> The young clients, practically all of them have disproportionately high demands. Even the school leavers demand at least 15000 roubles. That is about what most of us earn here with real good training and after 15-20 years of employment [...].

> Before the crisis the labour market was over-subscribed. People received excessive wages and demands on employers were very high. The crisis gave it a good dressing down, especially to the young. Now their demands are much more adequate.

Employment service officers also noted unwillingness of the young applicants to take up real sector jobs, especially blue collar ones, and their orientation towards more rewarding services sector. Thus, their area of job search remains limited.

---

[20] We have conducted 18 interviews with officers of local employment services in six regions of Russia.

5. Measures to Combat Youth Unemployment

State employment services have never been particularly popular with the majority of jobseekers, especially with educated and ambitious ones. During the period of reforms the registered unemployment rate always kept 3-4 times lower as compared to the overall unemployment rate obtained from LFS in accordance with ILO methodology. As far as the young unemployed are concerned, the gap is even higher: only one of five applies to the state employment service for registration. However, since youth have always been recognized as a vulnerable labour market group, regional employment services have designed programmes targeted at the young unemployed. With the beginning of crisis four special programmes were elaborated: the Programme of Subsidized Temporary Employment, the Programme of Forward-Looking Retraining, the Programme of Promoting Self-Employment, and the Interregional Labour Migration Programme. As a part of subsidized employment programmes a special sub-programme targeted at university graduates was introduced. Under this sub-programme, the government reimbursed employers an amount that is equal to minimum wage for each newly-hired graduate.

According to the assessments of employment service officers, with the introduction of special programmes, the popularity of employment services among young jobseekers went up. However, according to the results of our survey of jobseekers who applied to district employment offices,[21] the share of young applicants (15-29 years) was 28%, while according to the LFS the share of the same age category in total unemployment in 2009 was 1.5 times higher (42.4%). Moreover, almost half of the young applicants (46.3%) prefer avoiding official registration and using the employment service as just one of many information sources for finding a job.

Among the young applicants, 26.3% have university education with another 12% having incomplete university education which usually means they are still studying. However, the majority of employment service clients have less than university education and this stands for all age groups including the young.

[21] The survey covered all clients applied to local employment services in 6 regions of Russia during two days (Tuesday and Thursday) of the first week of June 2009.

Fig. 1-7. Educational Profile of Employment Service Clients by Age Group.

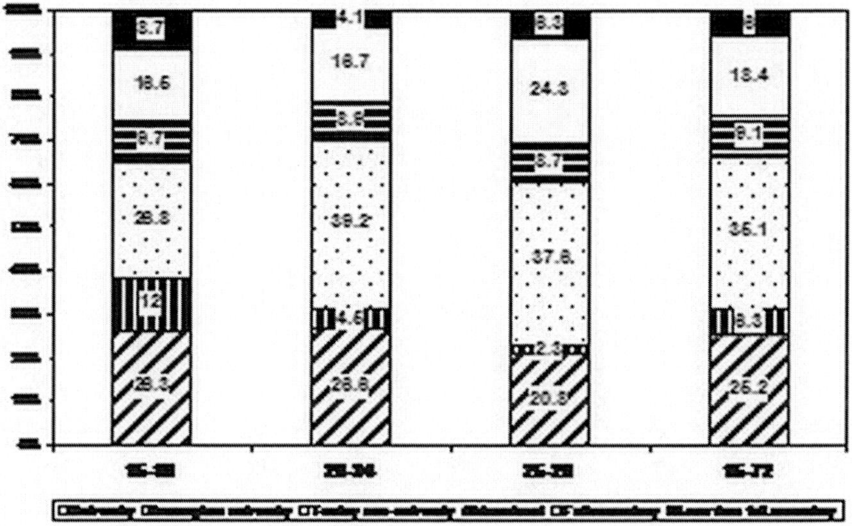

The survey revealed that the young applicants actively participated in a variety of employment service programmes. Only 6% stated that the employment service failed to assist them in any way. Eighty-two percent used the vacancy base available at employment services, 67% received consultations from the service officers during their job search. Ninety-six percent of applicants who at least once received a vacancy offer from employment services failed to obtain the job. The main reasons were "vacancy occupied" (50%), "too low wages" (22%) and "unsatisfactory working conditions" (18%). Only 10% of failures were due to "poor match with professional qualifications". About 1/3 of young applicants (37%) were offered retraining and 13% were offered assistance in starting a business of their own.

Regretfully, in most cases the programmes offered by the employment service either appeared to be in short supply or found little popularity with the young. Thus the popularity of the Adolescent Temporary Employment Programme went up with the beginning of the crisis, while the capacity of employment services in providing jobs for adolescents sharply declined. On the contrary, the graduates subsidized employment programmes proved to poorly match the demands of the targeted groups. The programme was only welcomed in small towns and rural areas having experienced a "return home" migration of recent graduates from the big cities where employment opportunities suddenly became scarce. However, the majority of experts are of the opinion that the programme is not appealing to both the graduates and the employers. Employers have little incentive to hire the young, when mature workers with experience become available on the labour market.

> A graduate needs close supervision; he needs a trainer to guide him. And this subsidized hiring entails a lot of red tape. Now there are lots of experienced people who are looking for work. Why bother with such a programme?

The university graduates, on their part, are reluctant to take poorly paid jobs even when they entail fairly good career prospects.

> The state reimburses employers just the minimum wage which is not much. The employers are unwilling to pay more even for "promising" graduates. Of the young jobseekers hardly 30% agree to such conditions but mainly not the ones with university education [...]

To sum up, both the regular labour market policies and special measures in combating youth unemployment during the crisis were not very successful. On the one hand, with an abundant supply of experienced mature workers, employers lost their interest in recent graduates and raised their demands for new hires. While on the other hand, growing unemployment compelled regional employment services to redistribute their effort in favour of the traditionally most vulnerable categories like elder workers, workers with disabilities, and family heads with many dependants.

6. Conclusion

The analysis reveals that the crisis-related rise of the youth unemployment rate to a large extent is caused by neo-liberal reforms in the system of vocational education lowering the employability of new labour market entrants. Commercialisation of vocational education has set in motion mechanisms reproducing human capital mismatches and quality erosion. The structure of the education system has been increasingly shaped by the demand of families possessing little information on the trends in labour market development. The result has been the gradual destruction of VET and an exacerbation of human capital mismatch. The national economy has become over-saturated with economists and lawyers and experiences a shortage of engineers, technicians and skilled workers.

Until recently, the mismatch was mitigated by the artificial bias in labour demand engendered by the rapidly-spreading Dutch disease. With the break of the crisis, markets for "quasi-professionals" shrank quickly and many recent university degree holders experienced unemployment.

During the crisis, only minor shares of the young unemployed were covered by employment service activities. Both the regular labour market policies and special measures in combating youth unemployment during the crisis were not very successful. However, at least two factors may lead to a decline of youth unemployment in the near future: 1) lowered aspirations of the young could reduce the discrepancy between superfluously high demands on employers and their actual skill level; 2) a rise in oil prices is bound to generate a new wave of demand for low- and mid-level office personnel. In the long run, demographic factors will contribute to strengthening competitiveness of youth due to smaller sizes of the new cohorts entering the labour market. The crisis may also have some positive long-term consequences. First, it may force the redundant second-rate university graduates into further education or retraining. Second, it can cut down the previously common practice of combining university education with full-time employment, and hence, it may lead to improved educational outcomes in universities.

References

Alekseeva, O., and I. Gahova. 2010. *Making Money on Redundancies* [In Russian]. http://wap.gazeta.ru/financial/2010/05/31/3377696.shtml (accessed May 31, 2011).

Avraamova, E., Kulagina E., and E. Vurpahovskaya. 2007. "Behaviour of Graduates on the Labour Market: New Trends [In Russian]," *Chelovek i Trud* No. 9:48-55.

Barro, R., and J. Lee. 2001. "International Data on Educational Attainment: Updates and Implications," *Oxford Economic Papers* 53, No. 3:541-563.

Bell, D., and D. G. Blanchflower. 2010. "Youth Unemployment: Déjà Vu?" IZA Discussion Paper No. 4705.

Belzil, C. 1995. "Unemployment Duration Stigma and Reemployment Earnings," *Canadian Journal of Economics* 28, No 3:568-585.

Blanchflower, D.G., and R. Freeman. 2000. *Youth Employment and Joblessness*. Chicago: University of Chicago Press.

Bolotov, V. 2003. *Malogo EGE ne budet* [The Uniform State Exam Postponed]. *Izvestia*. August 28.

Fund "Public Opinion". 2005. *Survey on Educational Research* [In Russian]. http://bd.fom.ru/report/map/education/educat_mom/obzres1 (accessed May 31, 2011).

—. 2010. *Investment in Education and Social Mobility* [In Russian]. http://bd.fom.ru/pdf/edmom10.pdf (accessed May 31, 2011).

International Labour Organization. 2010. *Global Employment Trends for Youth: August 2010: Special Issue on the Impact of the Global Economic Crisis on Youth*. Geneva: ILO.

Nikolaeva, E. 2011. "Development of the System of Training of Engineers and Skilled Workers for the Russian Economy [In Russian]." Paper presented at Expert Group "Labour Market, Professional Education and Migration" in the NRU HSE, Moscow, Russia. April 2.

Roschina, Y.M. 2006. "Social Differentiation of Youth in Professional Education" [In Russian]. Otechestvennie Zapiski, 3, No. 30. http://www.strana-oz.ru/?numid=30&article=1266 (accessed May 31, 2011).

Roschina Y. M., and M. A. Drugov. 2003. "Sotsialnie determinanti neravenstava doctupa [Social Determinants of Inequal Access]," in *Problemi doctupnosti visshego obrazovaniya,* ed. Shishkin, S.V. (Moscow: IISP).

Scarpetta, S., Sonnet A., and T. Manfredi. 2010. "Rising Youth Unemployment During the Crisis: How to Prevent Negative Long-term Consequences on a Generation?" OECD Social, Employment and Migration Working Papers No. 6, Paris: OECD.

Schultz, T. W. 1970. *Investment in Human Capital: The Role of Education and of Research*. New York: Free Pr.

Shishkin, S. V. 2005. "Funktsionalnaya i socialnaya differentsiazia rossiiskoi sistemi visshego obrazovania [Functional and Social Differentiation of University Education]," in *Problemi doctupnosti visshego obrazovaniya,* ed. Shishkin, S.V., (Moscow: IISP).

Skans, O. N. "Scarring Effects of the First Labour Market Experience." IZA Discussion Paper No. 5565. Bonn: IZA.

Skutneva, S. V. 2006. "Youth Strategies for Self-Realization in the World of Work" *Sociologic Research,* No. 3: 89-92.

Trud. 2010. "Useless Education [In Russian]," 16 August. http://www.trud.ru/article/16-08-2010/248401 (accessed May 31, 2011).

Verbitskaya, L. 2006. "Interview of the Day," *Moscow News,* No. 22.

CHAPTER TWO:

THE TRANSITION FROM EDUCATION TO THE LABOUR MARKET: WHAT MAKES FOR BETTER TRANSITIONS?

LABOUR MARKET TRANSITION POLICIES AND WELFARE STATE MODELS IN EUROPE

LUÍSA VELOSO, LUÍSA OLIVEIRA, HELENA CARVALHO AND SÉRGIO ESTEVINHA

1. Introduction

This article sets out to discuss how education, training, employment policies and placement systems in Europe join forces to achieve the political goals of promoting young people's integration in society and, indirectly, reducing educational failure and early school leaving.[1]

These two phenomena are closely related, in that the former tends to be the cause of the latter, affecting mostly young people. This reflection includes a debate on national employment programmes[2] and on European social models,[3] and it also discusses their differences in terms of employment and education policies.

Our methodology is based on a documentary analysis of official studies and materials from the European Union (EU) countries in the period 2005-2009, and includes an investigation of statistics drawn from the Statistical Office of the European Union (Eurostat). The purpose of a survey of this kind is to consider the latest available information for all the EU countries. Overviews of the education systems and of national policies

---

[1] The analysis is part of the research project "Impact of Lower and Upper Secondary School Attainment on Young People's Employability".

[2] Bosch, G., Lehndorff, L., and J. Rubery. 2009 "European Employment Models in Flux: Pressures for Change and Prospects for Survival and Revitalization," in *European Employment Models in Flux: A Comparison of Institutional Change in Nine European Countries,* eds. Bosch, G., L. Lehndorff, and J. Rubery, (London: Palgrave Macmillan), 1-56.

[3] Ferrera, M. 1996. "The 'Southern Model' of Welfare State in Social Europe," *Journal of European Social Policy* 6, No. 1:17-37; and Esping-Andersen, G. 1990. *The Three Worlds of Welfare Capitalism*. Oxford: Polity Press.

designed to support young people in their transfer to the labour market are also provided, which are available via the Eurydice network (Eurybase).[4]

We also surveyed some other relevant documentation, such as laws, government reports and further publications.[5] Our study also considered unemployment, employment and temporary work rates among young people, also by means of an intra- and inter-country analysis.

The paper begins with a discussion of the theoretical framework, considering welfare state models and transition systems. Due to the vast amount of information available, we narrow our research focus to four countries—Denmark, France, Portugal and the United Kingdom—each of which are representative of the four welfare state models in the EU. The paper concludes with a characterisation of the four transition systems, which shows the impact of government decision-making on the transition from the education system to the labour market.

2. European Social Models and Young People's Transition to the Labour Market

In order to appreciate the policy systems adopted in the European countries, the point of departure of our analysis has been a macro approach to national social models, which are characterised by a different economic organisation and welfare regimes.[6] This choice was made on the assumption that the models guide state action, by definition, function along with society and the economy, orienting policy planning in a variety of fields, including education and employment. Drawing on the proposals

---

[4] The Eurydice Network (http://eurydice.giase.min-edu.pt/index.php?option=com_content&task=view&id=1&Itemid=1) has been one of the strategic pillars set up by the European Commission and the EU Members States since 1980, facilitating cooperation and a better understanding of education systems and policies.

[5] E.g.: The Danish Government 2009. *Denmark's National Reform Programme — First Progress Report*. Herstedvang: Schultz Distribution. http://arenas.itcilo.org/countries/denmark/case-studies/denmark2019s-national-reformprogramme (accessed October, 24 2010). Wright, I., Knight, J., and K. Brennan 2009. *Investing in Potential—Our Strategy to Increase the Proportion of 16–24 Year Olds in Education, Employment or Training*. Annesley: DCSF Publications. Rubery, J., D. Grimshaw, R. Donnelly, and P. Urwin. 2009. "Revisiting the UK Model: From Basket Case to Success Story and Back Again," in *European Employment Models in Flux: A Comparison of Institutional Change in Nine European Countries*, eds. Bosch, G., L. Lehndorff, and J. Rubery, (London: Palgrave Macmillan).

[6] Hall, P., and D. Soskine. 2001. *Varieties of Capitalism: The Institutional Foundations of Comparative Advantage.* Oxford: University Press.

put forward by Esping-Andersen[7] and Ferrera[8] of four European social models, and because of the difficulty to address all the countries, we decided to focus on four countries—Denmark, France, Portugal, and the United Kingdom—since these countries exemplify each of the four models. The analysis looked at their public policies which, either directly or indirectly, aimed at the inclusion of young people in the labour market.

2.1. Social Models in Europe

Modern welfare states are considered to be the political expression of enshrined social rights. In this sense, they are supposed to ensure inclusion and true equality of opportunity in the different spheres of life, also safeguarding individuals' right to participate in economic and social activities. Since the late 1970s, the matrix of the welfare state has undergone changes, moving towards the institutionalisation of private and complementary schemes in the social domain. The private sphere is gaining independence, with sectoral interests that are increasingly giving priority to the definition of collective orientation. The common traits of the welfare state models in the EU countries contributed to the formation of a "European social model". This model is based on certain pillars, such as the promotion of economic well-being and full employment for all, in an attempt to distribute resources more equally. The model is, however, not homogeneous. Thus, on the basis of the comparative principle, Esping-Andersen carried out research into how the different European welfare states were structured. He constructed a framework model, illustrated in 1990 in his work, *The Three Worlds of Welfare Capitalism*, which explains the different types of welfare states in Europe.

This typology is based on the concept of "decommodification", in which individuals can aspire to have a socially acceptable standard of living, independent of market participation. State intervention in the social sphere should be aimed at redistributing wealth more equally, thereby providing for higher levels of decommodification. As far as access to the labour market is concerned, the notion of decommodification seems to clash with the basic principles of the human capital theory, as it argues that finding a job compatible with the specialty acquired in university is not an individual decision and may therefore require state intervention.

---

[7] Esping-Andersen, G. 1990. *The Three Worlds of Welfare Capitalism*. Oxford: Polity Press.

[8] Ferrera, M. 1996. "The 'Southern Model' of Welfare State in Social Europe," *Journal of European Social Policy* 6, No. 1:17-37.

In the opposite direction, "commodification" implies that access to better services is the effect of greater economic power. Finally, whereas family is in charge of providing social protection, the state only intervenes to make up for shortcomings in fulfilling this task. It is at the time of examining this third point that Santos,[9] while focusing on Portugal, develops the concept of a "welfare society", to describe the set of relations and social practices that—by means of informal exchanges of goods and services—ensures the economic well-being and social protection that are supplied by the welfare state in other countries. He makes mention of small farms in Portugal that allow many households to neutralise the negative effects of developments in macroeconomic, political and administrative matrixes by way of resistance, adaptation and readjustment that are effective enough to prevent serious ruptures in the forms of social reproduction.[10]

Esping-Andersen[11] suggests three types of European social models, which are defined on the way the supply of social protection is distributed between the state, the market and the family. Each of these institutions plays a role in the allocation of resources. The three models are of a social-democrat nature and protection and absorption of risks rely on factors such as a universalist state, a liberal model that favours market deregulation, and a conservative model—in the literature termed "continental"—that prioritises the role of the family.

There is fairly broad consensus as to Esping-Andersen's typology, though his proposal has generated a lively debate. Since the publication of *The Three Worlds of Welfare Capitalism*, other scholars have commented on his work, and some of them developed other theoretical models with the same goal as Esping-Andersen's.[12] Ferrera stands out among others, as

---

[9] Santos, B. S. 1995. "Sociedade-Providência ou Autoritarismo social?" *Revista Crítica de Ciências Sociais* 42:1-7.

[10] Santos, B. S. 1985. "Estado e Sociedade na Semiperiferia do Sistema Mundial: o Caso Português," *Análise Social* 87/88/89:869-901.

[11] Esping-Andersen, G. 1990. *The Three Worlds of Welfare Capitalism*. Oxford: Polity Press.

[12] Authors such as Leibfried, Castles and Mitchell, Bonoli and Korpi and Palme have put forward new typologies. See Leibfried, S. 1992. "Towards a European Welfare State? On Integrating Poverty Regimes into the European Community," in *Social Policy in a Changing Europe*, eds. Ferge, Z., and J. E. Kolberg, (Frankfurt: Campus Verlag), 120-143. Castles, F. and D. Mitchell. 1993. "Worlds of Welfare and Families of Nations," in *Families of Nations: Patterns of Public Policy in Western Democracies*, ed. Castles, F., (Aldershot: Dartmouth Publishing Company), 93-128. Bonoli, G. 1997. "Classifying Welfare States: A Two-dimension Approach," *Journal of Social Policy* 26, No.3:351-372. Korpi, W., and J. Palme.

in 1996 he devised a similar typology but with a new model that he named "the southern model".

2.2. Transition Systems and Support Policies

The prolonged social condition of young people is not merely the result of extended time in education, but it also mirrors the struggle that they experience in finding a job. They start working late and their transfer to the labour market ends up in precarious employment, as is evident in their trajectories.[13]

The frontiers between education and the labour market are becoming increasingly fluid and we are witnessing an increase in education and training opportunities. Fewer jobs mean that young people are faced with a series of insecure and temporary occupations, interspersed with periods of unemployment. This state of affairs results in difficult living conditions, as young people find it hard to take such important steps as settling down or starting a family. It is precisely young people entering the labour market for the first time who suffer the most from these changes[14], as shown in Fig. 2-1. The increasing rate of youth unemployment is common to all countries.

It takes longer for first-time entrants to the labour market to find employment, and they move between different labour market states—unemployment, training, underemployment—more often.

The recent changes that have occurred in the world of work have led young people to be placed in different segments of the labour market that depend on a number of factors, from social background to educational attainment.

As evidenced in Fig. 2-1, there is a higher level of youth unemployment among people with only nine years of schooling, particularly

---

1998. "The Paradox of Redistribution and Strategies of Equality: Welfare Institutions, Inequality and Poverty in the Western Countries," American Sociological Review 63:661-87.

[13] Rose, J. 1996. "L'Organisation des Transitions Professionnelles: Entre Socialisation, Mobilisation et Recomposition des Rapports de Travail et d'Emploi," *Sociologie du Travail* 1:63-79. Oliveira, L., H. Carvalho, and L. Veloso. 2011. "Youth and precarious employment in Europe," in *Young People at Work in the Developed World,* eds. Price, R., P. McDonald, Bailey, J., and B. Pini, (Farnham: Ashgate).

[14] Guerreiro, M. D., et al. 2006. *Os Jovens e o Mercado de Trabalho: Caracterização, Estrangulamentos à Integração Efectiva na Vida Activa e a Eficácia das Políticas*. Lisbon: DGEEP.

in countries such as Germany, Austria, Denmark, Spain, The Netherlands, Malta, Portugal and Sweden, a trend that is in stark contrast to those who possess tertiary education.[15]

Fig. 2-1. Unemployment Rates in the EU by Age Group and Country (2008).

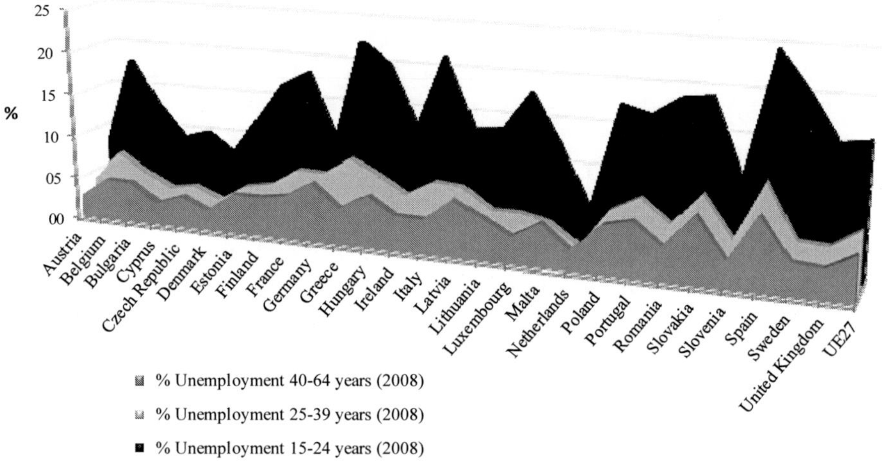

Source: Own calculations based on Eurostat, 2008.

In view of the ongoing changes that are taking place in employment, the aim is now to discuss how education and employment policies are central to the understanding of the attempt on the part of EU countries to adapt their strategies to this new reality.

Since the 1970s, a great deal of research in Europe has been directed towards employment and social inclusion strategies, and educational pathways addressing young people. The increased interest in the matter is mainly due to the constantly high youth unemployment rates (see Fig. 2-

[15] Eurostat makes use of the UNESCO International Standard Classification of Education (ISCED): ISCED 0-2: pre-primary, primary—first stage of basic education (the start of compulsory education) and lower secondary education—second stage of basic education; ISCED 3-4: upper secondary and post-secondary non tertiary education; and ISCED 5-6: first and second stages of tertiary education. Source: UNESCO. 1997. *International Standard Classification of Education I S C E D 1997.* http://www.unesco.org/education/information/nfsunesco/doc/isced_1997.htm (accessed October 11, 2009).

1), and the complex transition and inclusion of recent graduates in the labour market.[16]

Fig. 2-2. Educational Structure of Youth Unemployment in the EU by Country (2008).

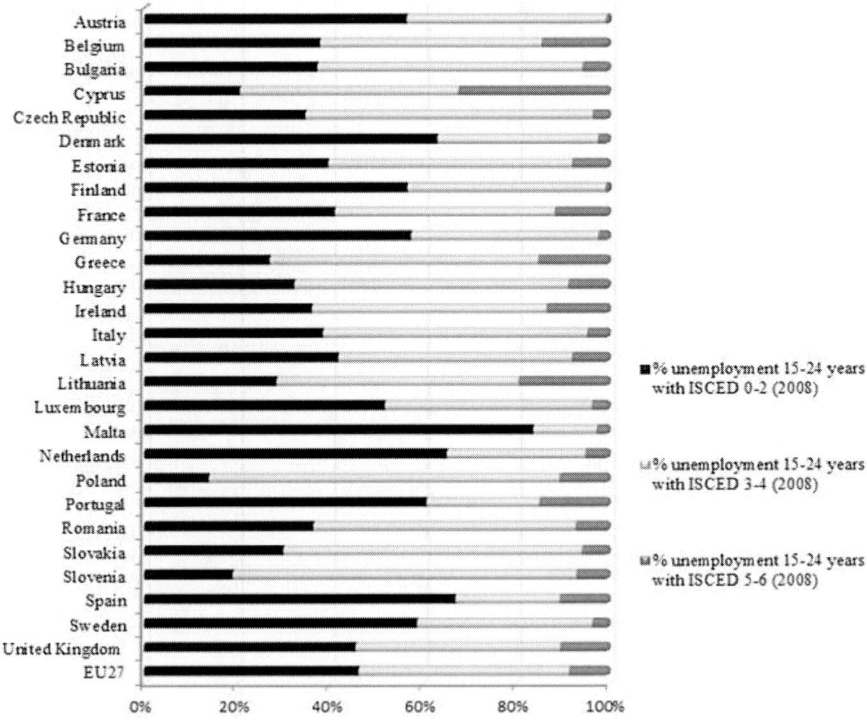

Source: Own calculations based on Eurostat, 2008.

Many scholars have devoted themselves to appreciating how the characteristics of national education and training systems, labour market structures, institutions in charge of inclusion and their socioeconomic

[16] Van der Velden, R., R. Welters, and M. Wolbers. 2001. *The Integration of Young People into the Labour Market within the European Union: The Role of Institutional Settings.* Working paper. http://arno.unimaas.nl/show.cgi?fid=9956 (accessed July 2, 2009).

contexts determine "transition systems", that is the shift from being a student to becoming a worker.[17]

A significant number of the analyses have been developed focusing on the interconnection between education and training systems and the labour market, particularly those including attempts at typifying results.[18] Schroeder[19], for example, conducted a study comparing programmes to help young people's transition to work in a number of European labour markets. His investigation covered five countries, namely Sweden, The Netherlands, Ireland, Scotland and France. According to Schroeder, the difference between these programmes lies in the way they are regulated, the interplay between education and labour market policies, and their coverage, which depends on unemployment rates, particularly when adopted as a counter-cyclic measure. The author argues that young people with no upper secondary education were much more likely to be at risk, with this probability that was also dependent on the employment situation of their family members. In the countries surveyed, the author found that for young people with at least one of the parents in employment such risk was less likely.

In considering the regulation of the labour market and the relationship between education systems and the labour market, Schroeder groups the five countries according to three "transition schemes". The first scheme—which includes France and Sweden—involves a considerable degree of state intervention in the shift from school to work in countries where markets are highly regulated and the barriers to young people's inclusion are not mitigated by a close relation between the education system and the business sector. The Netherlands and Ireland experience a different type of transition, in which the share of young people in the programme is considerably lower. Scotland falls into the third type of transition scheme.

---

[17] Raffe, D. 2001. "La Construction Sociale de la Recherche Transnationale sur l'Insertion Social et Professionnelle: le Réseau Européen de Recherche sur l'Insertion Professionnelle des Jeunes," *Éducation et Sociétés* 7:111-129.

[18] See, e.g., Allmendinger, J. 1989. "Educational Systems and Labour Market Outcomes," European Sociological Review 5, No. 3:231-250. Heinz, W., ed. 1999. *From Education to Work: Cross-National Perspectives*. Cambridge: Cambridge University Press. Coupiée T., and M. Mansuy. 2000. "La Place des Debútants sur les Marches du Travail Européens," BREF, CEREQ, No. 164. Hartkamp J., and H. Rustjes. 2000. *A Route to Skills, Rapport pour l'Atelier du TIY.* Antwerp, September. Schroeder, L. 2000. "The Role of Youth Programmes in the Transition from School to Work," in *A Comparative Analysis of Transitions from Education to Work in Europe—Based on National School Leavers Surveys*, ed. Hannan, D. (Dublin: Economic and Social Research Institute), 118-148.

[19] Ibid.

Although here the labour market is poorly regulated, the percentage of youth regarded as being at risk in the programmes is higher than that in France. This state of affairs might be determined by major shortcomings in the national education system with regard to vocational training.[20]

We will now address the policies supporting young people's transfer to working life in the period 2005-2009 in the four countries under investigation, in order to understand whether public policy assessments in these countries are in line with the welfare state models that—according to the typology developed by Esping-Andersen[21] and Ferrera[22] —characterise them.

2.3. Transition Systems and Welfare State Models

The EU currently promotes the regulatory and ideological principle whereby education and training play a role in the construction and consolidation of a knowledge-based economy, in that they help improve people's level of qualifications. At the same time, they help to strengthen social cohesion and active citizenship in European societies. In order to achieve positive results in the social and professional inclusion of young people, the EU allocates massive investments in education, while highlighting the urgent need for action to smooth the transition from education to work. Against this background, people in general and young people in particular, are entitled to an education, which translates into the right to acquire skills and abilities required in a knowledge-based economy. In this sense, education and vocational training are the keys to making this possible. Member states are encouraged to take measures to foster the development of essential skills from primary school, and to strengthen the relationship between education and the labour demand—e.g. favouring partnerships between educational bodies and employers.

2.3.1. Denmark

The social-democratic model is peculiar to the Scandinavian countries, with Sweden, Finland and Denmark that are suitable examples in this connection. "Decommodification", which is people's ability to live

---

[20] Ibid.

[21] Esping-Andersen, G. 1990. *The Three Worlds of Welfare Capitalism*. Oxford: Polity Press.

[22] Ferrera, M. 1996. "The 'Southern Model' of Welfare State in Social Europe," *Journal of European Social Policy* 6, No. 1:17-37.

without depending on market resources, is one of the main features of this model.

Denmark's case is a paradigmatic one, because here the "flexicurity" model has been reported to have the greatest impact on policy measures,[23] particularly from 1994 onwards, that is when the labour market was reformed. High state intervention is predominant and this can be seen in social protection, that is supplied in the form of universal coverage—e.g. generous social security systems and low levels of social inequality. Expenditure on the education system is the highest in Europe and this system is regarded as outstanding in today's intensive-knowledge economy. It also provides a wide range of social and personal services and active employment measures, which explain high activity and employment rates among both men and women. Countries that adopt this model are regulated by labour market policies that usually characterise the active welfare state. In order to bear the relative costs, this model provides for the highest taxes in Europe and high-quality forms of social protection.

The year 2009 was important as new legislative measures to deal with the issue of youth unemployment in Denmark were laid down. In this sense, education was given priority to support the young unemployed without adequate qualifications. The expected outcome should be that the youth population will have new opportunities in education and employment, also in terms of on-the-job training. Young people aged under 25 without any qualification will be obliged to enter education, unless they have dependants. They also have the right and the duty to receive training within six months of being unemployed, while being paid daily cash benefits. Eighteen and nineteen year-olds who leave school without starting upper secondary education will be immediately offered a job from a job placement centre.[24] Evidently, there is a commitment to supply education and to strengthen the connections between schooling and the labour market. This strategy has enabled young people to tackle the current recession better than their peers in most OECD countries.

---

[23] Madsen, P. K. 2002. "The Danish Model of 'Flexicurity'—a Paradise With Some Snakes," in *Interaction Between Labour Market and Social Protection*, ed. European Foundation for the Improvement of Living and Working Conditions. http://samba.fsv.cuni.cz/~kotrusov/Social%20Policy/Seminars/Seminar%203/Seminar%203%20-%20text%201.pdf (accessed April 13, 2010). Madsen, P. K. 2004. "The Danish Model of Flexicurity: Experiences and Lessons," *Transfer* 10:187-207. Bredgaard, T., L. Flemming, and P. K. Madsen. 2006. "Opportunities and Challenges for Flexicurity—the Danish Example," *Transfer* 12, No. 1:61-83.

[24] Source: http://arenas.itcilo.org/countries/denmark/case-studies/denmark2019s-national-reform programme (accessed September 24, 2010).

However, youth unemployment is still on the rise, as it increased from 7.2% in 2008, to 12.4% in the fourth quarter of 2009. By comparison, the average youth unemployment rate in OCED countries rose from 13.2% to 21% in the corresponding period.[25]

More recently, in 2010, Denmark allocated funds to 5,000 apprenticeship and training bodies to face a 24% decrease in hiring of apprentices in the first eight months of 2009, against the same period in 2008. But there is still a high drop-out rate in vocational employment and training.

Denmark is pursuing its activation programmes with active labour market policies (ALMPs), such as job-search assistance, training, and employment incentive schemes, which are crucial to the transfer to the labour market, though the economic downturn has significantly reduced job opportunities for new entrants. It is important to know how to make use of ALMPs effectively to devise measures aimed at "preventing youth poverty, disengagement from the labour market and human capital depreciation".[26]

2.3.2. The United Kingdom

The liberal European model is essentially found in the United Kingdom and, to a lesser extent, in Ireland. The coverage provided by these social protection systems is poor, as high degrees of inequality, poverty, and low demographic growth are usually reported. The social state is of a residual nature, with low levels of "decommodification". This model provides moderate protection and there are strong incentives towards the "commercialisation" of social rights.

The labour market is highly deregulated and there is no universal coverage in terms of social security. Neither the unemployed nor those who are employed whose earnings are below a certain level have access to the benefits of the national social security system, that are more modest than those in the Scandinavian countries. Since the 1980s, the real value of universal benefit schemes has deteriorated, and a number of restrictive measures concerning social protection against unemployment have been devised, particularly for young people. In applying this model, state intervention is limited to providing protection to people who are unable to

---

[25] Source: http://www.oecd.org/document/55/0,3746,en_21571361_44315115_44666999_1_1_1_1,00.html (accessed September 24, 2010).

[26] Source: OECD. 2010. *Jobs for Youth/Des Emplois pour les Jeunes: Denmark 2010*. http://www.oecd-ilibrary.org/employment/jobs-for-youth-des-emplois-pour-les-jeunes-denmark-2010_9789264075160-en (accessed September 24, 2010).

do so by way of internal market mechanisms. As a result, taxation is kept fairly low and any risks related to the funding of this social model are eluded. However, the way the market operates generates inequality and multiplies exclusion mechanisms. Poor public provisions and the increasing privatisation of the social security system are cause of "commodification" and educational inequalities. Following an extension of compulsory education and training, young people in the United Kingdom have to remain in school or commit to combining employment and training—e.g. apprenticeship—until the age of 18. In 2008, the United Kingdom government introduced courses for young people aged 14 to 19, where theoretic and practical learning were supplied together. In 2011, 17 new subjects were available nationwide. Northern Ireland is devising a new school improvement plan too, the aim of which is to ensure that all children leave the education system with adequate skills and qualifications to enter the labour market. In 2008, literacy and numeracy strategies were launched to increase educational attainment levels, especially among pupils at higher risk of failure. Concerning policies directly aimed at fostering youth inclusion in working life,[27] it is essential for young people aged 16 to 24 to be in education, employment or training, in order to boost the national economy and increase people's career prospects. In this sense, the UK government has endeavoured to integrate education with employment, so that young people obtain their qualifications while also gaining the practical experience they need for entering the world of work. All young people who are not in education, employment or training should be helped in this connection. The strategy entails monitoring and individual support for people in this age group.[28] However, what actually happens is that young people with higher levels of education tend to apply for jobs for which they have no special qualifications. Academic education is of a general nature. Only when they are in employment, can they receive the special training they need.[29] The idea is to bring employers and universities closer, particularly with regard to arranging education and

---

[27] Employment policies are generally applied nationwide, although provisions laid down in England, Scotland and Wales might differ in important respects.

[28] Wright, I., J. Knight, and K. Brennan 2009. *Investing in Potential—Our Strategy to Increase the Proportion of 16–24 Year Olds in Education, Employment or Training*. Annesley: DCSF Publications.

[29] Rubery, J., D. Grimshaw, R. Donnelly, and P. Urwin. 2009. "Revisiting the UK Model: From Basket Case to Success Story and Back Again," in *European Employment Models in Flux: a Comparison of Institutional Change in Nine European countries*, eds. Bosch, G., L. Lehndorff, and J. Rubery, (London: Palgrave Macmillan).

training programmes. The State has also encouraged young people to develop their entrepreneurial skills, which are essential in boosting the country's economic growth.

The government funded the "Make your Mark" campaign in order to build up young people's entrepreneurial spirit. The campaign is designed to introduce mechanisms to change their attitude to entrepreneurship and foster the principle whereby starting a business can constitute an alternative to salaried employment. "Jobcentre Plus" also provides job placement service and related information to help them in their inclusion in the labour market. Those who are unable to find an occupation within the first six months after graduation are given guaranteed access to training, an internship or assisted in self-employment. In addition, the programme "The Young Person's Guarantee" was established in 2009, offering jobseekers aged 18 to 24 years old a wide range of job opportunities. Some other programmes have been set up, such as "Routes into Work" to help prepare young people for jobs in high-growth sectors and "Care First Careers", with the same goals in the health care sector. This strategy requires all young people to take a place in one of the options mentioned. In other words, doing nothing is not an option.[30] In the aftermath of the 2008 recession, young jobseekers were eligible for the same support measures introduced at the time to help people claiming unemployment benefits. This included recruitment subsidies and sponsorship of self-employment for a six-month period.

2.3.3. France

The continental model is found in countries such as France, Germany, Belgium, The Netherlands, Austria and Luxembourg, where intermediate levels of "decommodification" are reported that are unevenly distributed among the population. Social protection coverage is fairly inclusive, although not as uniform as in the countries where the social-democrat paradigm applies. Social rights and the entitlement of benefits are dependent on individual social and employment status, and family situation. The underlying principle is that only those who contribute should be entitled to benefits. Labour legislation is highly protective of workers, with this aspect that has hindered job creation, widening the gap between the insiders—people in employment—and outsiders—people

[30] Wright, I., J. Knight, and K. Brennan 2009. *Investing in Potential—Our Strategy to Increase the Proportion of 16–24 Year Olds in Education, Employment or Training*. Annesley: DCSF Publications.

without work—particularly among young people. Individuals with limited resources have developed strong reliance on social protection schemes, especially subsidies, and this state of affairs has led to high taxes, as a result of problems associated with financial sustainability at a national level. In addition, the continental model places great importance on the role of the family, which is also held responsible to solve some problems independently. The school-to-work transition process is long and difficult in France, especially for early school-leavers. The government has introduced a number of policies designed to meet the needs of the youth, particularly for those aged between 16 and 25 years old.

Policy-makers have sought to cooperate with a number of bodies — known as "local missions"—operating at a local level in different regions in order to facilitate young people's entry into the labour market, also taking advantage of their connection to local people.[31] However, the goal should not be expressed only in terms of access to employment but also—and more comprehensively—in the establishment of transition paths. Local missions are also involved in helping young people solve their personal problems.

In 2005, France introduced the social integration contract (CIVIS), which mainly addresses young people. Over the same year, a national agreement was also signed between Adia, which is a temporary work agency, the Ministry of Labour, the National Council of Local Missions (CNML), and the National Employment Agency (ANPE) to set out guidelines for a new strategy supporting the transfer to work. These guidelines include experimental training programmes co-funded by the government and the Adia, which provides social and technical knowledge, and behavioural skills, also supplying in-house vocational training on a temporary basis. In 2008, the social partners concluded a national agreement on the modernisation of the labour market, which is currently being examined by relevant authorities and might soon turn into a law. This agreement specifies that unemployed people under the age of 25 should be paid a certain amount of money—funded by the National Professional Union for Employment in Industry and Trade (UNEDIC)—in accordance with terms laid down in a following unemployment benefit scheme.

---

31 See http://www.mission-locale.fr/. Local missions also provide individual assistance to young people in employment, training, health and housing.

2.3.4. Portugal

As for the southern model, it can be seen as the poorer version of the continental model and characterises the welfare state of countries such as Italy, Greece, Spain and Portugal. Levels of "decommodification" are very low in these countries, while the education system tends to maintain some selection mechanisms which hamper the full integration of social groups with more limited resources.[32] Unemployment rates are high, especially among young people.[33] As occurs in the countries that are influenced by the liberal model, the workfare principle is also dominant in these labour markets. Access to social services, which are often unavailable in the market, is insufficient. This phenomenon is particularly relevant in these countries because the concept of a welfare state was never fully developed. In southern European societies, a welfare state is combined with some other forms of social assistance—based on family ties and neighbourhood networks—that make up for some of its shortcomings.[34] Ferrera, Hemerijk and Rhodes[35] even argue that family serves as a provider of social security in these countries. Portugal stands out as a country that supplies high rates of under-qualified workers and cheap labour.[36] According to 2009 data, only 15.3% of the working population has higher education qualifications, while 67.8% of people—the overwhelming majority—have completed compulsory education, at most.[37] Regarding the democratisation of the Portuguese education system, Sebastião[38] maintains that much scholarly work provides a picture of a country that still has a highly unequal education system, even though it is possible to identify a tendency towards change in this field, with a positive impact also in social terms. In the author's view, there has been a recent and significant increase in the

---

[32] Abrantes, P., "Causas e Consequências da Distância entre Ciclos do Ensino Básico," Paper presented at the VI Congresso Português de Sociologia, Lisbon, Portugal, June 2008.

[33] Ferrera, M., A. Hemerijk, and M. Rhodes. 2000. *O Futuro da Europa Social—Repensar o Trabalho e a Protecção na Nova Economia*. Oeiras: Celta Editora.

[34] Santos, B. S. 1995. "Sociedade-Providência ou Autoritarismo social?" *Revista Crítica de Ciências Sociais* 42:1-7.

[35] Ferrera, M., A. Hemerijk, and M. Rhodes. 2000. *O Futuro da Europa Social—Repensar o Trabalho e a Protecção na Nova Economia*. Oeiras: Celta Editora.

[36] Capucha, L. 2005. *Desafios da Pobreza*, Oeiras: Celta Editora.

[37] Source: INE. *Inquérito ao Emprego; Estimativas Anuais da População Residente*.

[38] Sebastião, J. 2009. *Democratização do Ensino, Desigualdades Sociais e Trajectórias Escolares*. Lisbon: Fundação Calouste Gulbenkian/ Fundação para a Ciência e Tecnologia.

overall rates of educational attainment in Portugal. However, this process is taking place slowly and is characterised by low levels of achievement, with high rates of early school-leaving and educational failure. Without underestimating the significant progress that has been made by the democratic regime in recent decades, the democratisation of Portuguese education will take longer than elsewhere. This means, on the one hand, that students who in the past would have been excluded from the education system now have access to schooling and, on the other hand, that even today the national education system is characterised by high shares of students entering higher education, yet without completing it. Portugal's case is particularly interesting because of the attempt on the part of the government to reduce educational failure and the number of early school-leavers, by revisiting the national schooling system. In this sense, the period 2005-2009 witnessed a more active involvement of the State in educational matters. The first outcome was the expansion and diversification of vocational training, and an increase of the number of training opportunities at public and private levels. Vocational training courses have been introduced in public upper secondary schools—until then they were supplied only by private entities—in order to make them attractive to some younger strata, and the number of students attending them more than quadrupled in four years.[39] As for policy measures helping young people during the transition to the labour market, some of them were introduced in 2009 as part of the programme "Investment and Employment initiative" (IIE). In some cases, they were developed to assist young people in accessing employment by setting up more than 12.000 vocational internships, and other important measures involved supporting employers who recruit young people. In this respect, measures introducing internships took the form of financial support for private and public organisations to provide qualified young people with work experience, thus smoothing their transition to work and increasing permanent employment.

To stimulate entrepreneurship and the creation of self-employment, a joint initiative of the Institute for the Support of Small and Medium-sized Enterprises and Innovation (IAPMEI) and the Portuguese Youth Institute (IPJ) led to the establishment of the "FINICIA Youth Programme".

Regarding vocational training, mention should be made of training schemes targeted at young people, such the "New Opportunities Initiative" introduced in 2005. The aim of these schemes was to deal with low school

---

[39] Rodrigues, M. L. 2010. *A Escola Pública Pode Fazer a Diferença.* Coimbra: Edições Almedina.

performances of many young Portuguese. The initiative promotes diversification in the supply of education and training and has significantly increased the number of training opportunities. It is expected that it will be possible not only to improve the pass rates but also to boost youth employability, also awarding vocational certification. Another set of measures directly related to vocational training as a way of fostering the school-to-work transition, reducing early school-leaving and promoting academic achievement has to do with technical and financial support for vocational qualifications, resulting in academic and vocational certification. Accordingly, one might argue that Portugal stands out because of its attempt at filling the existing gap between the education system and job market, by setting the conditions to facilitate the transition to the labour market and fostering self-employment. Clearly, the role of the state in education has been re-established, yet a number of critical indicators point to large inequalities in the school system, that somehow mirror those taking place in society.

3. Discussion

The present study made it possible to discuss the set of policy initiatives addressing the inclusion of young people in the labour market, and stressing the importance of the state in the two fundamental areas of education and employment. The analysis shows that welfare state models are reflected in mechanisms for young people entering the labour market, with public investments in education that also play a major role. It is no surprise that in 2008, public spending as a percentage of GDP on labour market policies (training, employment incentives, job creation, and so forth)[40] was reported to be the highest in Denmark (around 2.4%), followed by France (2%), with Portugal lagging way behind (1.5%). In the United Kingdom, a more "commercial" approach in this field was adopted and only 0.5% of national GDP was channelled into meeting the needs of the labour market. This type of intervention in the United Kingdom tends to occur mainly within the scope of private strategies, while public policy plays a secondary role.[41] One can argue that Denmark, with its social-democrat welfare state, provides a transition system characterised by higher levels of protection and flexibility. The state is concerned with

[40] Being general measures, they do not address specifically young people.

[41] Eurostat. 2010. *Employment and Unemployment (Labour Force Survey), LFS series—Detailed Annual Survey Results.* http://epp.eurostat.ec.europa.eu/portal/page/portal/statistics/search_database (accessed December 3, 2009).

guaranteeing everyone's access to the labour market, but has a stake in education and active measures. This requires a more structured coordination with the production system based on the "flexicurity" model. Therefore, notwithstanding the important role played by the state, the levels of flexibility in the labour market may be a gauge of job insecurity. In France, the transition system is characterised by high levels of dependence on the state, although not providing extensive protection, because young people experience highly heterogeneous situations conditioned by other variables, and such an approach is traditionally marked by interventionist policies that safeguard young graduates more from job insecurity.[42] Even though the role of the state is more prominent, there are still social inequalities that are difficult to deal with, especially in the shift from school to work on the part of young people. The institutional framework that oversees aspects such as minimum wage and social protection is part of a deeply unequal society and the younger strata of the population are particularly affected. As stated by Berrebi-Hoffmann,[43] "[...] being young in France is regarded as being dependent on family solidarity". Due to increasing levels of privatisation, a move from state-led to state-enhanced capitalism has been reported.[44]

In the United Kingdom, a transition system marked by liberalised flexibility is adopted, in which state intervention is found particularly in tertiary education. At first sight, it seems like a highly market-oriented model and the state play an important role in access to the labour market. This is also visible in the fact that the United Kingdom is one of the countries with the lowest rates of temporary youth employment in the EU. However, compared to other countries in northern and central Europe (such as Denmark, Germany, Austria, Finland or Sweden), high rates of early school-leaving have been reported nationwide, with individuals who are already in employment who are also willing to enter into lifelong

---

[42] Oliveira, L., and H. Carvalho. 2010. *Regulação e Mercado de Trabalho: Portugal e a Europa*. Lisbon: Edições Sílabo.

[43] Berrebi-Hoffman, I., F. Jany-Catrice, M. Lallement, and T. Ribault. 2009. "Capitalizing on Variety: Risks and Opportunities in a New French Social Model," in *European Employment Models in Flux: A Comparison of Institutional Change in Nine European Countries,* eds. Bosch, G., L. Lehndorff, and J. Rubery, (London: Palgrave Macmillan), 178-199.

[44] Bosch, G., L. Lehndorff, and J. Rubery. 2009 "European Employment Models in Flux: Pressures for Change and Prospects for Survival and Revitalization," in *European Employment Models in Flux: A Comparison of Institutional Change in Nine European Countries,* eds. Bosch, G., L. Lehndorff, and J. Rubery, (London: Palgrave Macmillan).

training.[45] This model has been a neoliberal one only since the late 1970s, and starting from 2008, there has been growing state involvement, particularly in health care and education.

Finally, in Portugal there has been a move to reform the education system and promote mechanisms for transfer to the labour market. A concern for certifying people's formal or informal qualifications is also one of the ways to foster access to the labour market and tackle the existing unemployment trends that lead to social exclusion. However, a highly flexible labour market prevails. This is therefore a transition system characterised by flexibility and dependence on the state. The state has heightened its intervention in employment, particularly in education. With an increase in unemployment among the working population and difficulties in providing stable employment, the provision of social assistance by civil society in general and by the family might be jeopardised.

These welfare state models and their specificities translate into policy measures aimed at helping young people access the labour market. After the crisis that broke out in 2008, a series of measures addressing young people have been put in place, while their situation in the labour market deteriorated. This is a case of protectionism versus flexibility. There remains the question and expectation of understanding whether European countries will go for "commodification" or "decommodification" and the consequent role of the state in the areas of employment and education.

References

Abrantes, P. "Causas e Consequências da Distância entre Ciclos do Ensino Básico," Paper presented at the VI Congresso Português de Sociologia, Lisbon, Portugal, June 2008.

Allmendinger, J. 1989. "Educational Systems and Labour Market Outcomes," European Sociological Review 5, No. 3:231-250.

Alves, N. 2008. *Juventudes e Inserção Profissional*. Lisbon: Educa.

Arcanjo, M. 2006. *Ideal (and Real) Types of Welfare State*, Lisbon, Working Papers from Department of Economics at the School of Economics and Management (ISEG), Technical University of Lisbon.

[45] Rubery, J., D. Grimshaw, R. Donnelly, and P. Urwin. 2009. "Revisiting the UK Model: From Basket Case to Success Story and Back Again," in *European Employment Models in Flux: A Comparison of Institutional Change in Nine European Countries*, eds. Bosch, G., L. Lehndorff, and J. Rubery, (London: Palgrave Macmillan), 57-80.

Berrebi-Hoffman, I., F.Jany-Catrice, M.Lallement, and T.Ribault. 2009. "Capitalizing on Variety: Risks and Opportunities in a New French Social Model," in *European Employment Models in Flux: A Comparison of Institutional Change in Nine European Countries,* eds. Bosch, G., L. Lehndorff, and J. Rubery, (London: Palgrave Macmillan), 178-199.

Bonoli, G. 1997. "Classifying Welfare States: A Two-dimension Approach," *Journal of Social Policy* 26, No.3:351-372.

Bosch, G., L. Lehndorff, and J. Rubery. 2009 "European Employment Models in Flux: Pressures for Change and Prospects for Survival and Revitalization," in *European Employment Models in Flux: A Comparison of Institutional Change in Nine European Countries,* eds. Bosch, G., L. Lehndorff, and J. Rubery, (London: Palgrave Macmillan), 1-56.

Bredgaard, T., L. Flemming, and P. K. Madsen. 2006. "Opportunities and Challenges for Flexicurity—the Danish Example," *Transfer* 12, No. 1:61-83.

Capucha, L. 2005. *Desafios da Pobreza*. Oeiras: Celta Editora.

Castles, F., and D. Mitchell. 1993. "Worlds of Welfare and Families of Nations," in *Families of Nations: Patterns of Public Policy in Western Democracies*, ed. Castles, F. (Aldershot: Dartmouth Publishing Company), 93-128.

CCE 2007. *Comunicação da Comissão ao Parlamento Europeu, ao Conselho, ao Comité Económico e Social Europeu e ao Comité das Regiões - Promover a Plena Participação dos Jovens na Educação, no Emprego e na Sociedade.* http://eur-lex.europa.eu/LexUriServ/LexUriServ.do?uri=COM:2007:0498:FIN:PT:PDF (accessed May 20, 2009).

Council for Employment, Income and Social Cohesion 2008. "A National Responsibility—The School-to-Work Transition of Young People Without Diplomas," *Revenus Cohésion Sociale*, Report No. 9. Paris: La Documentation Française.

Coupiée T., and M. Mansuy. 2000. "La Place des Debútants sur les Marches du Travail Européens," BREF, CEREQ, No. 164.

Esping-Andersen, G. 1990. *The Three Worlds of Welfare Capitalism*. Oxford: Polity Press.

—. 1999. "Um Estado-Providência para o Século XXI," in *Para uma Europa da Inovação e do Conhecimento,* ed. Boyer, R. (Oeiras: Celta Editora), 79-125.

—. 2000. *A Welfare State for the 21st Century*. Report to the Portuguese Presidency of the European Union, Lisbon: Portuguese Presidency of the European Union.

Eurydice. http://eurydice.giase.min-edu.pt/index.php?option=com_content&task=view&id=1&Itemid=1 (accessed July 12, 2009).

Eurostat. 2010. *Employment and Unemployment (Labour Force Survey), LFS series—Detailed Annual Survey Results*.

http://epp.eurostat.ec.europa.eu/portal/page/portal/statistics/search_database (accessed December 3, 2009).

Ferrão, J. 2000. "Saída Prematura do Sistema Educativo: Aspectos da Situação, Causas e Perspectivas em Termos de Emprego e Formação," *Estudos e Análises* 36:257-262.

Ferrera, M. 1996. "The 'Southern Model' of Welfare State in Social Europe," *Journal of European Social Policy* 6, No. 1:17-37.

Ferrera, M., A. Hemerijk, and M. Rhodes. 2000. *O Futuro da Europa Social—Repensar o Trabalho e a Protecção na Nova Economia*. Oeiras: Celta Editora.

Guerreiro, M. D., et al. 2006. *Os Jovens e o Mercado de Trabalho: Caracterização, Estrangulamentos à Integração Efectiva na Vida Activa e a Eficácia das Políticas*. Lisbon: DGEEP.

Hall, P., and D. Soskine. 2001. *Varieties of Capitalism: The Institutional Foundations of Comparative Advantage.* Oxford: University Press.

Hartkamp J., and H. Rustjes. 2000. *A Route to Skills, Rapport pour l'Atelier du TIY.* Antwerp, September.

Heinz, W., ed. 1999. *From Education to Work: Cross-National Perspectives*. Cambridge: Cambridge University Press.

Korpi, W., and J. Palme. 1998. "The Paradox of Redistribution and Strategies of Equality: Welfare Institutions, Inequality and Poverty in the Western Countries," American Sociological Review 63:661-87.

Leibfried, S. 1992. "Towards a European Welfare State? On Integrating Poverty Regimes into the European Community," in *Social Policy in a Changing Europe*, eds. Ferge, Z., and J. E. Kolberg, (Frankfurt: Campus Verlag), 120-143.

Madsen, P. K. 2002. "The Danish Model of 'Flexicurity'—a Paradise With Some Snakes," in *Interaction Between Labour Market and Social Protection*, ed. European Foundation for the Improvement of Living and Working Conditions. http://samba.fsv.cuni.cz/~kotrusov/Social%20Policy/Seminars/Seminar%203/Seminar%203%20-%20text%201.pdf (accessed April 13, 2010).

—. 2004. "The Danish Model of Flexicurity: Experiences and Lessons," *Transfer* 10:187-207.

Martins, S. C. 2009. "Uma Europa em Vários Andamentos: Padrões de Escolarização e Sistemas Educativosl," Actas do Encontro—Contextos Educativos na Sociedade Contemporânea (Lisbon: Secção de Sociologia da Educação da Associação Portuguesa de Sociologia), 47-62.

Merle, P. 2002. "Democratization ou Accroissement des Inegalités Scolaires?" *Population* 57:633-660.

Oliveira, L., H. Carvalho, and L. Veloso. 2011. "Youth and precarious employment in Europe," in *Young People at Work in the Developed World,* eds. Price, R., P. McDonald, J. Bailey, and B. Pini, (Farnham: Ashgate).

Oliveira, L., and H. Carvalho. 2010. *Regulação e Mercado de Trabalho: Portugal e a Europa*. Lisbon: Edições Sílabo.

OECD. 2009. *Education at a Glance*, Paris: OCDE Publishing. http://www.oecd.org/dataoecd/41/25/43636332.pdf.

—. *Jobs for Youth/Des Emplois pour les Jeunes: Denmark 2010.* http://www.oecd-ilibrary.org/employment/jobs-for-youth-des-emplois-pour-les-jeunes-denmark-2010_9789264075160-en (accessed September 24, 2010).

Prats, J., and F. Raventós. 2005. *Los Sistemas Educativos Europeos: Crisis or Transformación?* Barcelona: Obra Social Fundación "La Caixa".

Raffe, D. 2001. "La Construction Sociale de la Recherche Transnationale sur l'Insertion Social et Professionnelle: le Réseau Européen de Recherche sur l'Insertion Professionnelle des Jeunes," *Éducation et Sociétés* 7:111-129.

Rodrigues, E. V. 2000. "O Estado-Providência e os Processos de Exclusão Social: Considerações Teóricas e Estatísticas em Torno do Caso Português," *Sociologia* 10: 173-200.

Rodrigues, M. L. 2010. *A Escola Pública Pode Fazer a Diferença.* Coimbra: Edições Almedina.

Rose, J. 1996. "L'Organisation des Transitions Professionelles: Entre Socialisation, Mobilisation et Recomposition des Rapports de Travail et d'Emploi," *Sociologie du Travail* 1:63-79.

Rubery, J., D. Grimshaw, R. Donnelly, and P. Urwin. 2009. "Revisiting the UK Model: From Basket Case to Success Story and Back Again," in *European Employment Models in Flux: A Comparison of Institutional Change in Nine European Countries*, eds. Bosch, G., L. Lehndorff, and J. Rubery, (London: Palgrave Macmillan), 57-80.

Santos, B. S. 1985. "Estado e Sociedade na Semiperiferia do Sistema Mundial: o Caso Português," *Análise Social* 87/88/89:869-901.

Santos, B. S. 1995. "Sociedade-Providência ou Autoritarismo social?" *Revista Crítica de Ciências Sociais* 42:1-7.

Schroeder, L. 2000. "The Role of Youth Programmes in the Transition from School to Work," in *A Comparative Analysis of Transitions from Education to Work in Europe—Based on National School Leavers Surveys*, ed. Hannan, D. (Dublin: Economic and Social Research Institute), 118-148.

Sebastião, J. 1998. "Os dilemas da Escolaridade," in *Portugal que Modernidade?* Eds. Viegas, J. M., A. F. Costa, and A. Almeida (Oeiras: Celta Editora), 311-327.

—. 2009. *Democratização do Ensino, Desigualdades Sociais e Trajectórias Escolares*. Lisbon: Fundação Calouste Gulbenkian/ Fundação para a Ciência e Tecnologia.

The Danish Government. 2009. *Denmark's National Reform Programme —First Progress Report*. Herstedvang: Schultz Distribution.

UNESCO. 1997. *International Standard Classification of Education ISCED 1997*. http://www.unesco.org/education/information/nfsunesco/ doc/isced_1997.htm (accessed October 11, 2009).

Van der Velden, R., R. Welters, and M. Wolbers 2001. *The Integration of Young People into the Labour Market within the European Union: the Role of Institutional Settings.* Working paper. http://arno.unimaas.nl/show.cgi?fid=9956 (accessed July 2, 2009).

Wallerstein, I. 1984. *The Politics of the World-Economy*. Cambridge: Cambridge University Press.

Wright, I., J. Knight, and K. Brennan 2009. *Investing in Potential—Our Strategy to Increase the Proportion of 16–24 Year Olds in Education, Employment or Training*. Annesley: DCSF Publications.

HIGH FLIERS VERSUS UPSTREAM SWIMMERS: YOUNG RURAL WORKERS IN CANADA AND IRELAND

GORDON B. COOKE

1. Introduction[1]

There is broad consensus that labour markets have been evolving rapidly in developed nations. As a result, "good quality" employment is becoming more elusive to those lacking education, skills, and experience. The fact that younger workers, on average, have less work experience, places an even higher level of importance on the acquisition of valued skills. An additional complication is that education and employment options are likely to be more limited, and possibly of lower quality, for those living in rural locations.

The aim of this study is to explore the choice of 15 young adults (aged 18 to 29) in terms of their pursuit of education and employment options. Those views are augmented by the perspectives of two older individuals who are employed within a rural post-secondary education institution. The views of these 17 individuals were captured via semi-structured interviews conducted in communities throughout rural Ireland and the two Canadian provinces of Newfoundland and Ontario, between February 2009 and June 2011. The interviews were a subset of a much larger study involving employment and life satisfaction among urban versus rural workers in the three jurisdictions described above, and primarily, although not exclusively, involving individuals of at least 40 years of age. After analysing the

[1] This research is supported by a grant from the Social Sciences and Humanities Research Council of Canada. The research assistance from Deidre Hutchings (Memorial University), Kevin Allen (University of Guelph), and Mike MacDonald (McMaster University) is gratefully acknowledged. The author also acknowledges the insights and role of colleagues on the larger comparative study: Isik Zeytinoglu (McMaster University), Sara Mann (University of Guelph), Jimmy Donaghey (University of Warwick) and James Chowhan (McMaster University).

opinions of these young adults, a typology is presented of the career paths that seem to be emerging among them. Afterwards, some brief final remarks are offered. First, though, a brief review of literature is presented, followed by methodological details.

2. Literature Review

As has been thoroughly documented,[2] a characteristic of modern labour markets is the degree of polarisation. While a fortunate minority enjoys good pay, benefits, access to training and other attractive working conditions, many others are only able to acquire so-called "secondary market" jobs which tend to be lower paying, have few if any benefits, training, or promotion opportunities, and tend to provide less security and stability of working hours and employment itself.[3] It is an understatement to simply argue that labour markets continue to evolve in Canada and elsewhere. The brief review of literature that follows looks at the causes of labour market changes, and then at the issues faced by rural and/or youth workers in particular. Since the bulk of the 16 participants were from Canada, much of the cited research is Canadian, but is augmented by European and others sources.

A key catalyst for these labour market changes is the increasingly globalised nature of economies, in which the movement of goods and services occurs more quickly than the movement of labour. As a result, power has shifted away from "labour" (i.e. workers individually and collectively) and towards employers.[4] However, it has also been theorised

---

[2] Betcherman, G., and G. S. Lowe. 1997. "The Future of Work in Canada: A Synthesis Report," Canadian Research Policy Networks. Bosch, G. 2006. "Working Time and the Standard Employment Relationship," in *Decent Working Time, New Trends New Issues,* eds. Boulin, J.Y., M. Lallement, J. Messenger, and F. Michon, (Geneva: ILO), 41-64. Atkinson, J. S. 1987. "Flexibility or fragmentation? The United Kingdom Labour Market in the Eighties," *Labour and Society* 12, No. 1:87-105.

[3] Saunders, R. 2003. *Defining Vulnerability in the Labour Market.* Vulnerable Workers Series, No. 1. Canadian Policy Research Networks.
Vallée, G. 2005. *Towards Enhancing the Employment Conditions of Vulnerable Workers: A Public Policy Perspective.* Vulnerable Workers Series, No. 2. Canadian Policy Research Networks. Zeytinoglu, I. U. 1999. "Flexible Work Arrangements: an Overview of Developments in Canada," in *Changing Work Relationships in Industrialized Economies* ed. Zeytinoglu, I. U., Amsterdam: John Benjamins, 41-58.

[4] Chaykowski, R. P., and M. Gunderson. 2001. "The Implications of Globalization for Labour and Labour Markets," in *Globalization and the Canadian Economy:*

that there has been a strategic change in the way that many employers operate, and since employers are the most influential player, the result is changing employment conditions throughout much of the labour market.[5] Those authors further noted a trend towards more employee involvement, which is part of a broader trend towards enriched work and/or high performance work systems.[6] However, it would be foolhardy to presume that workers are universally benefitting from these trends. On the contrary, each employer has a range of strategic options available in response to the changing business environment, ranging from providing very favourable working conditions to having a cost-minimisation approach to labour.[7] The unstated corollary is that only some individual workers are able to find desirable employment conditions offered by certain employers, or are able to elicit favourable conditions of work from their current employer. Although the causes and effects are complicated, the essential point is that powerful workers are more likely to acquire favourable working conditions from employers, and to resist the implementation of unfavourable conditions.[8] While Bosch[9] suggests that even powerful workers are having trouble retaining their favourable treatment, it is nonetheless clear that their treatment is better, on average, than less powerful workers.

The Implications for Labour Markets, Society and the State, ed. Chaykowski R.P., (Kingston: School of Policy Studies, Queen's University), 27-60. Cooke, G.B., and I.U. Zeytinoglu. 2004. "Temporary Employment: the Situation in Canada," in *International Perspectives on Temporary Agency Work*, eds. Burgess, J., and J. Connell, (The Hague: Routledge), 91-111.

[5] Kochan, T. A., H. C. Katz, and R. B. McKersie. 1986. *The Transformation of American Industrial Relations*. New York: Basic Books.

[6] Messersmith, J. G., and J. P. Guthrie. 2010. "High Performance Work Systems in Emergent Organizations: Implications for Firm Performance," *Human Resource Management* 49, No. 2: 241-264.

[7] Verma, A., and R. P. Chaykowski. 1999. "Employment and Employment Relations at the Crossroads," in *Contract and Commitment: Employment Relations in the New Economy,* eds. Verma, A., and R.P. Chaykowski (Kingston: IRC Press, Queen's University), 1-20. Cooke, G. B., I. U. Zeytinoglu, N. Agarwal, and J. B. Rose. 2008. "Employee-friendly and Employer-friendly Non-standard Work Schedules and Locations," *International Journal of Employment Studies* 16, No. 2: 31-66.

[8] Zeytinoglu, I. U., G.B. Cooke, and S.L. Mann. 2009. "Flexibility: Whose Choice is it Anyway?" *Relations Industrielles/Industrial Relations* 64, No. 4: 555-574.

[9] Bosch, G. 2006. "Working Time and the Standard Employment Relationship," in *Decent Working Time, New Trends New Issues,* eds. Boulin, J. Y., M. Lallement, J. Messenger, and F. Michon, (Geneva: ILO), 41-64.

If globalisation and the subsequent strategic responses by employers to environmental changes are key factors affecting conditions of work in Canada and beyond, then one might wonder how workers can respond appropriately. Notably, education is the short answer. For half a century, it has been argued[10] that workers can improve their employment prospects by increasing their "human capital". Thus, it should not be surprising that, on average, individuals with higher levels of skills or education hold better quality employment in terms of pay, benefits, and work schedules compared to their lesser skilled counterparts in Canada.[11] Of course, a case can be made that progressive employers should provide training and skills upgrading to their employees, and that public policies should also have the same goal.[12] Nonetheless, the case is clear that, at an individual level, acquiring valued skills or education is likely to improve one's employment prospects.

While the changes to the labour market are occurring throughout Canada and Ireland, workers living in rural locations face additional complications.[13] Relative to urban options, employment quality tends to be poorer and with fewer and less diverse options in rural areas.[14] Even if

---

[10] Becker, G. S. 1962. "Investment in Human Capital: A Theoretical Analysis," *Journal of Political Economy*, 70, No. 5:9–49.

[11] Cooke, G. B. 2007. "Alternative Work Schedules and Related Issues among Atlantic Canadians," *The Workplace Review* 4, No. 2: 8-15. Sobey School of Business. Kapsalis, C., and P. Tourigny. 2004. "Duration of Non-standard Employment," *Perspectives on Labour and Income* 5, No. 12: 5-13. Statistics Canada Catalogue No. 75-001-XIE. Lin, J. 2008. "Trends in Employment and Wages, 2002 to 2007," *Perspectives on Labour and Income* 9, No. 9: 5-15. Statistics Canada Catalogue No. 75-001-X.Organisation for Economic Cooperation and Development. 2006. "Boosting Jobs and Incomes—Policy Lessons from Reassessing the OECD Jobs Strategy," in *OECD Employment Outlook 2006,* (Paris: OECD).

[12] Conference Board of Canada. 2008. *How Canada Performs 2008: A Report Card on Canada.*

Organisation for Economic Cooperation and Development. 2006. "Boosting Jobs and Incomes—Policy Lessons from Reassessing the OECD Jobs Strategy," in *OECD Employment Outlook 2006,* (Paris: OECD).

[13] Donaghey, J., G. B. Cooke, and I. U. Zeytinoglu. "Exploring Rural Job Stability and Employment Policy in Newfoundland and Ireland," Paper presented at the 2nd Island Dynamics conference, Valetta, Malta, May 2011.

[14] Kapsalis, C., and P. Tourigny. 2004. "Duration of Non-standard Employment," *Perspectives on Labour and Income* 5, No. 12: 5-13. Statistics Canada Catalogue No. 75-001-XIE. Matthews, R., R. Pendakur, and N. Young. 2009. "Social Capital, Labour Markets, and Job-finding in Urban and Rural Regions: Comparing Paths to

rural workers have a job, there could be fewer advancement opportunities, especially for those with lower skills or education levels.[15] It is also worth remembering that Ireland and Newfoundland have long endured weak economic conditions, including high unemployment, and poor working conditions in general.[16] That said, from the early 1990s, Ireland enjoyed economic growth, although one not fully felt throughout the rural corners of the island, until the economic crisis beginning in 2008.[17] Similarly, Newfoundland has also witnessed an economic boom in recent years, and is now growing faster than Ontario, the traditional economic engine within Canada.[18]

As with rural workers versus their urban counterparts, younger workers also tend to have lower quality education compared to older individuals. More specifically, younger people have difficulty acquiring quality employment due to a lack of experience and/or education.[19] However, notwithstanding the importance of education, it is also influential for these young workers to seek and acquire a good job, as well as receive enough

---

Employment in Prosperous Cities and Stressed Rural Communities in Canada," *The Sociological Review* 57, No. 2: 305-330.

[15] Vera-Toscano, E., E. Phimister, and A. Weersink. 2004. "Panel Estimates of the Canadian Rural/Urban Women's Wage Gap," *American Agricultural Economics Association* 86, No. 4: 1138-1151.

[16] Felt, L. 2003. "Small, Isolated and Successful: Lessons from Small, Isolated Societies of the North Atlantic," Research Paper for the Royal Commission on Renewing and Strengthening Our Place in Canada.

Fortin, P. 2000. *The Irish economic boom: Facts, Causes, and Lessons*. Industry Canada.

[17] Bank Of Ireland. 2010. *The Irish Economy: An Overview*. Bank of Ireland Economic Research Unit. Murphy, A.E. 2000. "The 'Celtic Tiger'—An analysis of Ireland's Economic Growth Performance," EUI Working Papers, Robert Schuman Centre for Advanced Studies, RSC No. 2000/16.

[18] Government of Newfoundland and Labrador. 2010. *The Economy, 2010*. Government of Newfoundland and Labrador. Industry Canada, 2010. *Ontario Economic Overview: February 2010 Update*. Industry Canada. Lin, J. 2008. "Trends in Employment and Wages, 2002 to 2007," *Perspectives on Labour and Income* 9, No. 9: 5-15. Statistics Canada Catalogue No. 75-001-X. Newfoundland and Labrador Federation of Labour in Partnership with the Canadian Centre for Policy Alternatives [NLFL]. 2009. "Newfoundland and Labrador—Weathering the Storm?" Discussion Paper. Tobin, S. 2009. "Adapting to Current and Future Labour Conditions in Newfoundland's Energy Sector: The Employers' View," Unpublished report, Memorial University of Newfoundland, MER Program.

[19] Organisation for Economic Cooperation and Development. 2005. *From Education to Work—A Difficult Transition for Young Adults with Low Levels of Education.* Paris: OECD.

social support.[20] That is, young workers do not make their employment and education choices in isolation. Rather, their decisions are shaped by those around them, for better or worse, in terms of the acquisition of valued skills.[21] As outlined by Shucksmith,[22] at an individual level, some young workers are choosing the path towards education and a career, but others are taking a different path, perhaps travelling or emigrating to a different location for work or adventure, or postponing career decisions.[23]

As one might expect, net emigration (i.e. leaving one location for another) is higher among younger, single workers than those more entrenched with work and family, as are those in areas with weak employment conditions relative to those in areas with stronger job markets.[24] Nonetheless, recent evidence from Tang[25] among impending Newfoundland university graduates indicates that almost half of the participants preferred that their first job after graduation was outside of the province, while others were willing to take any available local job, regardless of quality. It is also worth noting that a reality of Canada, and to a lesser extent, Ireland, is that almost all universities, and even many colleges, are located in larger towns, if not cities or urban areas. Thus, young rural individuals are lucky if there is a nearby post-secondary institution, thereby negating the need to commute or move to acquire education.

When looking at this literature as a set, it seems like the main options available to young rural workers are to:

---

[20] Simmons, L., B. Braun, D.W. Wright, and S.R. Miller. 2007. "Human Capital, Social Support, and Economic Well-being among Rural, Low-income Mothers: A Latent Growth Curve Analysis," *Journal of Family and Economic Issues* 28, No. 4: 635-652.

[21] Locke, A. 2010. "The Social Factors Affecting the Pursuit of Higher Education and Employment for Rural Students," Unpublished report, Memorial University of Newfoundland, MER Program.

[22] Shucksmith, M. 2004. "Young People and Social Exclusion in Rural Areas," *Sociologia Ruralis* 44, No. 1: 43-59.

[23] Nixon, A. 2010. "Youth Attitudes and Employment: Is the Emerging Workforce Changing?" Unpublished report, Memorial University of Newfoundland, MER Program.

[24] Bernard, A., R. Finnie, and B. St.-Jean. 2008. "Interprovincial Mobility and Earnings," *Perspectives on Labour and Income* 9, No. 10: 15-25, Statistics Canada Catalogue No. 75-001-X.

[25] Tang, X. 2009. "Career Choices for Current Post-secondary Students in Newfoundland and Labrador," Unpublished report, Memorial University of Newfoundland, MER Program.

i) move away to seek post-secondary education;
ii) attend whatever post-secondary institution and/or programme that is available locally or within a manageable commute;
iii) move away to seek better-quality employment opportunities;
iv) try to find local employment without seeking post-secondary employment. Needless to say, there are pros and cons with each option, although the last one on average would seemingly involve the poorest quality employment.

3. Methodology

This exploratory analysis is based on the responses of 15 young adults (aged 18 to 29) in terms of their choices regarding the pursuit of education and/or employment. Those views are augmented by the perspectives of two older individuals who are employed within a rural post-secondary education institution. The views of these 17 individuals were captured via semi-structured interviews conducted in communities throughout rural Ireland and the two Canadian provinces of Newfoundland and Ontario conducted between February 2009 and June 2011.

This analysis was undertaken as part of a much larger comparative study of the employment, lifestyle, and well-being issues among urban versus rural individuals in Ireland and the two Canadian provinces of Newfoundland and Ontario. That study involved a number of researchers from McMaster University, the University of Guelph, and the University of Warwick. In the main study, particular attention was paid to older rural individuals (40+ years of age), although we included any adults (18+ years of age) who volunteered to participate. The focus on older individuals was due to our presumption that, at some point in life, perspectives can change, with employment and career paths becoming less important with regard to issues outside of work, such as family, hobbies, and lifestyles. Implicitly, then, younger individuals necessarily must change choices in terms of the acquisition of skills, education, and the pursuit of work experience.

The larger study consists of 155 individuals (at last count), of which 80 reside in Newfoundland, 46 in Ireland, and 29 in Ontario, who participated in semi-structured interviews individually or in small groups. Participants in this study were located via newspaper advertisements, door-to-door flyers, and snowball sampling. In terms of location type, approximately 20% of participants were from urban locations, and about 80% were from rural communities of varying sizes and degrees of remoteness.

At the start of the study, individuals from rural Newfoundland were of particular interest since they were thought to be affected by the economic restructuring, declining populations, and the weak economic circumstances that have existed for many years. Due to their cultural connections and similar economic conditions prior to the economic boom beginning in the 1990s, rural Irish workers were also of interest for comparative purposes. The views of participants from Ontario were also of relevance to be able to search for similarities and differences between those in the industrialised central part of Canada with those in the relatively remote and less industrialised Atlantic region. Due to random chance, interviews began to be scheduled shortly after the global economic crisis, emerging late in 2008, significantly and negatively impacted employment conditions in Ireland and Ontario, but less so in Newfoundland.

4. Interview Findings

Due to the relatively small number of young adult interview participants (i.e. 15), each will be briefly described. Afterwards, the participants will be grouped according to their education, employment, and residential decisions. It should be noted that some respondents did not provide specific demographic information and/or answers to each interview question. As a result, reasonable inferences were made, where necessary. To help with those inferences, the interview findings from the two older participants, involved in the education of young people, proved to be insightful. Finally, it should be noted that, to protect participants' identities, some minor details were omitted, modified or camouflaged.

The participants:

P1: This male participant, who is in his mid-20s, participated in a group interview in rural Newfoundland. He had at most high school education, and had moved to other areas in Canada at least twice for several months. He would like to stay in his current rural location, but indicated that his lack of education is preventing him from finding much employment locally. Thus, he is reluctantly expecting to have to move again. He lives in a community where it is possible to commute to an urban area in approximately 45 minutes either way.

P2: This university-educated male participant, who is in his late 20s, was interviewed in rural Newfoundland. He had to move away to attend university, but has been lucky enough to find a permanent full-time job in his chosen field (in arts/culture) in his hometown. Upward mobility is limited, and work demands are high, but he has a rewarding job. He lives in a small community having a tangible seasonal tourism industry, but is otherwise small and isolated from urban areas.

P3: This male participant, in his mid-20s, was interviewed in rural Newfoundland. He had to move away from his hometown shortly after finishing high school to find steady employment (in landscaping and construction) elsewhere in Canada. Prior to the move, he had tried to commute from his rural hometown to a nearby urban area to make a living, but only sporadic unsocial work (i.e. featuring night and weekend hours) was available. He is actually starting a family in urban Ontario, since he and his partner have much better employment prospects (in terms of job security, pay, and benefits) in that location. From his original Newfoundland hometown, transportation/infrastructure issues consistently prevented him from travelling to an urban area in under an hour, each way.

P4: This female participant, who is in her late 20s, was interviewed in rural Newfoundland. Although she did not indicate her attained education, she is employed in a seasonal but full-time public sector job working in an administrative/clerical office job. She and her spouse had moved to Ontario, but wanted to return to Newfoundland after their children were born. She thinks that long-distance commuting is not feasible for those with children, yet she acknowledges that returning Newfoundlanders have a significant challenge to find acceptable employment in rural western areas. She lives in a small, isolated community having a tangible, but short, seasonal tourism industry.

P5: This female participant was interviewed in Ontario and is in her early 20s. She has completed high school, and has chosen to stay in her rural hometown. That essentially requires commuting for about 45 minutes each way to a large urban area for employment. Her work experience in high school had been in the secondary market, consisting of sporadic, retail jobs. However, after high school graduation, someone in her social circle was able to get her a job as a claims clerk within a large financial company. She feels fortunate to have a secure, full-time white collar job with daytime hours. Plus, with chances for overtime, she is satisfied with her earnings. She indicated that "better jobs" are for those with higher levels of education.

P6: This male participant, who is in his mid-20s, was interviewed in urban Ireland. He holds an apprenticeship in a technical/trades occupation, and had worked in his urban hometown after high school. Due to an urge to travel, he quit his job for an overseas adventure for work and pleasure. However, he returned to Ireland after the financial crisis had arrived. Because of a lack of employment locally, he moved to North America, and worked in a permanent, full-time well-paying urban position as long as he was legally allowed to. Recently, he reluctantly returned to Ireland due an expiring work permit, but plans to relocate, within Ireland or beyond, wherever he can find a comparable high-paying job, like the one he held in the past .

P7: This female participant, who is not yet 20, was interviewed in rural Ireland. She has already moved to an urban centre in Ireland, to get a university degree, and was visiting home temporarily. She has already travelled internationally for a short-term tourist job for the work experience and adventure. Although she likes her hometown, she is planning to start a professional career in the urban centre after graduation. She will only return to her hometown if having children, and if she can find comparable employment or the opportunity to be self-employed. She stated that she "will not just work in a shop or pub" to return home.

P8: This female participant, who is not yet 20, was interviewed in Ireland. She is very attached to her small, rural community, and is unwilling to move away to acquire post-secondary education. She freely admits that she is making a choice that could affect her career. She expects to have to take whatever employment opportunities are available locally, such as part-time, retail jobs. She feels that it is worth it, since it means that she gets to stay and enjoy the benefits of friends, family, and lifestyle.

P9. This female participant, in her early 20s, was interviewed in rural Ireland. She commutes daily to her job in an adjacent rural community about 20 minutes away, each way. She enjoys the drive and also prefers the privacy and freedom of working in a different place other than her small hometown. She works in a publicly-funded, short-term, low-paying, part-time job at a tourist site. She does not have post-secondary education. She said that there are very few, if any, paid full-time permanent jobs in the area that become available, especially for someone with her education. Since she does not want to relocate, even for part of a year, she is prepared to commute up to 90 minutes each day for work, if a better opportunity materialises. She admits that it is hard to manage her expenses given her low earnings.

P10: This female participant, in her mid-20s, was interviewed in suburban Newfoundland, in a small community adjacent to an urban centre. She is university-educated, and attended a local university and also attended university in a neighbouring province to complete a program not available in Newfoundland. She has a permanent, full-time job in her chosen field, in her hometown. She is satisfied with her job, and would not have been able to obtain it without her post-secondary education. That said, she is still in a rather low-paying job. She agrees that the choices are tougher for rural youth who have fewer local employment and education options.

P11: This female participant, who is in her mid-20s, was interviewed in rural Newfoundland. She is an immigrant but has worked briefly elsewhere in Canada prior to relocating for a permanent, full-time job in rural Newfoundland. She is university-educated in her home country. She relocated for better career options in Canada, and was attracted to the job offer in Newfoundland. While she enjoys her job, and is happy with her current employer, co-workers, tasks, and lifestyle, she notes that there are better employment prospects outside of Canada, perhaps, and will not stay unless her family joins her in her adopted community and country.

P12: This female participant, who is in her mid-20s, was interviewed in rural Newfoundland. She is also an immigrant, has worked briefly elsewhere in Canada prior to relocating for a permanent, full-time job in rural Newfoundland, and was university-educated in her home country. Like her colleague, P11, she is happy with her job and lifestyle in this rural location. She is inclined to stay in her current job within this rural community, but is also willing to consider available employment opportunities in other locations in the future as well, within and outside of the province and country.

P13: This male participant, who is in his mid-20s, was interviewed in rural Newfoundland. He is an immigrant, and was recruited to work in rural Newfoundland. He was university-educated in his home country, and upon his arrival in Newfoundland, began in a professional, permanent, full-time position. He is very happy with his job and the lifestyle in his adopted community. He wants to live in a rural community because he prefers the pace of life. If his partner finds local employment, then he/they are inclined to establish roots in this location.

P14: This female participant, who is close to 20 years old, was interviewed in rural Newfoundland. She is currently employed in a publicly-funded, full-time job at a tourist site for the summer season. She is currently a full-time student at a local college. She chose that institution to avoid having to relocate to acquire post-secondary education. Her plan is that, upon graduation, she will find the best available local employment to be able to live in, or very near, her childhood hometown. She recognises that she is potentially going to have to make some financial sacrifices (in terms of pay, benefits, security, and upward mobility) to be able to be in proximity with friends and family, and to enjoy the lifestyle she seeks.

P15: This male participant, who is close to 20 years old, was interviewed in rural Newfoundland. He is currently employed in a publicly-funded, full-time job at a tourist site for the summer season. He is also currently a full-time university student within the province during other times of the year. That program requires him to relocate to an urban centre. His plan is that, upon graduation, he will take the best available position (which he described in terms of pay and security), regardless of location. If that requires him to live elsewhere in Newfoundland, or elsewhere in Canada – urban or rural – he will take that path to maximise his career. At the same time, he admits that he would like to raise his children in Newfoundland if that materialises in the future, but he is unwilling at this point to make career sacrifices to be able to stay in his childhood hometown. Thus, he says that he will only be able to return to his hometown when-or if- he is able to get a comparable job in his chosen career in that location.

5. Typology

Consistent with expectations and the reviewed literature, several of these young participants are struggling with their employment and education choices, and those in rural areas appear to have extra complications. Moreover, the ones without post-secondary education have faced more uncertainty and have faced the decision whether or not to move. In other words, there are logistical hurdles facing young individuals, and especially rural ones, that essentially force them into one of a small number of rigid streams or categories. More specifically, after attending high school, the young rural workers who were interviewed had to decide whether or not to seek additional training/education, and whether or not to seek employment. If the answer was "yes" to either or both of those decisions, then a decision needed to be made as to where to pursue these goals. Due to the lack of local post-secondary education options, these young people were faced with commuting, or moving temporarily or permanently to another location. Thus, it seems like the plight of these young workers is at least loosely captured by the following typology of three categories.[26]

High Fliers are committed to pursuing university education, and, in many cases, want to enter a professional occupation. This often requires them to move to an urban area to pursue that education, and even if not required, individuals are likely to seek urban education options. Moreover, after graduation, there can be limited options in their chosen occupation within their hometowns. Thus, these individuals, who are arguably the "cream of the local crop", are unlikely to remain in rural communities. However, once they have attained education and experience, they are potentially in a position to find the elusive good quality rural jobs, if they so choose.

Mid Fliers are interested in upgrading their skills/education, but are intent on doing so while residing in, or near, their hometown. Often, these are the ones aspiring to attend available local college programs or apprenticeships, or to commute daily to be educated in a different location. Due to their loyalty and educational pursuits, these people have the potential to advance within the local labour market, if they successfully obtain those sought-after skills. Part of the reason is that people in this category are acquiring the types of blue-collar and/or practical skills that are valued by rural employers. Nonetheless, many will have to leave their hometown to seek experience or advancement opportunities and/or additional education.

Upstream Swimmers either do not finish high school, or do not acquire additional post-secondary skills. They are likely to be stuck in low-paid, "secondary market" jobs of a part-time, seasonal or transient nature. These individuals are also relatively likely to live at home (with parents or another relative) which allows them to survive despite low annual earnings. While some individuals move elsewhere to seek employment, the proportion willingly emigrating is seemingly lower than among high fliers. Simply put, workers in this category are prioritising non-work issues over work/career issues, in the sense that they are choosing their place of residence and then seeking available work, rather than seeking the best opportunity for work, regardless of location. On the other hand, it is

---

[26] For an earlier version of this typology, see Cooke, G. B., X. Tang, A. Locke, S. Tobin, and A. Nixon. "Retaining Skilled Young Workers in Rural Newfoundland," Paper presented at the 48th Annual Meeting of the Canadian Industrial Relations Association (CIRA), Fredericton, Canada, June 2011.

fair to say that the higher levels of pay, benefits, and security that are available by emigrating remain a temptation.

6. Concluding Remarks

The purpose of this exploratory analysis was to understand the choices that young adults in rural Canada and Ireland are making with respect to education and employment. The main finding is that there are distinct categories of individuals in terms of their initial career paths. As a general rule, it is difficult to find sufficiently good quality employment in these locations without acquiring post-secondary education and experience. However, the pursuit of those things frequently forces young people to make a decision whether or not to emigrate. It is also worth remembering that a tangible proportion of these young people will want to emigrate, possibly, but not necessarily, with the intentions of returning at a later date. The unfortunate irony, however, is that the ones who are so committed to their community that they will not move even to acquire education or employment experience are potentially going to be trapped in "secondary market" jobs. As a result, the decision to stay or go could be an ongoing one. On the other hand, those moving away to improve their employment prospects might be in a better position to find good quality employment in, or near, their hometowns in the future.

It was also interesting to find that, based on the participants interviewed in this study, the issues affecting young adults in rural Canada are essentially identical to those facing young adults in rural Ireland. While it would be highly imprudent to draw firm conclusions from a small, exploratory study like this one, an obvious public policy response that comes to mind is that it would be desirable for rural individuals had an affordable, practical, accessible way to obtain at least some post-secondary education without having to relocate. Whether that needs to be new institutions or satellite campuses of existing ones, or some system of distance-based education, is an issue for much further investigation and analysis.

References

Atkinson, J. S. 1987. "Flexibility or fragmentation? The United Kingdom Labour Market in the Eighties," *Labour and Society* 12, No. 1:87-105.

Bank Of Ireland. 2010. *The Irish Economy: An Overview*. Bank of Ireland Economic Research Unit.

Becker, G. S. 1962. "Investment in Human Capital: A Theoretical Analysis," *Journal of Political Economy*, 70, No. 5:9–49.

Bernard, A., R. Finnie, and B. St.-Jean. 2008. "Interprovincial Mobility and Earnings," *Perspectives on Labour and Income* 9, No. 10: 15-25, Statistics Canada Catalogue No. 75-001-X.

Betcherman, G., and G. S. Lowe. 1997. "The Future of Work in Canada: A Synthesis Report," Canadian Research Policy Networks.

Bosch, G. 2006. "Working Time and the Standard Employment Relationship," in *Decent Working Time, New Trends New Issues,* eds. Boulin, J.Y., M. Lallement, J. Messenger, and F. Michon, (Geneva: ILO), 41-64.

Chaykowski, R. P., and M. Gunderson. 2001. "The Implications of Globalization for Labour and Labour Markets," in *Globalization and the Canadian Economy: The Implications for Labour Markets, Society and the State,* ed. Chaykowski R.P., (Kingston: School of Policy Studies, Queen's University), 27-60.

Conference Board of Canada. 2008. *How Canada Performs 2008: A Report Card on Canada.*

Cooke, G.B. 2007. "Alternative Work Schedules and Related Issues among Atlantic Canadians," *The Workplace Review* 4, No. 2: 8-15. Sobey School of Business.

Cooke, G. B., and I. U. Zeytinoglu. 2004. "Temporary Employment: the Situation in Canada," in *International Perspectives on Temporary Agency Work*, eds. Burgess, J., and J. Connell, (The Hague: Routledge), 91-111

Cooke, G. B., I. U. Zeytinoglu, N. Agarwal, and J.B. Rose. 2008. "Employee-friendly and Employer-friendly Non-standard Work Schedules and Locations," *International Journal of Employment Studies* 16, No. 2: 31-66.

Cooke, G. B., X. Tang, A. Locke, S. Tobin, and A. Nixon. "Retaining Skilled Young Workers in Rural Newfoundland," Paper presented at the 48th Annual Meeting of the Canadian Industrial Relations Association (CIRA), Fredericton, Canada, June 2011.

Donaghey, J., G. B. Cooke, and I. U. Zeytinoglu. "Exploring Rural Job Stability and Employment Policy in Newfoundland and Ireland," Paper presented at the 2nd Island Dynamics conference, Valetta, Malta, May 2011.

Felt, L. 2003. "Small, Isolated and Successful: Lessons from Small, Isolated Societies of the North Atlantic," Research Paper for the Royal Commission on Renewing and Strengthening Our Place in Canada.

Fortin, P. 2000. *The Irish economic boom: Facts, Causes, and Lessons*. Industry Canada.

Government of Newfoundland and Labrador. 2010. *The Economy, 2010*.

Government of Newfoundland and Labrador. Industry Canada, 2010. *Ontario Economic Overview: February 2010 Update*. Industry Canada.

Kapsalis, C., and P. Tourigny. 2004. "Duration of Non-standard Employment," *Perspectives on Labour and Income* 5, No. 12: 5-13. Statistics Canada Catalogue No. 75-001-XIE.

Kochan, T. A., H. C. Katz, and R. B. McKersie. 1986. *The Transformation of American Industrial Relations*. New York: Basic Books.

Lin, J. 2008. "Trends in Employment and Wages, 2002 to 2007," *Perspectives on Labour and Income* 9, No. 9: 5-15. Statistics Canada Catalogue No. 75-001-X.

Locke, A. 2010. "The Social Factors Affecting the Pursuit of Higher Education and Employment for Rural Students," Unpublished report, Memorial University of Newfoundland, MER Program.

Matthews, R., R. Pendakur, and N. Young. 2009. "Social Capital, Labour Markets, and Job-finding in Urban and Rural Regions: Comparing Paths to Employment in Prosperous Cities and Stressed Rural Communities in Canada," *The Sociological Review* 57, No. 2: 305-330.

Messersmith, J. G., and J. P. Guthrie. 2010. "High Performance Work Systems in Emergent Organizations: Implications for Firm Performance," *Human Resource Management* 49, No. 2: 241-264.

Murphy, A. E. 2000. "The 'Celtic Tiger'—An analysis of Ireland's Economic Growth Performance," EUI Working Papers, Robert Schuman Centre for Advanced Studies, RSC No. 2000/16.

Newfoundland and Labrador Federation of Labour in Partnership with the Canadian Centre for Policy Alternatives [NLFL]. 2009. "Newfoundland and Labrador—Weathering the Storm?" Discussion Paper.

Nixon, A. 2010. "Youth Attitudes and Employment: Is the Emerging Workforce Changing?" Unpublished report, Memorial University of Newfoundland, MER Program.

Organisation for Economic Cooperation and Development. 2005. *From Education to Work—A Difficult Transition for Young Adults with Low Levels of Education.* Paris: OECD.

Organisation for Economic Cooperation and Development. 2006. "Boosting Jobs and Incomes—Policy Lessons from Reassessing the OECD Jobs Strategy," in *OECD Employment Outlook 2006,* (Paris: OECD).

Saunders, R. 2003. *Defining Vulnerability in the Labour Market.* Vulnerable Workers Series, No. 1. Canadian Policy Research Networks.

Shucksmith, M. 2004. "Young People and Social Exclusion in Rural Areas," *Sociologia Ruralis* 44, No. 1: 43-59.

Simmons, L., B. Braun, D. W. Wright, and S. R. Miller. 2007. "Human Capital, Social Support, and Economic Well-being among Rural, Low-income Mothers: A Latent Growth Curve Analysis," *Journal of Family and Economic Issues* 28, No. 4: 635-652.

Tang, X. 2009. "Career Choices for Current Post-secondary Students in Newfoundland and Labrador," Unpublished report, Memorial University of Newfoundland, MER Program.

Tobin, S. 2009. "Adapting to Current and Future Labour Conditions in Newfoundland's Energy Sector: The Employers' View," Unpublished report, Memorial University of Newfoundland, MER Program.

Vallée, G. 2005. *Towards Enhancing the Employment Conditions of Vulnerable Workers: A Public Policy Perspective.* Vulnerable Workers Series, No. 2. Canadian Policy Research Networks.

Vera-Toscano, E., E. Phimister, and A. Weersink. 2004. "Panel Estimates of the Canadian Rural/Urban Women's Wage Gap," *American Agricultural Economics Association* 86, No. 4: 1138-1151.

Verma, A., and R. P. Chaykowski. 1999. "Employment and Employment Relations at the Crossroads," in *Contract and Commitment: Employment Relations in the New Economy,* eds. Verma, A., and R. P. Chaykowski (Kingston: IRC Press, Queen's University), 1-20.

Zeytinoglu, I. U. 1999. "Flexible Work Arrangements: an Overview of Developments in Canada," in *Changing Work Relationships in Industrialized Economies* ed. Zeytinoglu, I. U., Amsterdam: John Benjamins, 41-58.

Zeytinoglu, I .U., G. B. Cooke, and S. L. Mann. 2009. "Flexibility: Whose Choice is it Anyway?" *Relations Industrielles/Industrial Relations* 64, No. 4: 555-574.

THE SCHOOL-TO-WORK TRANSITION IN MEXICO

MARÍA ASCENSIÓN MORALES RAMÍREZ

1. Introductory Remarks

Nowadays, global changes in the economy, productivity and work organisation have made it extremely difficult for young people to actively participate in society.

Education and employment are wide-ranging issues because of the scope of both notions, mainly in terms of objectives, rationale and dynamics.[1] The relationship between these two domains has always been a complicated one and has undergone continuous changes over the years. Moreover, there are a number of issues and outcomes that characterise this interaction, which can be looked into through varied, innovative and inclusive perspectives.[2]

In Mexico, the nexus between education and employment has witnessed profound transformations over the last twenty-five years. During this time, one might observe the establishment of new education strategies, institutions and actors, as well as the devising of a range of aid programmes. Today, however, the relationship between these two domains as a means for individual and social development is being seriously questioned. As participation rates have shown, a high percentage of young Mexicans are unable to enter the workforce, with many of them who, although occupied, engage in precarious and unstable employment without being entitled to social security benefits.[3]

In view of the above, this paper aims at identifying some of the factors that can explain the difficulties faced by young people to enter the labour

---

[1] Ibarrola, M. 2005. "Educación y Trabajo," *Revista Mexicana de Investigación Educativa* 10, No. 25:303.

[2] Vera, A. 2009. *Los jóvenes y la formación para el trabajo en América Latina.* Buenos Aires: CUPPEC, 12.

3 Saravi, G. 2009. "Desigualdad en las experiencias y sentidos de la transición escuela-trabajo," *Papeles de Población* 15, No. 59.

market.[4] In order to do so, a brief analysis of the policies intended to modernise education will be presented, which resulted in innovative government strategies concerning the schooling system. Subsequently, an examination of the trends in vocational training will be provided, followed by a review of the measures implemented to minimise the issue. Finally, some remarks about future developments with regard to the transition from school to work will conclude the present work.

2. Education Policy

In Mexico, the onset of globalisation in the late 1980s placed the concept of "modernisation" at the core of public discourse and policies.[5]

At the time, it was regarded as imperative for the country to modernise its education system, also in consideration of new ideas stemming from the knowledge society and the importance attached to grounding competitiveness on greater productivity owing to scientific and technological innovation.

Accordingly, this state of affairs led government authorities to carry out necessary reforms, with the aim to provide students with the tools needed to face foreseeable developments in the working world. In 1989 the government devised and implemented education programmes for this purpose.[6]

A number of education policies were adopted by the last four governments, denoting an attempt to either comply with or move away from what was previously done, especially in the period 2000 to 2006.[7]

[4] In Mexico there are some 20.2 million young people (between the age of 15 and 24), that is one-fifth of the overall population (108.4 million), comprised of teenagers (10.4 million) and adults (9.8 million).

[5] In 1989, Mexico became openly and intentionally involved in economic modernisation and globalisation in the aftermath of the "lost" decade, when the national economy collapsed in the wake of those of most Latin American countries. During this period, the North American Free Trade Agreement was concluded, and the country became a member of the Organisation for Economic Co-operation and Development (OECD). In a similar vein, several bilateral treaties with South American countries were concluded. Strategies in the economy were targeted at exports and open trade.

[6] Starting from the 1980s, new administrations are under the obligation to present a National Development Plan at the beginning of each term in office. This plan must include programmes for all sectors, including education.

[7] Between 1950 and 1988, the policies implemented by the different administrations were manifold and lawmakers did not show any attempt to provide continuation of those formerly in place.

Each administration put forward different measures to overcome serious inequalities and shortcomings in the national education system. Sectoral studies were carried out and revealed the same problems at different levels, from preschool to higher education: limited access and coverage of education, attempts to improve the quality of training for teachers, the establishment of infrastructure and systems of coordination. Long- and mid-term proposals were carried forward to deal with the foregoing questions, as were evaluation mechanisms.

In general terms, what emerged was that the problems were passed along from one programme to another and each administration found that the teachers' unions was one of the causes for the measures having a minor impact on rectifying the deficiencies in basic education. In this sense, unions seem to contribute more in the form of discourse and legitimisation.[8]

By way of example, two decades after its creation, the programme *Participación Social* did not yield the expected results due to educational, political, social and geographic factors, as well as fierce opposition from the groups holding power in basic education.

As for higher levels of education, the State moved away from the evaluation function it had played in public universities, and at this level the logic of the market was seen as a strategic steering mechanism.

To put it briefly, educational policies have attended to the issue of the coverage needed to satisfy the demand of increased enrolment, although different trends can be seen if one considers the several stages of education. Evidently, such a discrepancy has brought out the deficiencies of teaching,[9] especially in basic education.

Measures put in place to ensure equality—e.g. the use of new technologies and adequate training to satisfy the needs of the productive sector—have not produced the desired results, mostly because they have not been fully implemented and remained effective only in theory.

The lack of both education and social policies within a macroeconomic context is likewise apparent; a developed and equitable society cannot

---

[8] Guevara Niebla, G. 2011. "El rumbo perdido, El escándalo educativo," *Nexos,* No. 401:33-34.

[9] Ensuring quality education is a process of inclusion throughout one's lifetime, during which tools are acquired to face the different obstacles that exclude or discriminate against students, thus limiting learning and their potential development as individuals.

exist or aspire to be competitive in a globalised world if 70% of its population over the age of 15 lag behind.[10]

3. Training for Work

3.1. Formal Education

As far as vocational training is concerned, programmes were adopted to keep up with the modernisation of the productive sector and economic inclusion in a globalised world. Formal education—that is structured into levels and provides a degree—confirmed the increasing rapprochement between methodologies and strategies, and education and productive systems. The demand in the productive sector was met through higher levels of educational attainment among the population under the formal education system and a higher percentage of graduates from technical schools.

In the meanwhile, a range of vocational education programmes was set up in order to fill the vacuum between secondary and tertiary education[11], as well as to promote on-the-job training and technological innovation. More specifically:

a) High schools offer technical and vocational courses. Although similar in terms of duration, the difference between them lies in the nature of the subjects taught.[12]

---

[10] Díaz de Cossío, R. 2011. "La chapulinera, El escándalo educativo," *Nexos*, No. 401:41-42.

[11] It should be pointed out, however, that the reform process that took place over the last two decades mostly concerned secondary education, particularly vocational training.

[12] Among others, the National Technical and Professional School (*Colegio Nacional de Educación Profesional Técnica - CONALEP*) is worthy of mention. Once a decentralised body, this school is still run by the state, although under federal control and supervision. It is a three-year school where students acquire a set of trade-related skills in addition to basic knowledge through formal education. In other words, the aim is to train technical experts. In this connection, amendments have recently been made to this education pattern to make it more skill-based to meet the needs of the productive sector. This curriculum combines theoretical learning with practical skills, with each year corresponding to a qualification—e.g. assistant, basic, and professional technician. This system allows students to obtain a qualification also in cases in which they decide to interrupt their studies. Since 1994, these schools have established joint committees with the involvement of local businesses, the aim of which is to define the cooperation with

b) As for upper secondary school, in addition to university courses, a range of intermediate programmes and technical institutes, as well as special "technological" universities—which have been increasingly widespread in Mexico since 1991—were established.[13] The aim was to train at least 70% of those exiting the university[14] and 30% of students in vocational schools.[15] The promotion of both vocational and technological programmes in higher education in an attempt to modernise education has produced a number of outcomes:[16]

- major improvements in courses and programmes;
- diversification as well as the creation of new educational levels and courses to respond to the demand for schooling, mainly in technical subjects;
- the establishment of decentralised educational bodies nationwide, such as the Centres for Science and Technology Education (*Centros de Educación Científica Tecnológica*) and Technological Universities;
- in order to meet the companies' needs, the scope for educational bodies to provide documentation certifying vocational and technical skills is widened, also as a way to liken the qualifications obtained to those of traditional educational paths;
- the introduction of educational standards based on occupational skills;

---

companies, promote training activities, propose new subjects and courses and, whereas necessary, ask for the removal of school officials.

[13] Technological universities are government-run bodies that operate at the decentralised level and offer postgraduate studies that can be completed in two years. Terms usually have a duration from four to six months; the amount of hours making up the courses is 3,000 and combines theoretical (30%) and practical learning (70%), with in-company training that is carried out in several ways. Following the upgrading of the production processes, a number of new courses have been introduced: environmental technology, office automation, and marketing, among others, at the end of which students obtain the qualification of Advanced University Level Technician.

[14] Although this level of education has reported an increase in terms of enrolment, there are still a number of questions to overcome with regard to the entry requirements and relevance of the courses.

[15] Ibarrola, M. 2001. "Los cambios estructurales y las políticas de capacitación y formación para el trabajo en México. Un Análisis de la expresión local de políticas nacionales," in *Los jóvenes y el trabajo: la educación frente a la exclusión social,* ed. Pieck, E. (Mexico: ILO), 229.

[16] These innovations are in line with new modes of production.

- the planning of internships within companies while attending high schools;
- the introduction of certification attesting to skills that are recognised nationwide. Cooperation between companies and education providers has been strengthened, also by the devising of new courses.
- the setting of *ad-hoc* policies to improve and ensure the up-to-date quality of teaching;
- the planning of academic and individual assessment criteria in order to grant funds and pay rises.

3.2. Informal Education

Among the bodies that afford informal education at either public and private level, the Work and Training Centres—*Centros de Capacitación para el Trabajo (CECATI)*[17]—and the Work and Training Institutes—*Institutos de Capacitación para el Trabajo (ICAT)*[18]—stand out in terms of relevance. Whereas the former are federal entities, the latter are government-run institutions. They both prepare the workforce to perform in manufacturing and service sectors and they are also responsible for on-the-job training and lifelong learning. These programmes are universally recognised as the most adequate means for providing workers—especially operators—with practical skills.[19] Such training systems are tailored to those who have not completed education, and to students who have access to further levels of education. It can be seen as an option for the segment of the population that is excluded from the general education system and aims at easing the transition from school to work.[20]

3.3. Scope

The increasing recourse to vocational training demonstrates that now the education system covers a growing number of subjects, offering a wider range of degrees. However, one of the side effects of such a variety is the emergence of deep-rooted differences—chiefly within formal education—in terms of access, quality, and school attainment. They also

---

[17] Created in 1988, these centres are now well-established.
[18] There are more than 200 institutes in the country.
[19] Work and Training Institutes have devised a certified Work Skills Recognition system that evaluates and certifies knowledge, skills and abilities, regardless of how they have been gained.
[20] ILO. 2007. *Trabajo decente y juventud.* Lima: Regional Office for Latin America and the Caribbean, 73.

brought out a tendency towards technical subjects and a growth in non-formal education. The most serious outcome of these differences marked increased levels of social inequalities. On close inspection, one might note that:

a) with regard to access to education, the skills provided by the system of formal education are not standardised, thus heightening inequalities among young people from different social backgrounds. Arguably, those from low-income families find it harder to access higher levels of schooling;
b) in taking the completion rate into account, the number of years of education attained might differ in accordance with social status;
c) when it comes to quality, the system fails to provide adequate vocational skills, widening the occupational gap and the fragmentation in employment and training. As a result, graduates face more difficulties in entering the workforce and in achieving required levels of productivity, which, in turn, generate unemployment among professionals and income inequality.

In this sense, relevant studies pointed out that individuals, although highly educated, are unemployed or engage in temporary and low-paid jobs. Further, the activities they performed have little to nothing to do with what they have learnt at school.[21]

Therefore, the quality of education is one of the key issues in unemployment. As one can see, the lack of connection between these two worlds is such only to those who have a superficial understanding of the issue. Notwithstanding this, the gap between the levels of educational attainment and companies' needs is growing wider.[22]

Furthermore, extracurricular and historical factors that explain access to employment need to be taken into account at the time of examining the

---

[21] Vocational training is no longer a privilege; it has lost value and generates social imbalances in the job market. Although the productive sector calls for personnel to be more adequately prepared, one might note that the same positions were previously filled by people with no schooling. This aspect is to be considered also in the context of school-to-work transition. For some workers, it implies new opportunities for personal and career development, particularly in monetary terms; for some others this has come to mean growing job insecurity and higher levels of vulnerability that doom them to suffer severe social disadvantages.

[22] This state of affairs brings about structural unemployment, which is defined as a lack of correspondence between the skills of the workforce and those needed to satisfy the demand of the job market.

relationship between school and work. In fact, employers demand that applicants fulfil certain requirements concerning physical appearance, personality, gender, and family values, as interpersonal skills help one to graduate and find an occupation earlier. In a similar vein, the structural segmentation of the economy determines the differences in remuneration and working conditions.

The disparity between the skills required by employers and those provided by the national education system has come up against non-formal education provided in vocational training institutions. In other words, on-the-job training had until very recently marked little difference among vocational training institutions within the context of the education system and on-the-job training institutions that are usually run by the Ministry of Labour and Social Welfare. More importance has been given to technical subjects in secondary and higher education, leading the public opinion to think that technical schools provide more adequate skills, and advocating alternative education patterns that are in line with the new productive paradigm, causing formal education to come to disfavour. Hence the gap between what the education system delivers and the reality of the job market, a crucial issue in young people's lack of employability.[23] Equally troubling is the system of job creation that is dependent on economic cycles and lacks forms of tax advantages and incentives for companies that are willing to hire personnel.

4. Training Programmes Targeting Young People

The struggle that many young people face in entering the workforce is the result of shortcomings in the education system, and this is magnified by the economic inequality in the labour market.

Various programmes have been implemented to address these issues, but they are usually seen as providing partial and isolated answers to structural problems, since there is a lack of planning of training, and employment schemes targeting young people. [24] In this connection, mention should be made of the following:

---

[23] Young people experience higher rates of unemployment than the rest of the economically active population (EAP).

[24] There are some other training programmes in Latin America that are intended for young people: Bicentennial Youth (*Jóvenes Bicentenarios*), or the Young Chile Project (*Chile Joven*)—with the latter that has also been implemented in Peru, Colombia, the Dominican Republic, and Argentina (which runs the programme *Jóvenes con más y mejor poder,* too)—and the *Projoven* project in Brazil.

Training Scholarships—*Programas de Becas de Capacitación (BECATE)*

This programme[25] aims at encouraging people to enter the workforce by further enhancing their employability through short training periods, some of which take place at the employer's premises. Training courses are held only in certain regions depending on the availability of facilities, such as training centres, technical high schools and a National School for Vocational and Technical Education (*Colegio Nacional de Educación Profesional Técnica—Conalep*).

This training scheme is usually entered into by people over the age of 16 who are either unemployed or underemployed. It mainly consists of a learning period lasting one to three months, with students who are entitled to a scholarship amounting to three times the minimum wage.[26] Although this programme is not intended exclusively for young people, they account for 60% of those enrolled.[27] Five training methods are combined in this model: mixed training, on-the-job training, self-employment, productive employment and training voucher schemes. Mixed and on-the-job training are the most relevant forms of learning, to which 70% of available funds are allocated.[28]

In offering the mixed system of training, the employer pledges to subsequently hire at least 70% of the students participating in the programme. As for on-the-job training, there is no formal obligation on the part of the employer. Yet this mode of training allows students to learn in the workplace while being granted a scholarship.

On-the-job training has also introduced some major changes, in particular:

---

[25] Similar programmes were already in place in 1984, more specifically the Training Scholarship Programme for Unemployed Workers—*Programa de Becas de Capacitación para Trabajadores Desempleados (Probecat)*—and the Vocational Training System—*Sistema de Capacitación para el Trabajo (Sicat)*.
They were run under the supervision of the Ministry of Public Education (SEP) as part of the Employment Assistance Programme (*Programa de Apoyo al Empleo—PAE*) which comprised a set of active job market policies funded by the Inter-American Development Bank.

[26] The programmes are run by the National Employment Service (*Servicio Nacional de Empleo*)

[27] ILO. 2007. *Trabajo decente y juventud.* Lima: Regional Office for Latin America and the Caribbean.

[28] The mixed training system is mostly adopted by large companies, whereas on-the-job-training takes place in small and micro enterprises.

1) a closer connection with vocational training provided in formal education;
2) the establishment of an unemployment insurance system;
3) a tighter link between employment policies and training programmes.

The "Opportunities" Programme (*Programa Oportunidades*)

This programme can be seen as a conditional cash transfers programme in the sense that it provides financial support to both young people and education providers.[29] It involves several levels of education, ranging from elementary to high school. In order to apply for it, both students and educational bodies must meet certain eligibility criteria:

a) students should complete more years of education than their parents;
b) they should graduate from middle school by the age of 15;
c) as for institutions, the share of girls attending high school should comply with the national average, with sixty percent of them that should successfully complete high school.[30]

In this sense, the project "Young People with Opportunities"—*Jóvenes con oportunidades*—can be viewed as a follow-up programme, as it rewards students who finish high school. In addition, if they decide to attend the university, they can cash their scholarship—2/3 of it at the time of enrolment and the rest if they successfully move to the following year.[31]

The literature provides divergent views about the results of this programme, as in considering a number of educational indicators, much scholarly work showed no evidence of improvement over the last three years. If anything, a significant decline has been witnessed in the completion rates. This setback, reported at the stage of graduation, seems to indicate that the schooling system falls short of accomplishing its purpose. Failing to provide quality education, the programme might run the risk of being shut down.

---

[29] This programme was established in 1997 and it currently provides support to 5 million people.

[30] SEDESOL. 2010. *Oportunidades, un programa de resultados*. Estados Unidos Mexicanos: Gobierno Federal.

[31] If they are unable to continue their studies, their account will be blocked. Money can only be withdrawn once the term expires, that is after two years.

First Job Programme (*Programa del Primer Empleo*)

By means of incentives (e.g. rebates on social security contributions), this programme—which is run by the Mexican Institute of Social Security—is intended to encourage employers to recruit new workers and to tackle undeclared work.

The First Job Programme started in March 2007,[32] and is expected to end in November 2012. The federal government allocated $3 billion Mexican pesos to fund the creation of 300,000 permanent jobs. This training programme is concerned with employers, either individuals or corporations, and new workers.

Registering workers as permanent ones and creating positions that should last 21 months are two of the requirements. At the time of insuring their employees, employers are entitled to social security benefits for the first 12 months. Although not formally targeting young people, a significant share of new recruits consists of young workers who opted for this programme because of its main characteristics.

However, since its establishment, the programme exposed a number of shortcomings:

a) a limited impact in terms of job creation;
b) too many eligibility criteria to be met by the employers, which made the programme unattractive;
c) the attitude of employers, whose recruitment policy was based on their needs and not on the fact that hiring workers is now more affordable.

By 2010, less resources have been allocated to the programme. Experts in the field regarded it as a partial solution to the issue of youth unemployment—especially because no sign of economic growth was reported since its implementation—thus failing to meet its main objectives.[33]

---

[32] The programme directives were published in the Federal Official Gazette on 23 January 2007, and the operating guidelines were published on 27 February of the same year.

[33] On 3 January 2010, the head of the *Instituto Mexicano del Seguro Social* announced that the programme was no longer a priority on its agenda.

Young Entrepreneurs

Fundación ProEmpleo is another institution that offers vocational training,[34] with a focus on developing entrepreneurial skills in those attending the courses.

The approach adopted to help those who want to start a business—or who already have a microenterprise and want to further develop it—might be of different kinds. The profile of those resorting to the services provided by *Fundación ProEmpleo* is diverse, with the share of young people which has increased over time.[35]

The basic programme "Start up or Improve your Business" (*Inicie o mejore su empresa*), has a duration of four weeks—80 hours—and is certified by the Ministry of Public Education. The course addresses various aspects that are critical for small and micro enterprises. After completing the course, students should be in the position to develop a business plan. The foundation provides support and guidance by means of business incubators, who supervise the work through the Business Development Centre (*Centro de Desarrollo Empresarial*).[36]

Young People in Rural Areas (*Juventud rural*)

The fund called *Fondo de Tierras e instalación del joven emprendedor rural* stands out in this area. It is aimed at providing people in the 18 to 39 age group with technical and managerial skills, also granting them a scholarship amounting to the minimum wage in the covered sector for a period of up to 90 days. Young people who complete training have access to the Land Fund (*Fondo de Tierras*), through which they can finance special projects and obtain credit for renting parcels or purchasing rights on them.[37]

---

[34] The foundation was created in 1995 by a group of Mexican companies. Its services are funded by way of contributions made by the Ministry of Finance through the PyME Fund and its own resources. In order to ensure their commitment, participants pay less and are granted the ownership of their activities.

[35] ILO. 2007. *Trabajo decente y juventud.* Lima: Regional Office for Latin America and the Caribbean.

[36] Vera, A. 2009. *Los jóvenes y la formación para el trabajo en América Latina.* Buenos Aires: CUPPEC.

[37] ILO. 2007. *Trabajo decente y juventud.* Lima: Regional Office for Latin America and the Caribbean, 91

5. Education and Employment Prospects

Within a context of trade openness and competitiveness, as is the case of Mexico, economic growth depends on technological innovation and investment in human capital.

Reviewing the education system cannot represent the panacea for the problems faced by young people entering the workforce. Strategies in terms of job creation are the result of economic, political and social changes. Both the schooling and the production systems are, in turn, immersed in a society that conditions their dynamics and structural characteristics.[38]

As a consequence, national governments need to envisage measures in terms of education and economy at the macro level—economic stability, income distribution, social protection and employment—characterised by equality and social justice in all fields, to devise a coherent set of initiatives that will help to attain shared results. Only with a comprehensive policy will it be possible to establish a solid transition between the education system and the job market.[39]

5.1. Education Policies

Basic education—which lays the foundations for entering the workforce— is marked by serious deficiencies and thus requires structural changes that are intended to:

a) divide decision-making power among actors in the field of education: teachers, students, parents, educational bodies, and society more generally (active social participation);[40]

---

[38] The trend growth of global unemployment produces harder competition among the economically active population, long-term unemployment and a more constricted job market.

[39] This also involves reducing the "interval of transition", that includes the time between the moment the formative phase has ended—either as a result of a drop-out or school completion—and the time required to consolidate the skills that are necessary to face the demand and the uncertainties of the labour market with a reasonable amount of aptitude.

[40] With regard to the schooling system, instruments of democratic oversight via Social Participation Councils should be provided to social actors, in order to empower them to influence the workings of education effectively.

b) empower the teaching staff and the education providers with higher levels of authority, thus reducing the power of unions in this sense;[41]
c) achieve professionalism among teachers resulting from gradual training, a strict selection procedure, regular evaluation of their performance, and skills updating;[42]
d) provide education that is relevant and consistent with specific social and economic developments, with the curriculum that should be a reflection of societal needs.

Social participation mentioned above represents a key factor in improving the quality of education. This can also be done by reviewing the school evaluation criteria and by making provisions aimed at strengthening teaching and learning processes. In this sense, education might play an active role in democracy, marking the transformation of the country.[43]

Courses offered in middle schools and universities need to improve their quality and relevance. It is necessary to devise policies, and programmes in the formal education system to deal with these two aspects so that young people can enter the workforce easily and to provide them with tools to update their skills through life, also in consideration of the main characteristics of the information society they lived in.[44]

Quality and relevance can be handled by way of coordinated action between educational bodies and the productive sector, in order to deal with skills shortages that might jeopardise the trade-offs between education and work, young people's aspirations and company's needs, ambitions and reality.[45]

---

[41] It is essential to divest the teachers' unions of its exacerbated power to oversee education, in order to limit their role exclusively to negotiation and labour issues.

[42] That also includes educational and technical aspects in order to learn how to use devices and software applications, helping students to acquire communication skills and develop techniques such as problem-solving and searching for information.

[43] Gómez Nashiki, A., and U. Zurita Rivera. 2011. "Escuela sin sociedad, El escándalo educativo," *Nexos*, No. 401:52-54.

[44] It is necessary to rethink training in the fundamental areas of basic education, particularly with regard to reading, writing and maths skills. Special occupational and decision-making competences should be supplied, alongside the strengthening of personality traits like motivation, discipline, and perseverance.

[45] This should make the education system more effective so as to yield skills companies look for.

In-depth knowledge and trade-related skills are the best guarantee to enter the workforce and enjoy a satisfactory working life. Further, graduates will have the opportunity to perform a job and to make full use of the training received.[46]

This also calls for profound changes in attitude on the part of academia, for instance by incorporating the teaching of practical skills and becoming familiar with the workplace and labour issues before completing training. This would give young people not only specific abilities, but also useful skills to be used in various circumstances, allowing them to adapt to change so as to overcome their most serious disadvantage: the lack of expertise. The analysis of outcomes and experiences that are common to institutions of higher education in both the public and private sector will make it possible to understand what is needed for professional practice.

It is also sensible for each institution to have a coordinator that serves as a go-between in the shift from education to work, as well as a guidance counsellor.[47]

As for investment and efficiency, they should be enhanced by improving the state of the education facilities, the training of teachers, teaching materials, while innovating learning techniques. In addition, measures aimed at fulfilling the demand, reducing dropout rates[48] and smoothing access for those with fewer resources, should be devised.[49]

As far as the entrepreneurial culture is concerned, the general assumption is that young people need to be supervised by an employer and cannot be independent. This view needs to be changed. Formal education should not only develop learning skills, but it should also provide students with entrepreneurial skills so as to become familiar with business. In this sense, young people need to become the protagonists of development.[50]

---

[46] There are precedents for fostering ties between education and the world of work through advisory boards and task forces to define or update curricula and programmes. However, such an effort did not produce substantial changes in practical terms.

[47] It is necessary to consolidate the role of guidance counsellors and transition coordinators at different stages of education to link schools and companies, making access to the labour market easier and contribute to fighting unemployment.

[48] The Mexico City High School has devised a programme called "High School Yes" (*Prepa Si*). A certain amount of money (45 USD) is granted on a monthly basis to students who continue in education, as well as to those who obtain grades from 9 to 10 (roughly 65 USD).

[49] In terms of equity, this is done to include those who do not study or work and, whereas possible, prevent youth migration.

[50] One of the aims of the programme *Oportunidades* is to encourage an entrepreneurial spirit among young people by providing information on how to

5.2. Macroeconomic and Job Market Policies

With regard to macroeconomics, it is crucial to facilitate recruitment in the private sector, by lowering payroll taxes and promoting social benefits in order to increase the demand for labour—that is the creation of jobs that are more satisfactory in qualitative and quantitative terms—relax the eligibility requirements and thus widen the coverage of social security.[51]

With respect to production, simplifying the process to start up small- and medium-sized enterprises is fundamental, alongside supporting existing business to create new job opportunities.[52] Equally important is the establishment of production plants or activities that are labour intensive—e.g. tourism and low-cost housing—strategic activities and occupations closely connected with changes in technology.[53]

As for labour flexibility, efforts have been made to develop strategies for modern and flexible work arrangements in cooperation with social actors. This also implies the devising of new types of employment schemes as a way to respond to a wide range of jobs[54], new methods to deliver learning, and innovative ways of acquiring grades, thus further strengthening the link between labour legislation and social protection.[55]

As far as lifelong learning is concerned, it is sensible to invest in young people through vocational training programmes to be carried out within education institutions, also prioritising individual's career and life cycle.

Concerning youth entrepreneurship, it is necessary to promote adequate conditions for the development of entrepreneurs by means of measures that further establish and improve competitiveness while eliminating legislative and financial barriers for the setting up of companies, particularly for young people (business incubators, joint

---

start up a company or their own business. Such information is available on an ad-hoc website (*Vas*).

[51] In Mexico, 60% of the economically active population is found in the informal sector, the result of failings associated with public life, as well as an inefficient tax and social security system. Therefore, it is necessary to devise incentives to encourage companies to invest and help workers to leave the informal sector.

[52] ILO-IMF. 2010. "Challenges of Growth, Employment and Social Cohesion" Conference paper presented at Oslo, Norway, September 2010.

[53] In Mexico, the 2006-2012 National Development Plan indicated that 800,000 jobs are needed each year.

[54] Social dialogue based on compliance with labour principles and fundamental rights is vital.

[55] ILO 2011. *Studies on Growth with Equity. Making Recovery Sustainable: Lessons from Country Innovations*. Geneva: International Institute for Labour Studies.

bodies, IT, market access, financial services, business development services and formalisation programmes, among others). This calls for proper legislation, that is the elimination of impediments concerning taxation, financial system records, also within the workplace, as well as new innovations and technological development.[56] Of equal importance is the making of a social protection system which provides for mechanisms such as minimum wage based on economic conditions.

To conclude, the planning of complementary training is likewise important, along with adequate information and job placement or support to self-employment services. This means focusing on job service activities in order to provide people with the tools needed to enter the workforce.

References

Candia, J.M. 2006. "Políticas públicas de apoyo a la capacitación y empleabilidad de los jóvenes mexicanos," *Estrategias educativas y formativas para la inserción social y productiva,* Montevideo: CINTERFOR-ILO.

CONAPO. 2010. *La situación actual de los jóvenes en México*. Consejo Nacional de Población.

Díaz de Cossío, R. 2011. "La chapulinera, El escándalo educativo," *Nexos*, No. 401:41-42.

ECLAC. 2007. *Social Panorama of Latin America*. Santiago: ECLAC, United Nations.

Gómez Nashiki, A., and U. Zurita Rivera. 2011. "Escuela sin sociedad, El escándalo educativo," *Nexos*, No. 401:52-54.

Guerra Martínez, M.I. 2005. "Los jóvenes del siglo XXI, ¿Para qué trabajan?" *Revista Mexicana de Investigación Educativa* 10, No. 25:419-449.

Guevara Niebla, G. 2011. "El rumbo perdido, El escándalo educativo," *Nexos*, No. 401:33-34.

Ibarrola, M. 2001. "Los cambios estructurales y las políticas de capacitación y formación para el trabajo en México. Un Análisis de la expresión local de políticas nacionales," in *Los jóvenes y el trabajo: la educación frente a la exclusión social,*ed. Pieck, E. (Mexico: ILO).

Ibarrola, M. de. 2005. "Educación y trabajo," *Revista Mexicana de Investigación Educativa* 10, No. 25:303-313.

[56] While this solution may not solve the problems of unemployment and underemployment, it may take on an important role.

ILO. 2007. *Decent Work and Youth.* Lima: Regional Office for Latin America and the Caribbean.

—. 2011. *Studies on Growth with Equity. Making Recovery Sustainable: Lessons from Country Innovations.* Geneva: International Institute for Labour Studies.

ILO-IMF. 2010. "Challenges of Growth, Employment and Social Cohesion," Conference paper presented at Oslo, Norway, September 2010.

Martínez Rizo, F. 2001. "Las políticas educativas mexicanas antes y después de 2001," *Revista Iberoamericana de Educación*, No. 27.

Méndez Méndez, E., and J. Irepan Hacha. 2004 "La relación educación-trabajo," *Ethos Educativo.*

Mendoza Rojas, J. 2002. *Transición de la educación superior contemporánea en México: de la planeación al Estado Evaluador.* Mexico: UNAM Centro de Estudios sobre la Universidad and Miguel Ángel Porrúa.

Muñoz Izquierdo, C. 2001. "Implicaciones de la escolaridad en la calidad del empleo," in *Los jóvenes y el trabajo: la educación frente a la exclusión social,*ed. Pieck, E. (Mexico: ILO), 155-200.

Observatorio Ciudadano de la Educación. 2008. http://www.observatorio.org/comunicados/EducDebate8_febrero08PSE07-12.html (accessed May 10, 2011).

Ramírez, J. 2001. "Estrategias para generar una transición formativa escuela trabajo en los jóvenes pobres urbanos. El papel de los actores involucrados," in *Los jóvenes y el trabajo: la educación frente a la exclusión social,*ed. Pieck, E. (Mexico: ILO), 333-354.

Saravi, G. 2009. "Desigualdad en las experiencias y sentidos de la transición escuela-trabajo," *Papeles de Población* 15, No. 59.

SEDESOL. 2010. *Oportunidades, un programa de resultados.* Estados Unidos Mexicanos: Gobierno Federal.

Suárez, M. H., and R. Zárate. 1997. "Efectos de la crisis sobre la relación entre la escolaridad y el empleo en México: de los valores a los precios," *Revista Mexicana de Investigación Educativa* 2, No. 4.

Vera, A. 2009. *Los jóvenes y la formación para el trabajo en América Latina.* Buenos Aires: Centro de Implementación de Políticas Públicas para la Equidad y el Crecimiento.

Vera, A., and R. Castioni. 2010. "Los jóvenes en Latinoamérica. La transición escuela-trabajo como objeto de políticas públicas," *Revista Educación Profesional* 36, No. 2.

Zoraida Vázquez, J. 1997. "La modernización educativa (1988-1994)," *Revista Mexicana* 46, No. 4.

Chapter Three:

The Transition from Education to the Labour Market

THE REFORM OF THE EDUCATION SYSTEM IN POLAND: THE IMPACT ON YOUTH UNEMPLOYMENT IN LIGHT OF 1989 POLITICAL EVENTS

JANUSZ ŁYKO

1. Introductory Remarks

Across the world, unemployment is a major economic and social issue. In the aftermath of the Second World War when the socialist regime prevailed and following the political events that took place in 1989, the challenge of unemployment became a serious one in Poland. Indeed, unemployment was not even a problem before, for the right to work in Poland was safeguarded constitutionally. In practical terms, however, this state of affairs led to the question of unemployment being overlooked, and education and employment were viewed as two unrelated fields. In order to secure economic independence and provide stable incomes, people were only trained and assigned a task on the basis of the job to be performed, often without envisioning further stages of education.

Nonetheless, the reform that took place in 1989 altered this situation. The right to full employment was no longer guaranteed, and shortcomings in the economic system generated mass unemployment. From virtually zero, unemployment rates rose to 14.9% in 1993 and to 19.6% in 2003.

Table 3-1. Unemployment Rates in Poland between 1992 and 2009 (%)

Year	1992	1993	1994	1995	1996	1997	1998	1999	2000
%	13.7	14.9	13.9	13.1	11.5	10.2	10.6	15.3	16.0
Year	**2001**	**2002**	**2003**	**2004**	**2005**	**2006**	**2007**	**2008**	**2009**
%	18.5	19.7	19.6	19.0	17.7	13.8	9.6	7.1	8.2

Source: Author's own elaboration on the *Statistical Yearbooks of the Republic of Poland*, 1993-2010.

There are many reasons for this state of play, such as the winding-up of unprofitable plants, structural mismatch, the lack of experience of the workers made redundant, as well as their difficulty in retraining and finding new employment. Lack of work was a new and unknown phenomenon to all, and caused serious consequences.

Table 3-2. Unemployment Rates in Poland by Age Group between 1992 and 2009

Year	Unemployment Rates by Age (%)						
	15-19	20-24	25-29	30-34	35-44	45-54	55 - >
1992	36.4	26.1	16.9	13.1	11.3	9.1	5.9
1993	42.9	27.9	17.6	14.8	12.9	10.1	6.0
1994	45.3	27.6	16.3	14.7	11.2	8.6	5.0
1995	44.1	27.1	14.5	13.4	10.8	8.2	4.9
1996	35.0	23.9	12.6	11.8	9.7	7.4	4.4
1997	31.7	21.2	10.6	9.9	8.9	6.5	4.0
1998	34.5	21.0	11.1	10.1	9.1	7.5	5.3
1999	45.6	29.7	16.9	14.3	12.2	10.8	9.2
2000	41.8	32.4	16.9	15.3	13.2	11.4	8.4
2001	46.8	40.0	20.1	15.6	16.0	13.3	7.1
2002	50.2	42.5	22.6	17.1	15.8	15.3	8.0
2003	42.8	43.1	23.0	17.5	16.3	15.2	9.4
2004	35.2	41.5	22.7	16.0	15.3	15.6	9.7
2005	30.7	38.5	21.2	15.3	14.1	15.2	9.5
2006	30.8	29.6	15.3	11.6	11.3	11.7	7.3
2007	22.2	21.6	10.6	8.2	7.2	8.3	6.1
2008	20.1	16.9	8.2	5.9	5.2	5.8	4.8
2009	27.2	19.8	9.8	6.5	5.9	6.5	5.6

Source: Author's own elaboration on the *Statistical Yearbooks of the Republic of Poland*, 1993-2010.

Young people up to age of 24 with a different educational background are those who have been affected the most by the labour market reform. Accordingly, the role of education at all levels is pivotal in tackling unemployment. In this sense, jobseekers face a number of issues at the time of seeking work which are often dependent on their education. Furthermore, job applicants also need to deal with a lack of expertise, which is commonplace among this group.

3. The Polish Education System until 1989

Over the last century, the education system in Poland has undergone a wholesome reform, the result of both ongoing political issues and efforts to adapt education to the changing needs of both employers and employees. In this connection, a significant role was played by the Polish government, which, among others, further consolidated the idea of sovereignty. Here, independence was restored in 1918 and a number of schooling systems were inherited and adopted, often the consequence of political affiliation. This is because political parties had a say in the provision of education. An example in this connection is the length of compulsory education. In the Austrian partition, school attendance was compulsory for seven years, while in the Prussian partition[1] schooling was mandatory for eight years.[2]

Major differences were also reported in the level of education afforded, particularly between urban and rural areas. The universal and compulsory nature of education were such only on paper, as in practice many villages had no schools at all.

In order to make education accessible to all, significant measures were put in place starting from 1932. The Act on the System of Education[3] that was enacted in the same year introduced major innovations in the system of schooling. Thirteen new institutions supplying primary and secondary education were established, with both elementary and high schools that lasted four years. Vocational training was also re-designed and it involved three main stages. The first training period was four-years long and ended with a journeyman exam. If trainees wanted to become a specialised technician, they needed to stay in their position for five more years. On the whole, the highest level of expertise—that was that of technology expert—

---

[1] The Austrian partition refers to the former territories of the Polish-Lithuanian Commonwealth acquired by the Austrian Empire during the partitions of Poland in late 18th century. The Partitions of Poland or Partitions of the Polish-Lithuanian Commonwealth—refers to three partitions which took place in the second half of the 18th century and ended the existence of the Polish—Lithuanian Commonwealth.

[2] Kwieciński, Z., and Śliwerski, B. (eds.). 2005. *Pedagogika*. Warsaw: PWN.

[3] Act of 11 March 1932 on the System of Education. Journal of Laws of 1932, No. 38, 389.

could be achieved after twelve years of training.[4] It is difficult to assess the quality and the effectiveness of the foregoing measures, also because of their short implementation period. The outbreak of World War II and the Nazi occupation hampered the resurgence of the education system in Poland. In the areas annexed by the Reich—that is the former German state—the Polish education system at all levels ceased to exist. The closing down of schools was connected to the persecution of intellectuals and thinkers, especially teachers and university professors. This could be seen as part of the long-term process of destruction of the national and cultural identity of the Polish society. Although secretly, the schooling system mentioned above continued to exist.

At the end of the war, it took more than ten years to review the national education system. In 1961, the body of the Parliament with legislative powers—the *Sejm*—passed an important provision[5] setting forth that primary education lasted six years and was now made mandatory. After completion of elementary school, pupils could choose between entering a three-year vocational school, a four-year institution providing general education or a five-year technical school.

The final examination at the end of secondary school—a precondition to enter the academic career—was to be taken only by students in general secondary schools and technical schools. Graduates from vocational schools were able to take the final exams and graduate after completing three additional years in secondary school or two and a half to three years in technical institutions. This path was not particularly appealing, especially because it further extended the period of compulsory school attendance. However, it was recognised that this programme strengthened the skills base required in the working world. As a result—and also in consideration of the inefficacy of the provisions adopted at the time that were intended to help job applicants to access the labour market—it is not surprising that all the same this was regarded as a good alternative. Compounding the picture was the increasing demand for unskilled workers—chiefly in the construction industry—the central role of working class in political life, and the lack of cutting-edge technology resulting from low levels of qualifications. As it was, Polish society was little concerned with increasing the levels of education and skills. Statistics also confirm this viewpoint. In the school year 1985/1986, only 16.3% of those in the 19-24 age group received education. This situation caused the country to enter the reform period with poor levels of literacy and it

[4] Prucha, J. 2004. *Pedagogika porównawcza*. Warsaw: PWN.

[5] Act of 15 July 1961 on Development of Education System. Journal of Laws of 1961, No. 32, 160.

further contributed to the emergence of alternative education patterns. In the school year 1990/1991, some 238,100 completed vocational school, whereas only 92,500 graduated from schools providing general education.

Table 3-3. Percentage of students aged 19 to 24 years old in Poland between 1993 and 2010[6]

Years	1993/ 1994	1994/ 1995	1995/ 1996	1996/ 1997	2000/ 2001	2001/ 2002	2002/ 2003
% of Students	25.4	27.9	30.3	32.8	45.4	47.4	50.7
Years	**2003/ 2004**	**2004/ 2005**	**2005/ 2006**	**2006/ 2007**	**2007/ 2008**	**2008/ 2009**	**2009/ 2010**
% of Students	52.9	54.4	54.8	55.3	55.8	57.9	56.4

Source: Author's own elaboration on the *Statistical Yearbooks of the Republic of Poland*, 1993-2010.

Amendments to higher education legislation were made earlier. The Act on Higher Education of 1958[7] made provision for the establishment of institutions supplying tertiary education, such as polytechnics, academies and schools of arts. Customarily, the programmes run in these schools lasted five years and were free of charge, as was the case with all education in Poland over that period. Also by granting a wide range of benefits, the legislator made an attempt to provide free schooling to students from different social backgrounds. Unfortunately, the reasons mentioned above, alongside major social inequalities and widespread economic hardship, made such an effort unsuccessful.

4. The Reform of the Socio-economic System and Changes in Education in 1989

Rapid changes were reported in higher education following the downfall of socialism. A number of private institutions that supplemented programmes offered by state universities made this sector profitable. Evidently, profound transformations were needed in order to comply with

[6] It was not possible to collect data for the school years 1997/1998, 1998/1999, and 1999/2000.

[7] Act of 5 November 1958 on Higher Education. Journal of Laws of of 1958, No. 68, 336.

the requirements and standards set forth at European level.[8] One of the main aims of the reform was to offer distinct master's programmes. For instance, the Act on Higher Education of 1990[9] introduced a three-year Bachelor's degree in almost all the disciplines. In addition, those who wanted to carry on studying could stay in school two more years and take a Master's degree. The planning of Bachelor's and Master's as two distinct programmes was met with approval and soon implemented by private schools. This can be explained either by the increasing attention given to tertiary education and the ease it took to comply with relevant legislation. At least initially, the main consequence of this state of play was that private schools mostly offered bachelor's degrees. The disciplines for which they were provided were determined in accordance with the demand of the market and a consideration of the costs to run these programmes.

Clearly, the costs to be borne to set vocational courses were higher and this caused a lack of trained engineering staff in the second half of the following decade. The issue was overlooked, particularly in the mid-1990s and became evident when a considerable number of professionals—economists, lawyers, psychologists and educators—were absorbed by the labour market. Once the balance was restored and vacancies in the legal and economic areas were filled, educational providers failed to keep up with the new job market demand, preparing the youth for jobs that were no longer required. The share of graduates in economics out of the total number of graduates over the last decade exceeded 25%, while the percentage of those with a degree in humanities was a little lower, although significant. In the academic year 2008/2009, the graduation rate in economics and humanities accounted for 41.7% of all graduates. The reform of the system of higher education was completed in 2005, when the Act on Higher Education[10] was enforced. It put the necessary provisions in place that would bring Polish higher education into line with what was agreed in the Bologna Declaration, which was signed in 1999. In addition to two existing programmes—bachelor's and master's degrees—an additional level was set, that is that of the Doctoral school. Furthermore, learning in stationary and non-stationary environments was experimented on, with the latter that was supplied free of charge. Increasing levels of

---

[8] Banach, C. 1999. *Polska szkoła i system edukacji. Przemiany i perspektywy.* Toruń: Wydawnictwo Adam Marszałek.

[9] Act of 12 September 1990 on Higher Education. Journal of Laws of 1990, No. 65, 385.

[10] Act of 27 July 2005 Law on Higher Education. Journal of Laws of 2005, No. 164, 1365.

involvement in training programmes was reported on the part of private schools. After a pioneering phase, private education was now well-established. Institutions that failed to meet the expectations of the market were closed or sidelined, while the others further consolidated their position, offering a wider range of programmes. In 1998, reform in primary and secondary education began. Amendments were made to the Education Act[11] which regulated education in elementary and secondary schools, and the duration of the latter was extended to six years. Integrated teaching was introduced up to the third grade, and starting from the fourth grade, classes were divided into didactic units. After completion of primary school, students enrolled in lower secondary school (gymnasium) at the end of which they could choose between attending three years of high school providing both general or specialised education, or gaining vocational training in four-year or two-year institutions.

Vocational schools at this stage of the academic career are a novelty, and they usually combine the provision of practical skills with theoretical learning. Also in this case, students in these schools might take the final examination after completing two-year courses that provide specialised or general education. The requirement for a final exam is an important one, as it represents a valuable assessment tool to admit students to the next grade. In public schools, the final test is usually the only condition to move to the next year. Another relevant point in this period is a decrease in the share of graduates from vocational institutions, particularly in comparison to high schools.

In the school year 1998-1999, there were over 190,200 graduates from vocational schools, and 173,900 graduates from high schools, whereas in the academic year 2008-2009 the corresponding figures were 72,100 and 230,500 respectively. Even though one considers the demographic changes that took place within the first group, these data are significant and confirm, in some respects, the tendency away from the stereotypical assumptions about vocational education that were typical of the socialist society.

5. Youth Unemployment in Poland

Youth unemployment in Poland is a very important issue. Data from the Central Statistical Office points out that unemployment rates are higher among people under the age of 24. According to the Labour Force

[11] Act of 25 July 1998 on Amending the Education Act. Journal of Laws of 1998, No. 117, 759.

Survey (LFS), the unemployment rate for this age group in Poland was 22.3%. Table 3-4 shows some statistics as a point of comparison to other age groups, while Table 3-5 focuses on the evolution of this indicator in previous years.

Table 3-4. Unemployment Rates by Age

Age Group	25-34	35-44	45-54	over 55
Unemployment rate (%)	32.5	34.1	41.1	43.6

Table 3-5. LFS Unemployment Rates in the 15-24 Age Group

Year	1999	2000	2001	2002	2003	2004
Unemployment rate	32.5	34.1	41.1	43.6	41.1	37.3
Year	**2005**	**2006**	**2007**	**2008**	**2009**	
Unemployment rate	34.6	27	18.7	17.1	22.3	

Source: Author's own elaboration on the *Concise Polish Statistical Yearbooks*, 2000-2010.

The fact that there has been a decrease in the unemployment rates in the following years is highly encouraging. This was, however, the result of a change in the demographic trends which led to an overall reduction of the population. Therefore, one should be careful in dealing with these data.

In considering the working active population, one might note that the share of workers in this age group is the smallest of all age cohorts. This trend has been illustrated in Table 3-6 with regard to the years 1999 to 2009.

Table 3-6. Individuals Aged 15 to 24 Years Old as a Share of the Active Working Population (%)

Year	1999	2000	2001	2002	2003	2004
	11.3	10.5	9.6	8.9	9.3	9.3
Year	**2005**	**2006**	**2007**	**2008**	**2009**	
	9.3	9.7	9.5	9.2	8.6	

Source: Author's own elaboration on the *Concise Polish Statistical Yearbooks*, 2000-2010.

Levels of participation lower than ten percent are considered to be unsatisfactory. Also in consideration of their lack of work experience, the situation of young people in this age cohort is disheartening if compared with individuals in different age groups. More importantly, there appears to be a need to provide them with further levels of expertise, even if this means postponing their entry into the labour market. The issue is highly debated in the literature, but no action has been taken in practical terms.[12]

The seriousness of the problem is also recognised by lawmakers. In this sense, the Employment and Unemployment Counteraction Act[13]—which was in force until 2004—set forth that those who graduated should be initially classed as unemployed. Following a number of amendments made to the Act,[14] drafters referred to this category as "unemployed under the age of 25", while special provisions were adopted also for people up to the age of 27 that were still in search of employment 12 months after graduation. In both cases, the focus was on groups of people who were unable to find work one year after completing education. Table 3-7 shows the share of registered unemployment in this age group. One might note that the unemployment rates for this group remain steady—with a variance that is equal to 5%—although a downward tendency has been reported among graduates. Since 2005, we have surveyed data on registered unemployment within twelve months after completion of higher education. Officially, statistics reported that the share of graduates not in employment for the years 2005 to 2009 was 23%, 25%, 29%, 30%, and 28%, respectively. It was difficult to extrapolate these figures due to a lack of data on the educational background of the graduates entering the labour market. What emerges, however, is an increase in the unemployment levels one year after graduation if compared to overall unemployment rates. This aspect points to a decrease of the demand for this category of workers.

---

[12] Skórska, A. 2004. *Młodzież na rynku pracy w Polsce i Unii Europejskiej*. Poznań: Wydawnictwo Wyższej Szkoły Bankowej.

[13] Act of 14 December 1994 Employment and Unemployment Counteraction Act. Journal of Laws of 1995, No. 1, 1.

[14] Law of 20 April 2004 on Promotion of Employment and Labour Market Institutions. Journal of Laws of 2004, No. 99, 1001.

Table 3-7. Registered Unemployed and Unemployed Graduates (thousands)[15]

Year	1999	2000	2001	2002	2003	2004
Total of the registered unemployed.	2349.8	2702.6	3115.1	3217	3175.7	2999.6
The unemployed registered within 12 months from graduating.	149.8	167.9	180.7	166.8	157.9	-
Year	**2005**	**2006**	**2007**	**2008**	**2009**	
No. of registered unemployed.	**2773**	**2309.4**	**1746.6**	**1473.8**	**1473.8**	
No. of registered unemployed within 12 months from graduating.	139.7	102.4	72.2	77.9	120.3	

Source: Author's own elaboration on the *Concise Polish Statistical Yearbooks*, 2000-2010.

The same conclusions can be drawn from an analysis of the data provided in Table 3-8.

The lowest unemployment rates have been reported among people with higher levels of education. However, the recent years have witnessed an upward employment trend, particularly among individuals with vocational education providing basic skills. Unfortunately, the share of graduates in this class is decreasing, too, with blue-collars workers who therefore have not benefited from this situation.

[15] It was not possible to collect data for the year 2004.

Table 3-8. LFS Unemployment Rates by Type of Education

Year	Higher Education	Post-secondary and secondary vocational Education	General post-secondary Education	Basic vocational Education	Local secondary/ primary/ incomplete primary Education
1999	4.8	24.5	19.2	18.4	19.2
2000	4.8	13.6	19.6	19.2	20.2
2001	6.4	16.1	22.9	22.4	22.6
2002	7.5	33.8	24	23.8	25.4
2003	7.7	33.7	22.9	23.5	26
2004	6.9	32.4	20.4	22.4	24.8
2005	7.3	29.2	21	20.6	25.1
2006	5.8	10.9	16.1	14.5	18.8
2007	4.5	7.6	11.5	10	13
2008	3.6	6.5	9.6	7	11.4
2009	5	8	10.3	9.3	15.9

Source: Author's own elaboration on the *Concise Polish Statistical Yearbooks*, 2000-2010.

6. Concluding Remarks

The Polish labour market was marked by a widespread and structural mismatch, the result of major changes inherited from the previous political system.[16] In a number of cases, overstaffing, particularly among blue-collar workers operating in unprofitable branches of heavy industry caused unemployment to increase. Amendments to the students' assessment scheme and the reform of the education system at different levels turned the focus on the relationship between the youth and schooling, particularly with regard to tertiary education. An attempt was therefore made to help people enter the labour market earlier, also taking account of younger generations that should gain increased levels of skills. Indeed, this state of play provided a reflection of the labour market needs, which required more professionals than manual workers. Clearly, this was associated with changes in economy, which was no longer based on heavy industry but

[16] Kwiatkowski, E. 2002. *Bezrobocie. Podstawy teoretyczne*. Warsaw: PWN.

rather on financial services. Bearing this in mind, one can offer a positive assessment of the changes that took place in education in the 1990s, also taking account of a rise in the overall educational levels and a decrease in the mismatch mentioned above. Of equal significance are the growth in the share of students under the age of 24 and the fall in those attending vocational schools. With regard to the last point, however, there will be a need to make technical schools more appealing. At present, there is a trend towards high rates of students willing to graduate in economics and law in private institutions, increasing the number of experts in these areas and reducing their chances to find employment due to increasing competition. To match the demand and supply of labour, the government issued a list of the most needed majors (e.g. sciences and technology), also as a way to increase the likelihood of being hired for graduates in these disciplines. Naturally, it would take time to evaluate the workability of this initiative. To be truthful, a number of actions have been taken to help young people enter the job market, particularly at national level (e.g. *First Job. First Business. Graduate*). Today, internships and training are the most realistic forms of support for the youth. As pointed out in the Act on Employment Promotion and Labour Market Institutions, attending an internship means to acquire practical skills by operating in the workplace without establishing an employment relationship with the employer. As for training, it is defined as outdoor activities aimed at obtaining, completing or upgrading specialised or general skills required to perform a working activity, including the ability to find employment. A survey carried out by the Ministry of Labour and Social Policy showed that only 30% of trainees find employment after completing these training programmes, with this percentage that however rises to 50% in the case of internships.

Indeed, at present, internships are attractive to employers. It has been estimated that half of the positions available are offered in the form of internships. They might last up to 12 months without any obligations upon the employers. Ideally, this contractual scheme seems workable, but it does not produce the desired outcomes, as it is often used to deal with labour shortages. As a result, the only instrument to tackle the issue of youth unemployment is to devise flexible education patterns. While acknowledging the difficulty in anticipating skills needs in the labour market, an attempt should be made to avoid the struggle that many graduates face in finding employment.

References

Banach, C. 1999. *Polska szkoła i system edukacji. Przemiany i perspektywy*. Toruń: Wydawnictwo Adam Marszałek.
Kwiatkowski, E. 2002. *Bezrobocie. Podstawy teoretyczne*. Warsaw: PWN.
Kwieciński, Z., and Śliwerski, B. (eds.). 2005. *Pedagogika*. Warsaw: PWN.
Central Statistical Office of Poland. 2000-2010. *Polish Concise Statistical Yearbook*. Warsaw: GUS.
Prucha, J. 2004. *Pedagogika porównawcza*. Warsaw: PWN.
Central Statistical Office of Poland. 1993-2010. *Statistical Yearbook of the Polish Republic*. Warsaw: GUS.
Skórska, A. 2004. *Młodzież na rynku pracy w Polsce i Unii Europejskiej*. Poznań: Wydawnictwo Wyższej Szkoły Bankowej.

THE INTERPLAY OF EDUCATION AND THE LABOUR MARKET IN MEXICO: AN OVERVIEW

GABRIELA MENDIZÁBAL BERMÚDEZ

In the labour market, training is the main component required of young workers. In this respect, common sense tells us that those who are adequately prepared or have graduated from widely renowned institutions should have privileged access to employment. However, at the time of examining the interplay between education and the labour market, one might note that many highly educated young people often swell the ranks of the unemployed. On the basis of these considerations, the present study provides an analysis of the socio-demographic and legal framework of youth and the labour situation in Mexico, focusing on aspects such as higher education rates, wage levels, and data regarding young migrants. As a parallel, it is pointed out that some European countries give priority to academic subjects that differ from those offered to Mexican students, in an attempt to diversify their labour force and provide graduates with high levels of social security protection from the early stages of education.

1. Youth in Mexico: A Reference Framework

In order to explore topics such as education and school performance of the youth in a given country, it is important to begin by defining what is meant by youth in the context surveyed. In considering the Western population, the notion of youth has been dealt with in terms of biological age, as the period of life between childhood and adulthood. However, it is down to national cultures to specify when youth starts and finishes. The complexity of this conceptualization lies in the fact that this notion implies a transition from a state of total dependence—which characterizes childhood—to full autonomy, that is typical of an adult.

It must be acknowledged at the onset that this process does not always go through the same stages in one's lifetime, and each government sets its lower and upper age limit in accordance with its own criteria.

In 1985, the United Nations (UN) proclaimed the Year of the Youth and in 2010, on occasion of its 25th anniversary, it further reinforced its relevance.[1] According to the UN, youth is the period involving the transition between two stages: childhood and adulthood. In other words, it is a period over which children undergo a transformation into autonomous individuals[2] and it refers to the population between 14 and 25 years old. Pursuant to the Political Constitution of the United Mexican States, young people are protected by the anti-discrimination principle. Article 1 of the Political Constitution, which safeguards young people's civil and social rights, states that:

> In the United Mexican States, every individual shall enjoy the guarantees granted by this Constitution [...]. It is hereby prohibited all discrimination motivated by ethnic or national origin, gender, age, disabilities, social status, health conditions, religion, opinions, preferences, civil status or any other violating human dignity and with the purpose of nullifying or impairing the rights and freedoms of individuals.

Art. 2 refers to the multicultural composition of the state, and Section B points out that, in order to reduce shortages and lags facing minorities—e.g. indigenous people—the relevant authorities are under the obligation, among others, to supply special education and nutrition programmes to migrant children and youth. This is an important point to make if one considers that in Mexico 4 out of 10 migrants are adolescents.[3] Further on in the same article, it is specified that "the programmes, services and actions within the Institute should address the share of population between 12 and 29 years old, because of its strategic importance for the development of the country".[4] Therefore, in Mexico, youth are young people

---

[1] UNO, 2010. *Proclamation of 2010 as the International Year of the Youth: mutual dialog and understanding 64/134.* Resolution passed by the General Assembly, based on the report of the Third Commission (A/64/432). http://www.un.org/es/comun/docs/?symbol=A/RES/64/134, (accessed May 10, 2011).

[2] CISC, 2011. *Youth: a concept or a category.* http://www.cisc.org.mx/sitios/ant/index.php?option=com_content&view=article&id=146:juventudconceptocategoria&catid=21:articulos&Itemid=74 (accessed June 10, 2011).

[3] La jornada, March 14, 2011, At http://www.jornada.unam.mx/2011/03/14/index.php?section=economia&article=024n1eco (accessed May 5, 2011).

[4] Ley del Instituto del Instituto Mexicano de la Juventud http://info4.juridicas.unam.mx/ijure/tcfed/99.htm?s= (accessed May 5, 2011).

in the 12 to 29 age group. In this connection, there are a number of legal provisions that refer to age issues and ensuing entitlements, from the Federal Labour Law—which sets certain limitations at the time of employing minors—to the Civil Code, which fixes the minimum age to get married. Notwithstanding the above, and with a view to framing the problems arising from the relationship between youth, the labour market, and education, it seems useful to provide a socioeconomic framework which allows one to become familiar with the context young Mexicans operate in, to understand their needs and outline existing legislation. With a population of 112.3 million inhabitants, Mexico can be viewed as a country of contrasts.[5] According to the National Institute of Statistic and Geography (INEGI), the population of young people in the 15-29 age group in Mexico is 29,706,560—15,167,260 females and 14,539,300 males[6]—and reports an annual growth of 0.85 percent.[7] This means that the young population amounts to roughly a quarter of the total population (26.2%). As for education, the share of illiterate individuals in the same age cohort is about 1.7%. On average, young people have completed school up to the first grade of senior high school, meaning that they usually remain in education for ten 10 years.[8] Further, 15.7% of them have completed elementary school, 37.6% of them have obtained a junior high school diploma or equivalent, and 27.9% have entered baccalaureate education—with 15.5% of them enrolling in courses in higher education and only 0.4% taking part in postgraduate studies. If one looks at the statistics, what emerges is that men usually fare better than women in all levels of schooling. Attention should also be drawn to the relationship between the birth rate and the levels of education, which is always inversely proportional, as the lower the education, the higher the number of children women give birth to.[9]

---

[5] Demographic and population indicators 2011. At http://www.inegi.org.mx/Sistemas/temasV2/Default.aspx?s=est&c=17484 (accessed June 13, 2011).

[6] Knowing us all, 2011. At http://www.inegi.gob.mx/inegi/contenidos/espanol/prensa/contenidos/Articulos/sociodemograficas/mexico-jovenes.pdf (accessed June 13, 2011).

[7] Ibid.

[8] Ibid.

[9] *Fertility is associated with education says INEGI, 2011.* At http://www.noticiasnet.mx/portal/principal/45832-fecundidad-asociada-escolaridad-dice-inegi (accessed June 23, 2011).

2. Employment and Youth in Mexico

The precarious nature of employment in Mexico is well-known, and one of the consequences of this state of play has been an overall impoverishment of a significant number of workers nationally. In this sense, Kurczyn has pointed out that "the exclusion from the economically active population (EAP), and the formal sector—due to the fact that many households are not covered by social security—alongside job insecurity, inter-union problems associated with national policies, and the current economic crisis at both domestic and global level, have caused poverty, and social marginalization".[10] The effect of globalization on employment has made it increasingly difficult for young people to enter and remain in the labour market, as confirmed by some indicators provided by the INEGI survey. In investigating the data on youth and labour, what emerges is that the economically active population of Mexico is equal to 57.8% of the total population and includes 50.4%[11] of young people (14 to 29 year-olds). In addition, 5.36% of the overall EAP is unemployed,[12]

---

[10] Kurczyn Villalobos, P. 2001. *Work Relationships in the 21st Century.* Ministry of Labour and Social Welfare and National Autonomous University of Mexico: Mexico, 30.

[11] Occupation, INEGI, 2011. At: http://dgcnesyp.inegi.org.mx/cgi-win/bdiecoy.exe/603?s=est&c=13033 (accessed June 13, 2011).

[12] The unemployment rate used by INEGI is calculated through the method employed by the Latin American Association of Integration. More specifically, "The unemployment rate is calculated as the number of unemployed people divided by the Economically Active Population (EAP), being this population either in working age in the referred period, occupied in producing economic goods or services (Occupied), or not actively looking for a job (Unemployed). The Unemployment Rate is often referred to as Open Unemployment Rate." Latin American Association of Integration at:
http://www.aladi.org/nsfaladi/indicadomacro.nsf/vtiposindicadorescat/Tasa%20de%20Desempleo (accessed June 13, 2011) and at
http://www.finanzas.com/economia/paro/ (accessed June 13, 2011). In considering the way the share of unemployed is obtained, it is understood that both the street vendors and, in general, all the workers in informal economy "have an occupation in which they produce economic goods or services." Therefore, they do not count as unemployed; otherwise it is unexplainable why we have lower unemployment rates than some European countries. For instance, in Spain the unemployed account for 20.6% of the population (Spanish Economy in Review: Regional Analysis of the Labour Market and Inflation 2011, 21), while in Mexico only they are only 5.36% of the total population. Youth unemployment in Spain is over 40% and in Mexico it is 8%.

according to the data of the INEGI for the first quarter of 2011,[13] with this percentage that increases for young people, especially in comparison with the rest of the unemployed (8.6%).[14] Further, 47.1% of youth is in employment and 26.7% of them is in education, while the remaining 26% neither studies nor works, in the sense that they are in an unproductive situation, even though they should benefit from the demographic bonus. One might also note that many people in the 15-19 age group are in education, irrespective of their gender. As for 20 to 24 year-olds, males are usually in employment, while 42.2% of women are engaged in housekeeping. In this age cohort, the percentage of women and men in education is almost similar (roughly 17%). Finally, with reference to those in the 25 to 29 age-group, an age in which people usually face family commitments, 88.4% of males and 45.3% of females engage in a working activity, with 48.8% of the latter who are devoted to household responsibilities. [15] At this stage of life, there is an attempt to access the labour market, yet it is the young who find themselves in a position of disadvantage with respect to more skilled workers, the long-term unemployed and even more experienced workers who have not met retirement requirements. Low remuneration is a further obstacle to their independence. This aspect, along with the struggle to find employment, leads a growing number of youth towards emigration or, what is worse, engagement in illicit activities (e.g. drug trafficking). Concerning migration, one should note that, according to the National Population Council, 816,000 Mexicans out of a total of 994,000 leave the country every year, and more than 30% are young people.[16] Their main destination is the United States of America, for a number of reasons: higher wages, geographical closeness, existing migration chains that allow for a more rapid access to employment than in Mexico, family reunion and fewer opportunities in their place of origin, notwithstanding their professional expertise. In the past, migration was confined to those in a particular social strata—e.g. workers, ideally men with little schooling. Things are different today, and the migration process involves individuals from different social backgrounds, and likewise different levels of education. As a result,

---

[13] Occupation, INEGI, 2011. At: http://dgcnesyp.inegi.org.mx/cgi-win/bdiecoy.exe/603?s=est&c=13033 (accessed June 13, 2011).

[14] Ibid.

[15] Ibid., 4.

[16] *Four out of every 10 Migrants are Adolescents and Young,* INEGI. At http://www.jornada.unam.mx/2011/03/14/index.php?section=economia&article=024n1eco (accessed June 28, 2011).

1,039,898[17] higher education graduates live in the United States and perform jobs for which they are overqualified.

3. Education and the Labour Market

An impressive number of programmes are being developed in Latin America to smooth young people's transition to employment, particularly after recent trends in Latin America have been brought to the fore, primarily concerning their struggle to find employment, even though they are adequately prepared.[18]

In this connection, the main questions are: Where are individuals with higher education placed? And, above all, which sectors are in demand of recent graduates?

With regard to the first question, and according to the data released by the National Association of Universities and Higher Education Institutions (ANUIES), the number of professionals in employment in 2010 was 5,966,350,[19] which is 13% of the national workforce.[20] More specifically, they were occupied in a number of areas such as accounting (648,900), administrative sciences (614,500), law firms (544,400), computer and IT engineering (328,200), and teachers' training for elementary education (287,900), making up 41.6% of employed professionals.[21]

Fewer people were employed in mining and metallurgical engineering (5,000), geophysics and geology (6,800), theology and religion (7,000), naval and aeronautics engineering (7,400) and the music industry (9,000), with these groups that accounted for barely 0.6% of professionals employed in the country.[22] This does not necessarily mean that they are the least needed in the country—or the least employed—in relation to the

---

[17] *One out of every 10 Mexicans with B.A. / B.S. Degree Migrates to the USA: Tuirán*. At http://www.jornada.unam.mx/2011/06/17/sociedad/040n1soc (accessed July 5, 2011).

[18] Vera, A., and R. Castioni. *Youth in Latin America*. School-to-work transition as the aim of public policies. At: http://www.senac.br/BTS/362/artigo1.pdf, (accessed June 23, 2011).

[19] Employed professionals, by region 2000 and 2010. At: http://www.anuies.mx/e_proyectos/html/parte%204/cuadro%2014%20%28b%29.htm, (accessed June 14, 2011).

[20] National Overview of Careers. At: http://www.observatoriolaboural.gob.mx/work/sites/ola/resources/LocalContent/809/3/ResumenEjecutivo.pdf (accessed June 14, 2011), 5.

[21] Ibid.

[22] Ibid., 6.

corresponding share of graduates. In fact, if one looks at the national occupancy rates, 20 to 24 year-olds represent 6.3% of professionals in employment, whereas those between 25 and 34 years old constitute 35.1%.[23] Of relevance is also the average monthly income in Mexico that amounts to $9,961.00 Mexican pesos.[24] Concerning the future needs of the labour market, the Labour Observatory of the Ministry of Labour and Social Welfare (STPS) has singled out a number of industries that will be characterised by an increase in labour demand: environmental sciences and geomatics, genomics, pharmacogenomics and gene therapy, radiology, biotechnology, mecatronics, telematics and cybernetics, nanotechnology and molecular engineering.[25] Notwithstanding these career prospects, serious questions are raised in relation to whether Mexico is preparing professionals considering both the needs of the labour market in the sectors just mentioned and the prospective growth at a national level. Currently, there are 3,923,822 students who are in baccalaureate programmes and 2,705,190 in higher education, more generally.[26] This data becomes alarming if compared with the number of university graduates per year—about 450,000—that struggle to have access to employment,[27] also because of the insufficient labour absorption capacity. By way of example, statistics from the Ministry of Labour and Social Welfare reported that in 2010 the national economy fared well in terms of job creation—750,000 jobs[28] were created, the best performance since 1996. However, this figure might be misleading, as it also considers the number of jobs lost in the previous year. As a result, this outcome is not as significant as it seems, particularly when considering the number of unemployed, which in Mexico is 3.5 million people. In passing, while examining the interplay between education and the labour market, there are two additional points that need to be looked at:

---

[23] Ibid., 8.

[24] Ibid., 9.

[25] Labour Observatory of the STPS, *How is Expected to be the Work in the Future?* At: http://www.observatoriolaboural.gob.mx/wb/ola/ola_como_se_espera_que_sea_el_trabajo_en_el_futuro?page= (accessed June 23, 2011).

[26] Registration and school processes, INEGI 2011. At: http://www.inegi.org.mx/sistemas/sisept/default.aspx?t=medu17&s=est&c=21788 (accessed June 14, 2011).

[27] Hernández V. *Mexican University Students Face Challenging Job Market.* At: http://spanish.peopledaily.com.cn/31617/7023786.html, (accessed June 28, 2011).

[28] Inconceivable not to pass the labour reform, At http://www.jornada.unam.mx/2011/05/02/politica/012n2pol, (accessed June 10, 2011).

- the increasing number of overqualified professionals (e.g. graduates in medicine and law) that the labour market does not absorb is an indication that the school-to-work transition paths are lacking, or fail to adapt to the ever-changing economy.[29]
- Clearly, the education system is intended to keep up with major developments in the labour market, yet this is not always the case, as recent graduates often provide little to no contribution to national economic growth, particularly because labour market policies are poorly implemented.

4. Technical and University Education in Mexico with respect to the Labour Market Needs

A close reading of the labour market-education relationship points out an attempt on the part of the government to diversify the education supplied and make it more attuned to employers' needs. In this sense, growing importance has been placed on technical schooling. The Latin American and Caribbean Centre for Demographics (CELADE) which operates under the supervision of the Economic Commission for Latin America (CEPAL) released data showing that during the 1990s, numerous programmes promoting youth employment were put in place at a sectoral level, particularly in the aftermath of the national reform of higher education.[30] This was accompanied by the allocation of massive investment and the devising of a number of training schemes targeted at young people. Mexico was no exception, and funded several initiatives nationally, especially in tertiary education, for instance by setting up two curricula at this level. In this sense, Ibarrola speaks of " [...] studies of propedeutical or technical nature in higher education, as well as vocational schools that have defined the two modalities in which this level is divided into."[31] The intention was to supply technicians of varied levels of expertise,

---

[29] Cfr. Schmid, Günther, "*Strukturwandel des Arbeitsmarkts und seine Folgen für Übergänge aus dem Bildungssystem*" Diskussionsbeitrag für den Workshop zum Schwerpunktthema des nationalen Bildungsberichts 2008 in Berlin en http://www.bildungsbericht.de/daten/schmid-txt.pdf , (accessed June 18, 2011).

[30] CELADE, Youth, population and development in Latin American and Caribbean, CELADE-CEPAL, Santiago, 2000. At: http://www.eclac.org/publicaciones/xml/3/4973/lcl1424.pdf (accessed June 13, 2011).

[31] Ibarrola de, María and Bernal, Enrique, *Perspectives of Technical Education and Professional Training in Mexico,* at:

skilled workers, and professionals to serve as middle managers. However, despite the proliferation of vocational schools (e.g. technical colleges), the public opinion still regards traditional education as the best option in finding employment. According to the INEGI survey, there were 3,923,822 senior high school students in 2010; 366,964 of them attended technical studies, while the rest of them pursued a baccalaureate degree. In addition, out of as many as three million students in higher education, only 91,530 were in vocational schools.[32]

As seen, vocational training for the development of the workforce has been offered through several initiatives, but it was poorly implemented. All in all, training for the labour force should be aimed at:

- providing technicians with the necessary skills to perform quality jobs so that they can be handsomely remunerated and plan both their working and family life;
- supplying professionals with practical knowledge in order to increase their competitiveness, particularly recent graduates from higher education.

A system that is worth investigating is the one adopted in Austria, Germany and Switzerland, which is known as the dual training (*Duale Ausbildung*) system. Of special interest is that put in place in Germany, as it differs slightly from those implemented in other countries. It is termed "dual" because it combines on-the-job training with theoretical learning.[33] By entering into this form of training, young people in technical positions[34] are instructed in the company (*Lehre-* means learning in German) over a period from two up to three years and a half, depending on their occupation. While learning, they also receive an allowance amounting to 300 to 550 euros per month and, more importantly, they are

---

http://www.cinterfor.org.uy/public/spanish/region/ampro/cinterfor/publ/boletin/141/pdf/bol141h.pdf, (accessed May 1, 2011).

[32] Enrolment and school processes, INEGI 2011. At: http://www.inegi.org.mx/sistemas/sisept/default.aspx?t=medu17&s=est&c=21788, (accessed June 28, 2011).

[33]At: http://www.bildungsxperten.net/wissen/so-funktioniert-die-fachhochschulreife/ (accessed June 28, 2011).

[34] In Mexico, a distinction should be made with regard to the relationship between the levels of qualification and educational attainments. Graduates from higher education perform "professions"—for which a licence is necessary—while those in technical programmes study in order to be engaged in "trades". On a general basis, the former position entails higher remuneration than the latter.

registered for social security, a prerequisite to enter into a training contract with the employer. However, trainees are also under the obligation to attend school (*Berufsschule* stands for vocational schools) for one day or 2 days in a week, or in blocks of three up to eight continuous weeks, in order to get the necessary theoretical education. All training activities are supervised by a state-run educational centre and at the end of the programme students must sit a final written examination. If approved, certification will be issued proving their ability to carry out a given task, and they will also be entitled to higher pay.

One of the main disadvantages of this training system is its reliance on employers' willingness to host trainees, which also depends on the fluctuations of the labour market. For instance, 4,500 training opportunities were cut in 2010, amounting to a number of training contracts concluded that was lower than that in 2009, the year of the worldwide economic downturn.[35] Notwithstanding this aspect, dual training is still the most effective system to help graduates to shift from education to the world of work. Finally, another difference with the German case can be seen in terms of remuneration between graduates from technical schools and colleges in Mexico (Table 3-9).

[35] Bundesinstitut für Berufsbildung (BIBB) En
http://www.bildungsxperten.net/wissen/wie-funktioniert-eine-duale-ausbildung/
(accessed June 28, 2011).

Table 3-9. National Income in Germany and Mexico

Country	Year	Profession	Annual salary	Monthly salary	Monthly equivalence in USD[36]
Germany	2008	Architect	Between 29,000 € and 69,000 €[37]	2,416.66 € and 5,750 €	1,666.66 and 3,965.51[38]
Germany	2008	Cook	22,600[39]	1,883.33 €	1,298.84[40]
Mexico	2010	Architect	$128,064.00	$10,672.00[41]	897.80
Mexico	2010	Cook	$46,572.00	$3,881.00[42]	326.33

Source: Author's own elaboration based on http://www.gehalt.de and www.observatoriolaboural.gob.mx.

5. Social Security and the Youth

One aspect that escapes the investigation of the way young people enter the labour market is their situation in terms of social security. In Mexico, there are certain criteria to comply with in order to be eligible for social insurance. The status of a worker must be recognized, in the sense that by way of an employment contract, a legal relationship of personal subordination between the employer and the employee should be acknowledged, in both the private and public sector. This relationship

[36] As of June, 29 2011, one dollar equals to $11.83 Mexican pesos. Exchange rates at: http://www.sat.gob.mx/sitio_internet/asistencia_contribuyente/informacion_frecuente/tipo_cambio/, (accessed June 29, 2011).

[37] According to the experience and size of the company. At: http://www.gehalt.de/statistik/Architekten-und-Bauingenieure-nach-Firmengroesse-und-Berufserfahrung-2008, (accessed June 13, 2011).

[38] One euro is equivalent of 1.45 USD at the Exchange rate as of July 4, 2011. At: http://www.euroresidentes.com/finanzas/tipo_de_cambio_euro_dolar.htm, (accessed July 5, 2011).

[39] At: http://www.gehalt.de/ , (accessed June 28, 2011).

[40] One euro is equivalent of 1.45 USD at the Exchange rate as of July 4, 2011. At: http://www.euroresidentes.com/finanzas/tipo_de_cambio_euro_dolar.htm, (accessed June 28, 2011).

[41] *Best paid careers; 2010. At:* http://www.empleo.gob.mx/wb/BANEM/BANE_cuales_son_las_carreras_mejor_pagadas_/_rid/1724/_mod/edit, (accessed June 28, 2011).

[42] Fast food preparers. At: http://www.observatoriolaboural.gob.mx/wb/ola/ola_ocu_cuanto_ganan, (accessed July 5, 2011).

must be established in accordance with relevant legislation and takes place in the formal economy.[43]

Young people could be beneficiaries of an insured person, or take part in voluntary insurance schemes. This state of affairs entitles more than 52%[44] of the population to benefits granted by the social security system or to enjoy the contractual rights entitled by social security in the sphere of formal employment. The remaining population is entitled to limited social assistance, basic coverage for certain issues concerning health, housing and retirement. Against this background, it is important to understand the functioning of social welfare for young people in Mexico. Children of individuals who are already covered by a social security scheme are entitled to benefits that include childcare and sickness in the event of their parents' death. It is up to the Mexican Institute of Social Security (IMSS), the Institute of Social Security and Social Services of the Employees of the State (ISSSTE), the Institute of Social Services of the Mexican Armed Forces (ISSFAM), and the Institute of Social Security of the State of Mexico and Municipalities (ISSEMYM) to administer and provide this service. As far as students are concerned, they can enrol in an optional insurance plan funded by the IMSS—which supports them in the event of sickness or pregnancy—provided that they are in last year of public high school or state-funded institutions of higher education and that they are not already covered by any other social security scheme.[45] There is also a special insurance scheme targeted to families[46] which allows individuals to benefit from health insurance supplied by the IMSS. One might note that coverage provided to young people is only with respect to health issues. For this reason, it might be the case that educational bodies decide to offer private life and accident insurance plans that supplement the foregoing schemes, which however provide limited coverage (e.g. serious injuries),

---

[43] To know more, see: Mendizábal Bermúdez, Gabriela, *Social security in Mexico*, Porrúa, Mexico, 2007.

[44] *Right-holders and the use of health services, INEGI, 2010.* At: http://www.inegi.org.mx/sistemas/sisept/default.aspx?t=msoc01&s=est&c=22594, (accessed June 28, 2011).

[45] Article 1 of Decree of 14 October 1998 makes provision for compulsory social security scheme with respect to sickness and maternity benefits for those in the last year of public high schools or institutions of higher education not already covered by similar social security schemes. At: http://info4.juridicas.unam.mx/ijure/nrm/1/207/2.htm?s=iste, (accessed June 29, 2011).

[46] Article 242 of the Social Security Law.

or have limited application (major medical expenses, indemnity in case of death).

The lack of protection for the youth which characterizes the Mexican social security system is particularly overt if compared with the benefits granted to young people in other countries. By way of example, in Austria, students are fully supported in the event of occupational accidents, irrespective of their educational level or institution, and this also includes those who volunteer in communities and suffer work-related injuries.

Accordingly, Austrian social security provisions cover a wider range of subjects than in Mexico.[47] Clearly, funding these schemes is the key issue. Students have limited resources and it is up to the state to bear the relative costs. In Mexico, if students suffer an accident on their way to school or while performing training activities, they are only entitled to first medical assistance. As a result, they are not protected in the event of permanent impairment, making them dependent on their family or social welfare.

6. Concluding Remarks

On the basis of the foregoing considerations, the present work will conclude by putting forward some proposals with regard to the interplay between education and the labour market:

- in order to solve youth-related problems, existing data (e.g. unemployment rates) needs to be looked at taking account of more specific variables, as current indicators do not seem to reflect the actual situation;
- vocational training must be given priority in the process of economic development at national level, while providing youth with the opportunity to have a better life resulting from higher remuneration;
- the reality of the Mexican education system and of its youth points out the need to make the transition from school to work smoother, in keeping with social, economic and demographic changes;
- it is necessary to acknowledge the value and the professional nature of the trades—that is technical occupations—and to remunerate workers in these positions accordingly;

[47] Tomandl, T. 1999. Unfallversicherung. Austria: Universitätsverlag, 325-327.

- in legal terms, increasing the range of benefits trainees are entitled to might be a stepping stone to safeguard their individual right to training.[48]
- as occurs in other countries, youth in Mexico require higher levels of protection that should arise from a more comprehensive social security system, particularly at the time of engaging in training activities.

References

Aguilera Izquierdo, R. and García Piñeiro, N. P. 2010. *"La formación profesional para el empleo: reflexiones para su reforma," Revista Española de Derecho del Trabajo,* No. 147:485-494.

CELADE. 2000. *Youth, Population and Development in Latin America and Caribbean*. Santiago: CELADE-CEPAL.

Gómez Abelleira, F. 2002. "Labour Law is Trading Downward? An Important American Decision on the Labour Law and Illegal Migration*," Critical Review of Theory and Practice* 2, No. 17:1189-1194.

Kurczyn Villalobos, P. 2001. *Work Relationships in the 21st Century.* Ministry of Labour and Social Welfare and National Autonomous University of Mexico: Mexico, 30.

Mendizábal Bermúdez, G. 2007. *Social Security in Mexico.* México: Porrúa.

Tomandl, T. 1999. Unfallversicherung. Austria: Universitätsverlag.

Sánchez Castañeda, A. 2007. "Instruction and Training in Mexico: Regulation, Realities and Challenges*," UNAM Latin American Journal of Social Law,* No. 5.

Castillo Reynoso, C. 2007. "Notes on Training in Mexico," *UNAM Latin American Journal of Social Law*, No. 5.

Schmid, G. 2008. "Strukturwandel des Arbeitsmarkts und seine Folgen für Übergänge aus dem Bildungssystem," Discussion Paper for the Workshop on National Training Reports, Berlin.

---

48 For further information on the subject, see Aguilera Izquierdo, R. and García Piñeiro, N. P. 2010. *"La formación profesional para el empleo: reflexiones para su reforma," Revista Española de Derecho del Trabajo,* No. 147:485-494.

Legislation

The Political Constitution of the United Mexican States
The Federal Civil Code
The Mexican Youth Institute Act
The ISSSTE Law
The ISSFAM Law
The Social Security Law
The General Education Act
The General Youth Act
The National Youth Act

AGUSTAWESTLAND INVESTS IN YOUTH: A CASE OF BEST PRACTICE IN THE TRANSITION FROM EDUCATION TO THE LABOUR MARKET

MARIA TUTTOBENE

1. Introduction

The purpose of this paper is to provide food for thought on how the complex transition from education and training to the labour market can be improved and accelerated, a topic which is usually given little attention in the Italian debate. Here, youth unemployment has long been a problem of great importance and relevance which, in addition to stifling the enthusiasm of many willing and ambitious young people, hampers national economic recovery. It is commonly known that a nation is more dynamic and competitive if provided with a more motivated and competent workforce. That being said, what is striking about Italy's case—especially when compared with other countries—is the delayed and difficult entry of young talent in the labour market. On average, access to regular employment concerns those of 25 years and older, an age which however should mark the transition to adulthood, according to EU rules about state aid and employment incentives. Furthermore, it should be noted that Italian youth tend to find work later than expected, and without possessing marketable skills and knowledge. The reason for this is to be found in the prejudicial stance according to which those in education should not be engaged in any working activities and vice versa.

Clearly, lengthening the shift from education to work—in Italy, such transition lasts longer than in most of OECD countries, 11 years rather than 7 years, which is the OECD average—can only have negative repercussions on young people in terms of skills and motivation, as the longer the transition, the lower the opportunities to access employment by way of formal contractual arrangements. This negative trend might be attributed to several factors, such as shortcomings in the provision of training, education and guidance, a mismatch between training supply and employers' needs, sometimes even to a lack of personal initiative. In an awareness of this state of affairs, the Italian government has tried to deal with the issue, pointing out that, in order to achieve full employment for youth, it is necessary to establish a new and closer relationship between the education system and the world of work. In this connection, of relevance is the document issued by the Italian Ministry of Labour along with the Ministry of Education: "ITALY 2020. An action plan for young people's employability through the integration between learning and work", that was presented to the Regions and social partners in June 2010, before being further amended in January 2011.

Significantly, the document begins with the following statement: "The people before all, our young before anyone. This is our ambition". The ITALY 2020 plan sets the ambitious goal to review the policies targeting young people, by providing six lines of action, which include the setting up of a monitoring system for sought-after skills and those already available in the labour market, the provision of vocational guidance since the very beginning of the academic career, the supply of education and vocational training and, more importantly, a more effective connection between school and work, by reviving apprenticeship and on-the-job training while still in education. This might be the point of departure—for both Italy and other countries—to change the current status of the labour market. Yet providing a set of guidelines might not be enough, as notwithstanding the innovative and pragmatic nature of such an attempt, the risk is to remain tied to a theoretical dimension. Accordingly, it is also essential to know and disseminate examples of excellence, in order to facilitate the exchange of good ideas and better solutions. This is the reason that prompted me to write and disseminate this short article.

The Doctoral research programme I am on has given me access to a great company, the *modus operandi* of which is a good example of how the guidelines laid down by the Italian government with regard to youth employment should be implemented and tested in practice. The company I am referring to is AgustaWestland (also referred to simply as AW). This is an Anglo-Italian company, fully owned by Italian Finmeccanica. AW is the worldwide leader in high-tech production of helicopters, designed for both civil and military customers around the world. AW has its main operations in Italy, The United Kingdom, Poland and the United States of America: it currently employs over 15,000 people worldwide and offers younger people unique career opportunities in different areas. The company can be certainly regarded as a case of "best practice" with regard to the transition from education to the labour market, thanks to its training schemes and initiatives aimed at facilitating access to the working world on the part of young people.

2. The Case of AgustaWestland S.p.A.

2.1. Apprenticeship Opportunities in Italy and the United Kingdom

In AW, one of the most widespread instruments to accelerate the shift from school to the labour market is the apprenticeship contract, devised to meet both business needs and afford young people the skills and knowledge to succeed in the working world. The apprenticeship programme includes theoretical and in-house training in order to provide a fitting environment where trainees can practice what they learn in the classroom. In the context of this paper, I will not dwell on the way apprenticeship is structured, as it is not the main theme of my work. What I would like to highlight is the difference between AW Italy and AW UK at the time of implementing it. As far as Italy is concerned, only qualified 18 to 19 year-olds without any work experience are hired through apprenticeship contracts for a period up to 54 months (white-collar workers) or 46 (blue-collar workers).

This contractual arrangement consists of an individual training plan—the aim of which is to develop technical and personal skills to gain a vocational qualification—that is usually carried out under the supervision of a company tutor, who oversees the apprentice's training activities. This plan has to be signed upon hiring by both the apprentice and the tutor.

Training is undertaken in special areas within the plant that are separated from the production line, and the instructors are usually AW employees or former employees who are now retired with significant work experience and the willingness to share their expertise with the beginners. In the UK, the company seeks to attract people of the highest calibre to join its engineering, technician and business apprenticeship programmes, based at their Yeovil site in Somerset. AgustaWestland was recently awarded the "Outstanding" status, the highest award possible, which demonstrates its excellent training capability, offering a "good strategic planning of the apprenticeship programme to meet business needs". The different types of apprenticeship offered by AW UK, all of which require different profiles and interests, can broadly be classified into two categories: "Aeronautical Engineering" and "Business". "Aeronautical Engineering" covers design, manufacture and production of aircraft and it can be split into two fields:

- the Technician Apprenticeship Programme: it caters for those who are interested in the design, development and test elements of engineering. Over this period, apprentices are trained to become a mechanical or electrical technician.
- The Engineering Apprenticeship Programme, with specialisation in electrical, composite or transmission components manufacture, installation and repair: it addresses those who are interested in the more hands-on activities, such as production, repair, overhaul and test elements of engineering. Commencing in September, the "Aeronautical engineering" apprenticeship lasts 4 years. The first year is spent at the Yeovil College, learning the basics of engineering. During this phase, the apprentice undertakes the first year of the National Certificate in Mechanical or Electrical/Electronic Engineering course—or the City and Guilds Certificate, for those who have chosen the specialisation in transmission production—and the National Vocational Qualification (NVQ) Level 2 in Performing Engineering Operations (PEO). NVQs are work-based awards in United Kingdom that are achieved through training and assessments. They reflect the professional qualifications of a person, obtained in the workplace and/or with the support of University or College. To achieve a NVQ, candidates must prove that they have the ability and competence to carry out their job in a given area, according to the required standards. There are five levels of NVQ ranging from Level 1, with a focus on basic work activities, to Level 5 for senior management.

In the remaining three years, apprentices work on-site and full time at AgustaWestland at Yeovil-Somerset, but the significant element is that they spend time working in 3- to 6-month placements—according to the programme followed—in different engineering departments, under the direct supervision of a tutor, gaining excellent experience and learning to become skilled in a particular discipline. The functional skills acquired in these departments can be assessed for the NVQ Level 3 in aeronautical or mechanical engineering, depending on the training scheme.

During the three years, or in the second year only if the programme is "Engineering Apprenticeship", and for one day a week, the young apprentice is on day-release to Yeovil College, in order to complete the national certificate course—or the city and guilds certificate—and to follow, in the last two years, the higher national certificate course in mechanical or electrical/electronic engineering. The latter is reserved to technician apprenticeship programmes. The second major type of apprenticeship, as previously mentioned, takes place in the business area: the "business" concerns management's choices in order to collectively achieve goals and maximise profit from the sale of goods and/or services.

This apprenticeship scheme has two secondary routes: the first is the "Business Administration Apprenticeship Programme", while the second is the "Business Support Advanced Apprenticeship Programme". The business administration apprenticeship programme is intended for those who would like to continue with academic learning while at the same time receive important business experience in a work environment. Business Administration apprentices spend 2 years working in 3-month placements in different departments of the organisation (HdR, Trainee Development, Employee Development, Procurement, Customer Support and Service and so forth), learning from their supervisor(s) and gaining essential business skills. Academically, the trainees undertake different qualifications: Technical Certificate in Principles of Business and Administration, National Vocational Qualification (NVQ) Level 2 in Business Administration and, on the second year, the BTEC (Bio-manufacturing Training and Education Centre) Award in Business. This, finalised to complement the NVQ programme and raise their academic level, is a 2-year training programme, so it will be completed by trainees during the first year of their permanent position. On successful completion of the business administration apprenticeship the trainee has, indeed, a real possibility to gain a permanent position within the company, often in administrative, secretarial, clerical or junior officer roles or he/she may apply for further academic sponsorship to commence studying for a Foundation Degree in Business and Management. The business support advanced apprenticeship programme is a higher-level entry route into a career in business, particularly suited to those who are keen to progress both academically and practically in a top-level multinational organisation.

Business support apprentices spend 18 months working in 3 six-month placements and they benefit from studying part-time for a Foundation Degree in Business and Management, fully sponsored by AgustaWestland and which will be completed after the conclusion of the training scheme. Furthermore, the trainees embark on National Vocational Qualification (NVQ) Level 3 in Business and Administration. They have excellent career prospects: most of them gain a permanent position within the company, often in officer level roles. The entry requirements to access above apprenticeship programmes are 5 GCSEs (General Certificates of Secondary Education, grades A-C), including Maths, English and Science—this lasts only for "Aeronautical Engineering Apprenticeship Programmes". If the training route followed is "Business Support Advanced

Apprenticeship Programme", it is also requires3 A levels (General Certificate of Education Advanced Level, grades A-C) or equivalent.

2.2. Training and Orientation Internships—sites of Italy and United Kingdom

Another important tool facilitating the transition from education to the working world is represented by training and career guidance, by way of which on-the-job learning is provided through temporary placements in the company, with the goal of allowing individuals to become familiar with and experience the world of work, while helping them in their future professional choices. These schemes cater to both graduates and undergraduates and to students of secondary schools. On the basis of agreements with local schools and within the project called "school-work alternation", AW also hosts some secondary students for a number of weeks, to motivate and guide them in developing their future careers, and providing them with vocational training at the workplace. Further, AgustaWestland is constantly looking out for the best young people who have successfully completed their education and who are interested in job opportunities. Internships are generally related to specific projects in different departments within the company and last about six months. Job placements can be considered the main channels of entry into the labour market and this is particularly evident in the UK. AgustaWestland UK offers brilliant undergraduates industrial placements covering a 12-month period—usually from July to June of the following year—in the fields of Engineering and Business and based at their Yeovil site in Somerset.

The internships—within an undergraduate programme—are intended to monitor trainees' progress, giving them insight into a high-tech multinational and unique opportunity to gain technical and occupational skills, and valuable practical experience that will accompany their future careers. Throughout the programme, incumbents in these positions are supported by an ad-hoc employee development officer who supplies guidance and advice with the aim of promoting continuous growth. Furthermore, each year, AW UK seeks to attract the best Engineering and Business graduates to join the Graduate Programmes at the Yeovil site in Somerset. Starting in October, this programme lasts two years and consists of a series of specialised placements and development activities that have been designed to support graduates as they embark on the first steps of their post university career: the placements allow them to develop the knowledge, skills and attitudes required for a brilliant future in the working world. Graduate trainees have a pre-determined role/destination when recruited by the Company and the training programme provides a personalised placement plan to prepare them for this. The two-year programme is broken down into four 6-month structured placements, covering different and significant areas of engineering or business—depending on education—and that are tailored to trainees' interests and development. Graduates also benefit from a number of other training and development opportunities, including the enrolment into the "Finmeccanica Learning Induction Programme" (FLIP) where Agusta Westland graduates network with other graduates from the wider Finmeccanica population. The aim of this Programme is to ensure that Graduates joining any Finmeccanica Group Company around the world experience the same high standard of induction and development. To this end, participants have to complete various online modules, attend seminars and courses, and undertake projects via the Internet with their colleagues in other worldwide companies. FLIP culminates with an international graduate conference where all participants from around the world come together to celebrate their success of the programme and to define the next steps on their journey within the Finmeccanica Group.

2.3. School Liaison Activities in the UK

This section explains the AgustaWestland school liaison strategy, from the viewpoint of the current main activities run by AW in the local areas, in order to introduce the concept of engineering from a young age. Through a number of initiatives, AgustaWestland wants to further develop and increase the interest in Engineering, promoting it as a career and itself as an employer of choice. To do so, the company leads its focus on a number of institutions—called Priority Schools—and, according to the age of the students (from 5 to 13 years old), it runs different types of activities, with the purpose of generating an interest in engineering at a young age and instilling the presence of AgustaWestland in student's minds for the years to come. The activities cover a full set of initiatives, starting from the "Imagineering clubs" where classes of 5 to 6 year-olds are involved in the creation of working models that explain various engineering concepts.

Industry days and in-class presentations follow, in order to promote the company and its opportunities, relevant hands-on activities to students in the 9-10 age group, and careers speed dating sessions, with the aim of allowing students to meet employers who provide their personal and professional view of the various apprenticeship routes. One of the most effective methods of engaging with the immediate target market for AW apprenticeship programmes is to arrange in-class/lunchtime presentations, allowing students who are interested to take part in the event to "find out more". AW believes that work experience plays a substantial role in preparing young people for their future careers. It is a unique opportunity to gain necessary skills and knowledge to succeed throughout their working lives. For this reason, AW has also implemented a new programme lasting one week in summertime named "work experience periods". They are addressed to students—mainly of the age of 10—and they consist of a number of company visits and job-shadowing experiences, along with hands-on engineering activities and workshops which increase their levels of employability. The subjects involved in this initiative are educational bodies, students and employers. The school should brief students about the objectives of work experience, whereas the student should engage with the process and make the most of this opportunity. Finally, the function of the company is to provide a general introduction to the world of work and an insight into working for AgustaWestland, with the view to support the educational and professional career of young pupils. By resorting to this school recruitment strategy, AgustaWestland operates with local authorities providing career information and guidance to young people, and funding the West regional careers fair. Another significant activity towards the transition from school to work is the Flying Start Challenge, where 13-14 year-olds with an interest in engineering and in the aerospace industry are involved in designing and building an aircraft, competing with other students from all over the country to be awarded a prize. Other collaborations include that with Yeovil Federation, Science, Technology, Engineering and Manufacturing Network (STEMNET) links, EBP, Connect South West Somerset and Connexions Dorset, Industrial Trust and Engineering Education Scheme. The main goal of these organizations is to ensure that more young people in the UK make a choice to enter science-, technology- and mathematics-related careers at all levels. They also want to help companies and contribute to the wider economy by building bridges between companies and schools.

2.4. Recruiting Activities in Italy

In Italy as well, AgustaWestland is constantly looking out for the best young people who have brilliantly completed their education and who are interested in training opportunities. In order to make the recruitment procedures more successful, the company cooperates with the most important institutions (universities, business schools and technical high schools) specialized in different employer branding.

By way of example, AW arranges on-site visits for some local schools, to show students the manufacturing processes in the rotorcraft industry, and list the several career opportunities. It also participates in numerous job fairs, promoted by the most important Italian universities to bring together employers and the most talented students. Furthermore, it is important to note that AW line managers, teachers and professors from both universities and technical high schools work side by side to integrate academic programmes into special classes, and to supply strategic technological skills. The “High School Study Tour” is another initiative that is worthy of mention, as it aims at bringing together school and work through a series of meetings at different schools, over which representatives of AgustaWestland present the company and its career opportunities. An open day is held at the end of the year, and students from all schools in the nearby areas can take part. Finally, evaluation centres are arranged in some secondary schools. Here, career guidance is supplied to students and a selection procedure might also take place, with the company that meets young graduates who have made themselves available for job opportunities and interviews even before graduation.

2.5. Postgraduate Courses in Rotary Wing Technologies

AgustaWestland IT funds 10 scholarships to attend a Postgraduate Course in Rotary Wing Technologies, organized by the Department of Engineering of the University of Milan.

Beneficiaries of these scholarships are usually new graduates—with a master’s degree in science, aeronautical, space, aerospace, mechanical, electronic or electric engineering or with a three-year university degree in the aerospace or contiguous field and two-year experience in the same areas—selected by an admission board in accordance to their suitability for the available positions. This training programme offers students the opportunity to widen their knowledge in specific areas in the rotorcraft industry. At the end of the course, a selection of students will be offered a six-month apprenticeship at AgustaWestland, which is broken down into two phases. In the first phase, students are thoroughly instructed to perform different activities under the supervision of a tutor, such as rotorcraft description and utilization, design and structural analysis, helicopter certification, customer care and so forth. In the second phase, they are assigned to a department and they work on hands-on projects. This is a suitable example of how the transition from education to work can be smoothed in a pragmatic way, enabling new recruits or engineers already in employment to be quickly and effectively introduced into the company.

2.6. Master's Degree in Management for the Aerospace Sector

AgustaWestland Italy promotes and finances—along with other companies—a second level master's degree in management for the aerospace sector, granting participants a number of scholarships that cover the registration fees. Candidates are required to hold a degree in aerospace, aeronautical or management engineering. As far as higher education is concerned, the H&A Master's degree combines theoretical learning—provided by both academics and engineers from the company—with work experience, to develop technical and managerial skills of participants, in order to allow them to enter the dynamic sector of aerospace more rapidly.

3. Conclusions

The AW experience shows how the cooperation between educational institutions and employers allows for a better alignment of academic careers and company's needs. Activities such as those described above prevent the risk that the skills acquired at school are not line with the market demand and, consequently, that young people are not able to find a suitable job after completion of their studies. The worlds of education and employment should work together in order to satisfy their respective needs. Institutions in charge of schooling have to adapt the education supplied to business needs if they want to be appealing to students and employers. Only by bridging the gap between employment and education, it will be possible to positively impact on youth employment levels.

References

Gelmini, M. S., G. Meloni, and M. Sacconi. 2010. *Piano di azione per l'occupabilitá dei giovani attraverso l'integrazione tra apprendimento e lavoro.* Italian Government. http://www.lavoro.gov.it/NR/rdonlyres/56F52DEC-F9A1-4D48-BCF0-C3C444251A37/0/pianogiovani_print.pdf (accessed July 15, 2011).

AgustaWestland. Careers: http://www.agustawestland.com/content/careers (accessed July 15, 2011).

VOCATIONAL TRAINING IN PERU

RAÚL G. SACO BARRIOS*

1. Introduction[1]

Over the last years, lifelong learning[2] and personal development[3] have been widely-discussed issues. "Education and training are the key to making people employable, thereby allowing them to gain access to decent work and to escape poverty". More specifically, "In affording the working population with basic education, sought-after skills, and lifelong learning opportunities, national governments ensure that workers maintain and improve their levels of employability, contributing to a more skilled and productive workforce". In this sense, "Societies aiming to attain full employment and sustained economic growth need to invest in training and human resources development".[4] Accordingly, education should be supplemented with practical work experience under the direct supervision of an instructor, in order to gain valuable expertise.

---

* Full Professor of Law at the Pontificia Universidad Católica, Perú. He is member of the Ibero-American Association of Jurists of Labour Law and Social Security (AIJDTSS), and of the Peruvian Society of Labour Law and Social Security (SPDTSS) and the Peruvian Association of Labour Relations (APERT) rgsaco@pucp.edu.pe.

[1] Translation from Spanish by Martina Ori.

[2] Lifelong Learning "encompasses all learning activities undertaken throughout life for the development of competencies and qualifications" (ILO, *Human Resources Development Recommendation, 2004*).

[3] Pizarro Posse, R., 1995. "Rol y función de la gerencia de recursos humanos," in *Relaciones Industriales y Recursos Humanos en América Latina*, eds. Aldao-Zapiola, C. M. and Hermida Martínez, D. (Buenos Aires: Federación Interamericana de Administración de Personal), 121. The author regards training as being the same as "lifelong learning", since "every job requires the highest possible educational level".

[4] The last three quotations have been taken from:
http://www.ilo.org/global/standards/subjects-covered-by-international-labour-standards/vocational-guidance-and-training/lang--en/index.htm

For the purpose of this paper, it seems appropriate to make a distinction between job training (i.e. training for a job) and on-the-job training: the former is supplied in training centres that prepare youth for future jobs, while the latter refers to the set of skills provided at the workplace once full-time education and training have been completed. In this context, mention should be made of a number of vocational training arrangements that combine work and training (e.g. apprenticeship, vocational training, training for the youth, internship, and retraining to smooth the reinstatement of workers). In concluding one of the above mentioned accords, one signatory party pledges to supply training and remuneration, while the other undertakes to fulfil job assignments and to learn as per required. These training arrangements also play a fundamental role in social terms, for workers need training and skills upgrading throughout their life. In this sense, they serve as complementary tools to traditional full-time vocational education and training.[5]

The present study provides an outline of the vocational training arrangements listed above. First, the International Labour Standards on Vocational Guidance and Training will be investigated, with a view to bring out those features that are also common to traditional vocational training, followed by some insights into the research approach adopted. Afterwards, and drawing on this analysis, the rules governing vocational training in Peru will be looked into, as well as resorting to some statistical data analysis. Finally, some concluding remarks will be offered.

2. International Labour Standards on Vocational Guidance and Training

The regulatory system of the International Labour Organization (ILO) consists of the whole set of provisions issued by the ILO, such as conventions, recommendations, declarations and resolutions. The term "International Labour Standards" (hereafter simply as ILS) specifically refers to a number of Conventions, Recommendations and Declarations.[6]

---

[5] Training arrangements "must pursue a purely educational purpose and should not be too burdensome for employers. They should not become a simple and cheap way to recruit youth or people with no work experience" (Campana, D., and Prelle, H. 2000. "La reforma normativa de la contratación laboural durante los noventa: ¿Flexibilidad o precarización?" in *Estudios sobre la flexibilidad laboural en el Perú*, (Lima: International Labour Office), Working Paper No. 124, 64).

[6] In a more narrow sense: "[…] the ILO Constitution […] identifies in Conventions and Recommendations the two main tools to define International Labour

With regard to vocational training, special mention should be made of the Human Resources Development Convention, 1975 (No. 142), the Paid Educational Leave Convention, 1974 (No. 140) and the Recommendation concerning Human Resources Development: Education, Training and Lifelong Learning (No. 195), laid down during the International Labour Conference (Geneva, 2004).

By issuing the foregoing ILS on vocational training, the ILO aims at emphasising the fundamental role of training, education and lifelong learning.[7] First, the purpose of ILS is to foster social inclusion and a more balanced economic growth in a global economy, by giving priority to individual interests, as well as those of employers, and the society at large, with a focus on full employment and poverty reduction. Secondly, their aim is at a better connection between training, education and lifelong learning with social and economic policies and labour market programmes, by safeguarding fundamental rights. All of these factors are of particular importance for both social and economic development, sustainable economic growth and job creation. Thirdly, since education, training and lifelong learning have a major impact on encouraging personal development, they should contribute to promote access to knowledge and active citizenship. The significance and effectiveness of the ILO Conventions are not undermined by the fact that one of the ILO members might not ratify such conventions, once adopted.[8] Not only must conventions be ratified by the Member States, but they should also be taken as a point of departure to devise policies on education and training. This is particularly the case of Recommendation No. 195, adopted in 2004, that is to be taken into great consideration and fully implemented by ILO Members, all the more so in view of its all-important contents.

Standards. The basic difference between them is that Conventions are open to ratification by the Member States, whereas the ratification lays down legal obligations in terms of implementation and enforcement. A recommendation instead cannot be ratified and can only provide guidance to Member States on the actions to be taken in a specific area" (Von Potobsky G. W. and Bartolomei De La Cruz, H. G. 1990. *La Organización Internacional del Trabajo*, Buenos Aires: Editorial Astrea, 24).

[7] ILO. 2004. *Human Resources Development Recommendation,* par. 2, 4 and 6.

[8] This is the case of Peru, that has not ratified Conventions No. 142 and No. 140.

3. Regulation of Vocational Training[9] in Peru

In Peru, the Constitution sets forth that education "prepares for life and work" (Art. 14). Further on in the same document, it is maintained that "the State establishes the conditions for social and economic progress, especially through policies aimed at fostering productive employment and training for work". In this connection, particularly relevant is Law No. 28518 on Vocational Training implemented by Supreme Decree No. 7-2005-TR of 16 September 2005 that regulates apprenticeship, vocational training, training for young people, internship and retraining for the reinstatement of workers.[10]

3.1. Principles, Objectives and Scope of Application

The law sets forth the underlying principles of vocational training, which help interpret relevant legislation, particularly at the time of dealing with uncertain or controversial issues or with cases of legal vacuums[11] and

---

[9] In this context, the notion of regulation having the force of law may refer to: laws (passed by the Congress and enacted by the Government), legislative decrees (passed by the Government that is delegated by the Congress, the enforcement of which is similar to ordinary laws, in terms of enactment, publication, validity and effects) and decrees (approved by the Government). It may also refer to certain decrees and resolutions such as Supreme Decrees (the most relevant provisions issued by the Government, which are approved and signed by the President of the Republic and at least one of the Ministers) and Supreme Resolutions (issued by one or more Ministers with the approval of the President of the Republic).

[10] Although it refers to workers rather than to trainees, Law No. 29498 on the Promotion of Human Capital Investment of 16 January 2010 aims at "promoting human capital development by means of continuous training, increasing their [trainees] productivity as well as the competitiveness of national economy". This provision amended Law on Income Tax (Consolidated Act enacted by means of Supreme Decree No. 179-2004-EF), and sets forth that the costs of training can be deducted from the total costs borne yearly, up to a maximum of 5%. To apply for such training deduction, companies should submit to the Ministry of Labour and Employment Promotion a written statement indicating the training programme they have adopted. The submission is free of charge. The Ministerial Resolution of 30 December 2010 defines training as "any action taken by employers to increase workers' skills, in order to contribute to improving their employability as well as increasing the company productivity".

[11] Legal vacuum refers to "an event which is not covered by existing legislation and that must not necessarily be regulated by law but rather according to applicable hermeneutical principles" (Rubio Correa, M. 2007. *El Sistema Jurídico.*

regulatory gaps.[12] In addition, they are at the basis of most recent provisions on training. The law also specifies that rights and obligations "must be interpreted in accordance with the International Labour Organization Conventions". Consequently, vocational training programmes should be supplied considering three main aspects: the central role of the individual in the educational process; equal opportunities without discrimination in terms of access to vocational training, the attempt to re-shape training in order to adapt to effective market needs. As for the objective, the provisions considered above are intended to achieve a better match between labour demand and supply, to develop training programmes in line with production processes to further enhance employability and productivity, and to design training courses that supply valuable skills to achieve higher levels of flexibility and facilitate job swop. With regard to the scope of application, employers who operate in both the private and public sector can provide for training arrangements, on the ground that workers are subject to labour laws that govern private economic activities. However, training is not usually regulated by labour law provisions,[13] but, where applicable, by a special set of rules, which is the Law on Vocational Training or the General Law on Education. In a narrow sense, these training arrangements require special regulation. The Law on Vocational Training "does not expressly state that vocational training agreements do not constitute an employment relationship. They can therefore be considered as special employment relationships subject to specific

---

Introducción al Derecho, Lima: Fondo Editorial de la Pontificia Universidad Católica del Perú, 244).

[12] A regulation gap is defined as an event which is not covered by existing legislation, although requiring special regulation. In a narrower sense, a regulation gap arises when the law fails to regulate a given situation. In some cases, new provisions must be laid down to provide a solution to the case at issue. In this regard, Art. 139, par. 8 of the Constitution defines "principles and rights of the judiciary: […]. According to one of these principles, a lack of regulation on a particular issue should not prevent courts from administering justice. On these occasions, judges must apply the general principles of law and customary law. Still on the same topic, Art. 8 of the Introduction of the Civil Code provides that a lack of regulation on a particular issue should not prevent courts from administering justice and in such cases, judges should apply the general principles of law and in particular those that inspire national law.

[13] This means that training contracts are not regarded as an employment relationship, although guaranteeing special rights and obligations, as defined in the Law on Vocational Training (see Boza Pro, G. 2011. *Lecciones de derecho del trabajo*. Lima: Fondo Editorial de la Pontificia Universidad Católica del Perú, 2011, 55).

provisions".[14] However, the Law on Vocational Training provides that, under certain conditions—if the agreement is null and void, not properly implemented, or not signed by the parties—"a traditional employment relationship might be presumed", implying that a training scheme can turn into a standard employment relationship. One might ask how this is possible as it seems sensible that a special employment relationship is converted into an ordinary one, in accordance to labour law provisions. Indeed, and pursuant to Law No. 26636—Procedural Labour Law of 21 June 1996—labour courts are not empowered to settle disputes or to deal with matters pertaining to vocational training agreements. Subsequently, employment tribunals were given competence in this area as well, according to Law No. 29497—New Procedural Labour Law of 13 January 2010. Does the new provision acknowledge the special nature of this type of employment relationship? In order to emphasise the special character of these training programmes, the law governing such arrangements makes use of "agreements" and "allowances" rather than "contracts" and "remuneration".

3.2. Overview

Vocational training schemes constitute "special types of agreements providing for theoretical and practical learning by means of specific training tasks" (LMFL, Art. 5). Vocational training can be supplied through: apprenticeship, according to which on-the-job training is given in both companies or in vocational training centres to youth that are still in education and training; vocational training; youth training, in-house internships, also for instructors, and retraining for the reinstatement of workers. In order to provide vocational training successfully and to manage the different steps of training—structuring, supply, assessment, and certification—a number of institutions have been purposely set up to contribute to the full implementation of these programmes (save for youth training and retraining for dismissed workers). Among others, vocational training centres, that are authorised by the Ministry of Education, and services for vocational training at a sectoral level. There are also industry-wide vocational training services that are directly managed by companies, employers' associations and trade unions that certify training quality according to the guidelines included in the National Vocational Training Policy. Vocational training centres are in charge of concluding vocational

---

[14] Neves Mujica, J. 2009. *Introducción al Derecho del Trabajo*, Lima: Fondo Editorial de la Pontificia Universidad Católica del Perú, 51.

training agreements and monitoring their full enforcement. The Law on Vocational Training regulates a number of specific programmes, particularly with regard to apprenticeship, youth training (with a minimum duration of one year), youth vocational training, the national vocational training plan, internships (including special arrangements for the promotion of internships), and skills upgrading to help workers re-enter the labour market, in order to increase their employability.

The Law on Vocational Training also requires the drafting of a training plan that must respond to specific needs, e.g. it should list objectives and content of the programme, and a description of in-house training activities. The plan is to be included in the contract—except in those cases where the relevant authority has already given its consent—and serve as a starting point for the development of this form of on-the-job training. The plan should comprise the name of the programme, detailed information of the host company and trainees, the name of the training provider, the purpose of the programme (expected outcomes in terms of skill development), information on on-the-job training activities (tasks to be performed), duration (date of beginning and completion of the course, and training schedule), training environment (a brief description of health and safety standards, infrastructure, machinery, tools and materials) and monitoring and evaluation criteria (the name of the tutor or supervisor must be indicated). With regard to the programmes, the one addressed to young people and the supplementary training programme require minimum information concerning training activities, particularly if one compares it to the retraining scheme. On some occasions, the company should indicate the reasons for starting special training for young people, for instance, business or market developments, and this programme should have the same duration as the youth training programme carried out on an annual basis (see below).

The submission of a training plan to the relevant authority constitutes a prerequisite for the conclusion of the agreement. Although under the obligation to provide training, micro enterprises are not required to provide a detailed training plan.

As for the agreement, it involves three actors, the trainee, the employer,[15] and—in the cases of apprenticeship, vocational training and internship—also the vocational training centres. The accord, which is

[15] Although the legislator makes use of the terms "company" and "employer" to indicate the receiving entity in the case of company-based apprenticeship, in the present paper the terms "employer" and "company" are used with reference to all forms of vocational training. The law itself provides for such a broad interpretation.

concluded before entering training, should be in writing and include at least the following information: the name of the natural person or legal entity (the employer), name, age (date of birth) and further information on the trainees—or of their legal representative if under age[16]—their nationality, identification number, address, sex, marital status, job position, skills and tasks to be performed, the amount of the allowance they are entitled to, the duration of the programme (date of beginning and completion of the course), as well as reasons for amending, suspending or terminating the agreement. In addition, and although not explicitly stated, the agreement should also include special training obligations and should be submitted to the Ministry of Labour and Employment within 15 days upon conclusion. Later submission is allowed but only before the end of the training period. The Law on Vocational Training also specifies that the government, upon proposal from the Ministry of Labour and Employment, can introduce specific mechanisms to increase multi-sectoral coordination, with a view to ensuring the full enforcement of training agreements and the fulfilment of their goals, also through the definition of certain implementation criteria. Coordination takes place through a Multi-sectoral Training Commission that monitors the labour market demand. Health and safety is likewise important. In this respect, the employer should provide trainees with adequate instructions to prevent occupational risks, informing them of safety procedures to comply with during the training period. Where necessary, trainees should also be equipped with appropriate personal protection equipment (PPE). Evidently, in carrying out the training programme, the employer should comply with minimum health and safety requirements laid down in relevant legislation. In general terms, the Labour Inspectorate is responsible for monitoring compliance with the OSH regulation and can apply sanctions in the event of infringements. Inspections are carried out upon request of the trainee or of any other concerned party.

3.3. Legislation Applying to Vocational Training

Vocational training is subject to a set of common rules which lays down obligations on the part of trainees, employers and training providers, concerning the duration of training, monthly remuneration, registration of the agreement, supervision, terms limiting the conclusion of training

[16] Art. 45 of the Civil Code sets forth that legal representation for minors is exercised according to rules concerning parental authority or guardianship, whereas applicable.

agreements, conversion of training agreements into employment contracts, infringements and sanctions. Trainees are under the obligation to comply with rules, to fulfil the tasks assigned to them, and to actively participate to training activities. As for employers, they have to ensure that training is properly implemented, supply necessary technical supervision, allocate sufficient financial resources, and secure prompt payment of monthly allowance to trainees. They should also guarantee paid weekly rest periods and days off, as well as at least fifteen days of paid holiday every year.[17] An additional sum of money amounting to half the monthly allowance should be granted to training incumbents every six months, if training has been discontinued.[18] One should note that employers ought to supply training free of charge, as well as health and safety insurance coverage through the Social Security System (*EsSalud*)[19] or through private insurance arrangements, equivalent to 14 or 30 working days in cases of illness or accident, respectively.[20] The opportunity to join a retirement scheme should also be discussed. Finally, employers must draft reports which outline the training activity—to be submitted to the vocational training centre attended by the trainee—certification of the skills acquired and the tasks performed at the workplace. As far as training bodies are concerned, they are asked to design training programmes in line with the labour market needs,[21] cooperate with operators in the economic sectors involved, and support employers in supervising, assessing, certifying training, as well as monitoring the tasks carried out by trainees. Guidelines helping them fulfil these obligations are available for each sector. The duration of the training day is determined by the training needs of trainees and varies according to the different vocational training schemes. In the case of company-based apprenticeship, vocational training agreements, youth training agreements, internship agreements, retraining agreements the time devoted to training should not exceed 8 hours a day or 48 hours a

[17] These 15 days must be taken during the following 12 months, while the allowance must be paid before the holiday break. In cases in which the overall duration of the training agreement—or its extension—does not exceed 12 months, the trainee is entitled to full allowance.

[18] Extra allowances should be paid within 15 calendar days.

[19] The Ministry of Labour and Employment Promotion should cooperate with the social security system (*EsSalud*) to implement and develop special programmes regarding occupational health and safety.

[20] In the event of work-related illnesses or accidents, the employers who have not applied for any insurance shall bear full liability in terms of premiums.

[21] The term "labour market" refers to the interactions between labour demand and supply. A further explanation is however required: human labour is not a commodity.

week. As for centre-based apprenticeship, it can be carried forward for a period not exceeding 6 hours a day or 30 hours a week.[22] In both cases, the text of the Law on Vocational Training adopts the disjunctive "or",[23] meaning that the two possibilities are independent from each other. Nevertheless, junior doctors who carry out their apprenticeship in public health facilities are not allowed to work more than 6 hours a day, 36 hours a week or 150 hours a months, including night shifts (Supreme Decree No. 3-2008-TR of 20 May 2008).

Concerning vocational training contracts concluded with people under age, the duration of the training day should be calculated considering the restrictions laid down in legislation regulating child labour, namely the Child and Adolescent Code (*Código de los Niños y Adolescentes*).[24] Art. No. 56 of the Code sets forth that minors between 12 and 14 years old are not allowed to work more than 4 hours a day and for more than 24 hours a week, whereas 15-17 year-olds are not allowed to work more than 6 hours a day and 36 hours a week.[25] Students in the last year of secondary school can take part in internships, and the duration of the training day is defined by the Ministry of Education. According to the Secondary Education Learning Programme, the training day for interns lasts 2 to 4 hours a day and takes place twice to three times a week. In this case, the legislator uses

[22] Despite this general rule concerning the maximum number of working days for centre-based apprenticeship, Art. 2 of Supreme Decree No. 3-2008-TR of 20 May 2008 provides basically the same restrictions set for trainee lawyers, i.e. 6 hours a day or 30 hours a week. Unfortunately, the rules on apprenticeship are violated by companies, law firms and public bodies on a systematic basis (Boza Pro, G. 2011. *Lecciones de derecho del trabajo*. Lima: Fondo Editorial de la Pontificia Universidad Católica del Perú, 2011, 55).

[23] "The disjunctive 'or' expresses opposition or contrast" (REAL ACADEMIA ESPAÑOLA, *Diccionario de la Lengua Española*, 2001).

[24] Youth between 14 and 18 years old can undertake vocational training, provided they supply a medical certificate (that they can obtain free of charge from social security or health care services) certifying their physical, mental ability to carry out assigned tasks. The contract will be concluded by parents or guardians. Youth are not allowed to perform underground activities, work involving the handling of heavy weights and toxic substances, activities that jeopardize their safety and that of other people under their responsibility, as well as all the activities in the "list of dangerous jobs and tasks causing damages to youth physical and mental health" according to the provisions laid down in the Child and Adolescent Code (*Código de los Niños y Adolescentes*).

[25] Or 30 hours per week in case of centre-based apprenticeship.

the conjunctive "and",[26] thus meaning that both requirements must be met, with a maximum of 8 hours a day or 12 days. The Labour Department can also allow night time training, provided it responds to training needs, and shifts should not prevent trainees from attending training centres. Minors, however, are prohibited from working at night; in exceptional cases, night shifts may be authorised for youth between 15 and 18 years, for a maximum of 4 hours. Like other workers, trainees are also granted rest periods of at least 45 minutes a day,[27] but they are not allowed to work overtime (Supreme Decree No. 3-2008-TR of 20 May 2008, Art. 1).

As far as training allowances are concerned, they are paid in accordance with the company remuneration policy. As a general rule, trainees are not permitted to waive the receipt of their monthly salary, which cannot be lower than the statutory minimum wage[28] in the event of maximum duration of training days. For shorter training days, the amount of their wage is determined considering the actual number of hours worked. Pay-scales of those taking part in internship and retraining are fixed in accordance with special rules. Interns who are still in secondary school are entitled to a monthly remuneration that should be at least 50% of the minimum wage or, in special cases, at least 30% of such minimum. When the internship that is carried out in vocational training bodies is compulsory, students are not granted any allowances. In the case of retraining that help the re-insertion of workers, participants are granted a monthly allowance that amounts to at least twice the minimum wage. Training allowance is not regarded as salary in a strict sense, and is not subject to tax withholdings or to contributions on the part of the employer (unless the employer agrees to pay for social security contributions on a voluntary basis). Neither are tax deductions provided to employers for offering training places, unless they decide to join a retirement scheme. However, allowances can be deducted for tax purposes. Remuneration—or any other financial benefit agreed-upon or stated in statutory law, which is due at the end of the training period must be paid within 48 hours after

---

26 "A conjuction connects and coordinates" (REAL ACADEMIA ESPAÑOLA, *Diccionario de la Lengua Española*, 2001).

27 Legislative Decree No. 854 – Law on Working Time and Overtime Work, Consolidated Law enforced by Supreme Decree No. 7-2002-TR of 3 July 2002, establishes that during work, workers are provided with a meal break. Workers are entitled to at least 45 minutes of rest every day. Rest periods should not be counted as working time, unless otherwise provided in the applicable collective agreements.

28 Currently, the minimum wage is approximately S/. 675,00: which is about 250,00 US Dollars. (exchange rate as of 31 January 2012: S/. 2.70.).

termination of the contract. A recent proposal makes provision to repeal the obligation on employers to pay young workers and apprentices the minimum wage, with the intent of boosting formal employment, leaving employers and trainees the discretion of negotiating pay. The premise behind this reasoning is that young workers are mainly interested in acquiring experience and skills, while gaining the employer's trust in order to be hired at the end of training.[29] The name of participants to vocational training should appear in a special register set up by the employer and authorised by the relevant authorities, which also store training agreements in a special database. As for supervision, this is carried out by the Labour Department, which also monitors compliance with relevant legislation. In general, employers are not allowed to conclude training agreements with their employees. In a similar vein, temporary agencies are prohibited from sending workers who have entered into training agreements to host companies. Concerning the misuse of vocational training,[30] the improper use of vocational training[31] can cause the transformation of the training relationship into an employment relationship in the following cases:[32]

1) in a loose sense;

a) the agreement is null and void because a prerequisite for it to be valid is missing;

- if the agreement is concluded with someone who already holds an employment relationship—be it of a direct or an indirect nature;

---

[29] Briceño, H. 2011. "Remuneración diferenciada," *El Comercio,* Lima, 9.

[30] The law on vocational training simply refers to "misuse" of vocational training, without however mentioning the causes. For the purpose of the present research, "misuse in a loose sense" and "misuse in a narrow sense" will be used.

[31] This formulation indicates non-compliance with the relevant regulation, thus requiring the implementation of corrective measures (Neves Mujica, J. 2009. *Introducción al Derecho del Trabajo.* Lima: Fondo Editorial de la Pontificia Universidad Católica del Perú, 41).

[32] Campana and Prelle, previous legislation on Youth Vocational Training and Apprenticeship sets forth that in order to prevent illegal hiring practices and exploit cheap youth labour without providing training, it would be advisable to define appropriate guidelines prohibiting training agreements in low-qualified positions and encouraging companies to provide training, also by means of tax rebates and legal instruments preventing employers from unlawfully hiring youth in precarious jobs (Campana, D., and Prelle, H. 2000. "La reforma normativa de la contratación laboural durante los noventa: ¿Flexibilidad o precarización?" in *Estudios sobre la flexibilidad laboural en el Perú*, (Lima: International Labour Office), Working Paper No. 124, 66).

- if, in the case of a violation of labour legislation[33]—e.g. the employer has already hired the maximum number of trainees allowed by law, or submits forged documents to the Labour Department to unduly be able to employ more trainees than allowed and become eligible for the relative benefits;
- if temporary agencies employ workers to operate in host companies under vocational training contracts, or in the case of law infringements or fraud[34] which contravene the so called "principle of primacy of reality" in Labour Law[35]. The law clearly provides

---

[33] According to Art. 2 par. 14 of the Constitution, "Every person has the right [...] to conclude a contract for lawful purposes, provided it does not violate the relevant legislation". In addition, Art. 5 of the Introductory Section of the Civil Code states that: "the contract that violates law or morality is null and void". Among others, Rubio Correa defines a body of law that must be fully complied with both by natural persons and legal entities, and the authorities must ensure its enforcement also by means of coercive measures, whereas necessary" (Rubio Correa, M. 1986. *Título Preliminar, Para leer el Código Civil. Vol. III*. Lima: Fondo Editorial de la Pontificia Universidad Católica del Perú, 95). According to Mario L. Deveali, the special nature of Labour Law does not always allow for derogation, as deviations from statutory law are allowed only in favour of workers.
(Deveali, M. L. 1983. *El derecho del trabajo en su aplicación y sus tendencias*. Buenos Aires: Editorial Astrea, 138). Camerlynck G. H. and G. Lyon-Caen discuss the social function of labour law: "Labour Law consists of mandatory rules that have a specific social function, for they set minimum standards that negotiation can adjust only upward" (Camerlynck, G. H., and Lyon-Caen, G., 1974, *Derecho del Trabajo*, Madrid: Aguilar, 29). According to Américo Plá Rodríguez, "The social function of labour law is based on a principle that underlies rules that are more favourable to workers. This principle has a very broad scope of application, much broader than specific legal provisions" (Plá Rodríguez, A. 1998. *Los principios del Derecho del Trabajo*. Buenos Aires: Ediciones Depalma, 131).

[34] Fraud means avoiding to implement the relevant law, by enforcing a law that is not applicable in the specific case, regardless of the intention of the working person. If a mandatory law prohibits a certain action, such an action cannot be performed by virtue of a different law. Whereas possible, a broad interpretation might be given to the law that is being violated, to include the action improperly excluded, and the law that has actually been unlawfully applied can be interpreted in a strict sense, in order to locate the action under the applicable law. Fraud can be committed in a number of ways including fraudulent deception. When the fraudulent action is concealed the crimes committed include both fraud and deception. (Neves Mujica, J. 2009. *Introducción al Derecho del Trabajo*. Lima: Fondo Editorial de la Pontificia Universidad Católica del Perú, 44).

[35] Plá Rodríguez explains: "According to the principle of primacy of reality, in the case of inconsistencies between what happens in practice and what emerges from documentation and agreements, priority should be given to the former, that is

that the unlawful extension of the training day – or week – or the introduction of overtime work constitutes a violation of the law (Supreme Decree No. 3-2008-TR of 20 May 2008);

b) if the vocational training agreement is not in writing or it has not been unduly signed by the parties.

2) In a narrow sense, the agreement is valid but it is not implemented in practical terms – no training is provided, the trainee performs activities different from those agreed upon, the agreement has expired or exceeds the maximum duration.

By law, minor violations include failure to remunerate the trainees, and to comply with a number of terms, such as keeping track of trainees in a special register, avoiding submission of the agreement to the Labour Department, lacking the authorisation to extend training day duration beyond statutory limits or to night time work (between 10 p.m. and 6 a.m.), avoiding to pay insurance against illnesses or accidents, failing to bear liability in case of work-related diseases or accidents and, finally, neglecting to supply certification after completion of training. In this connection, the Regulation on the Law on Labour Inspection – as enforced by Supreme Decree No. 19-2006-TR of 28 October 2006 – sets forth provisions that apply in case of violations, classing them as minor, serious, and very serious. The Law on Vocational Training provides for a sanctioning mechanism in the case of non-compliance with terms considered above. In particular, the Regulation on the Law on Labour Inspection fixes the amount of money to be paid on the basis of the Peruvian tax units (*Unidad Impositiva Tributaria*[36]), depending on the seriousness of the violation and the number of people concerned.

3.4. Special Regulation Governing Vocational Training

The law lays down special provisions that regulate the different range of programmes supplying vocational training. The section that follows outlines the way vocational training is arranged in Peru.

---

reality" (Plá Rodríguez, A. 1998. *Los principios del Derecho del Trabajo*. Buenos Aires: Ediciones Depalma 313).

[36] The *Unidad Impositiva Tributaria* for the year 2012 amounts to S/. 3 650.00, approximately about 1,352.00. USD (exchange rate as of 31 January 2012: S/. 2.70).

Apprenticeship

Apprenticeship is carried out either at the workplace and in vocational training centres, in order to complement on-the-job training and enhance personal and social skills. The apprenticeship agreement should be signed by the employer, the training provider, and the apprentice. Apprentices must be at least 14 years old and must have completed primary education. The employer hosting the apprentices is in charge of supplying practical training, assigning them specific working tasks in accordance with the learning plan established by the vocational training provider, also taking account of complementary activities that are to be carried out at the training centres. Here, young people entering into apprenticeship agreements have their activities planned, assessed and certified. These tasks must be closely related to training and consistent with trainees' skills. On a general basis, there are two types of apprenticeship schemes: company-based apprenticeship and centre-based apprenticeship.

Company-based apprenticeship takes place at the employer's premises and is supplemented by a specific training programme carried out in a vocational training centre. The apprenticeship agreement is concluded between the employer, the apprentice—who must have completed primary education and be at least 14[37] years old—and the training provider that must be duly authorised to supply training. The duration of the agreement must cover the whole training period.

With regard to centre-based apprenticeship, the apprentice has the opportunity to use the skills acquired in a vocational training centre on the job, by completing training at the company for a definite period. For this purpose, it is necessary to conclude an apprenticeship agreement—between the employer, the apprentice and the training provider—the duration of which must be proportionate to the duration of training and to the job qualification. For apprentices studying abroad or taking part in exchange programmes, the apprenticeship agreement will be signed by a representative of the vocational training centre. Where absent, the agreement needs to be signed by the officers from the embassy of the hosting country—for company-based apprenticeship—or by the receiving vocational training centre, in the event of centre-based apprenticeship.[38]

---

[37] Youth can have access to vocational training after turning 14 years old.

[38] Overseas youth who are willing to enter vocational training programmes need to define their immigration status (e.g. Student), pursuant to Legislative Decree No. 703 of National Immigration Law.

Vocational Training

Vocational training is addressed to youth who are about to obtain a qualification at a training provider. It aims at consolidating the knowledge acquired in this position, by performing in a real work task scenario.[39] To this end, a vocational training agreement must be concluded between the employer and the trainee, and its duration must not exceed 12 months unless the vocational training body allows otherwise. A draft letter introducing the candidate to the company should be drafted by supervisors at the vocational training centre, who should also keep record of the number of times trainees have engaged in training. As occurs for apprenticeship, assignments must be in line with the training activities. Just before trainees—be they nationals or overseas trainees—start on-the-job training,[40] the administrators of the training centres will draft a letter certifying the training activity. If written in a foreign language, a simple translation in the official language should be provided including the name, personal details and signature of the translator.[41] Trainees who take part in exchange programmes abroad and who still want to enter this training programme are in need of a letter drafted by the receiving training provider.

Youth Training

Training for youth takes place at the workplace, where trainees are given the opportunity to learn on the job. These programmes are addressed to 16-23 year-olds who have not yet completed compulsory education, early school leavers, or those who do not continue into higher education—either vocational or traditional education—to give them theoretical and

---

[39] According to Guillermo Boza Pro, "It is particularly striking that, in this case, the law refers to youth who have completed training in a vocational training centre. Surprisingly, even when the training period is ended, the law still allows companies to hire young people through a vocational training agreement, in order to increase their levels of flexibility" (Boza Pro, G. 2011. *Lecciones de derecho del trabajo*. Lima: Fondo Editorial de la Pontificia Universidad Católica del Perú, 2011, 55).

[40] Also in this case, young people from abroad who intend to enter vocational training must define their immigration status, pursuant to Legislative Decree No. 703 of National Immigration Law.

[41] Art. 48 of the Constitution provides that: "the official languages are Spanish and, according to the different areas, Quechua and other indigenous languages as laid down in the relevant legislation".

practical skills required in a specific occupation. For this purpose, the company should sign a youth training agreement and provide those in this position with the necessary tools to acquire practical skills, by assigning them tasks that are in line with a special youth training programme previously defined.

Pursuant to the agreement, the employer is in charge of designing, developing, managing, assessing and certifying training activities. Trainees, for their part, must successfully carry out the assignments. In signing the agreement, and through an additional written statement, trainees certify they are not in higher education at the time of engaging in training, nor will they enter it for the whole duration of the programme, which must be modelled on the skills to be learned. For instance, training should not exceed six months for low-qualified or unskilled positions, and for occupations with a low degree of responsibility. Training can be extended for a further six months—in any case for no more than 24 months—in the event of occupations that require higher qualifications and that imply higher levels of responsibility. In no case can this form of training exceed the statutory maximum duration.

The number of young trainees enrolled in training programmes cannot exceed 20% of the total number of workers in a specific sector or occupation, or 20% of the company's total workforce. This figure includes only workers hired by the company, in other words it does not comprise temporary agency workers or cooperative workers.

The 20% limit can be increased by a further 10%, if this additional workforce is made up of people with disabilities or young mothers with family responsibilities. According to General Law No. 27050 on People with Disabilities, the disability status is certified by inclusion in the Register of Persons with Disabilities, established by the National Council for the Integration of Persons with Disabilities (CONADIS) or through a legal disability certificate. Young mothers with family commitments must provide a copy of the birth certificate of their children. It should be noted that companies with 3 to 10 employees can only employ one trainee. For information and registration purposes, companies are also required to draft an annual youth training plan to be presented to the Labour Department during the fourth quarter of the fiscal year. In case of market or business expansion, companies can devise a special youth training programme to be authorised by the same authority, which can verify the accuracy of the information provided. Information should be given as regards the type of working activity to be performed, the training plan that has to include at least 5 hours per week of specific training and the regular evaluation. This type of on-the-job training can be replaced by off-the-job training for the completion of vocational training programmes. The duration should consider the working activity, and the annual youth training plan should list the skills to be acquired to obtain the relevant qualification. Training for young people must comply with the general requirements envisaged in the national vocational training guidelines. Occupations for which it is possible to sign youth training agreements are usually low-skilled positions associated with low levels of responsibility, as well as high-level positions requiring higher qualifications and implying much responsibility. This classification has been developed by the Labour Department, which also groups the different occupations into a number of subcategories and provides a definition for each job.[42] The duration of the training agreements is established in advance according to the job category: for low-skilled occupations the maximum duration is six months extendable by further six months. For higher qualified occupations the maximum duration is 24 months. If the job is not included in the list, the company must submit a description of the main working tasks, in order for the Labour Department to classify the job in one of the categories mentioned above, and define its duration. It is advisable that training be provided on the job or, alternatively, in vocational training bodies or during in-company vocational workshops for young people who are still in education, with the support of the Ministry of Labour and Employment Promotion and educational providers. The training certificate will be issued by the Ministry of Education, upon compliance with a number of specific requirements, and enables the holder to obtain the relative job qualification[43]. In this respect, of particular importance is the definition of technical qualification as laid down in the regulation: "Technical qualification: training certificate granted by the Ministry of Education allowing for the validation of training corresponding to a secondary vocational qualification or higher education".

---

[42] This list has been approved through Ministerial Resolution No. 167-2010-TR of 19 July 2010. It is available online at the website of the Ministry of Labour and Employment Promotion: www.mintra.gob.pe (accessed January 31, 2012).

[43] The Peruvian Institute of Evaluation, Accreditation and Certification of the Quality of Basic Education (IPEBA) put forward a skill-based system, which certifies the work performed by a person according to standards established at a national level and on the basis of the labour market needs. In this way, people who obtain certification will have better job prospects and might increase their income. (see "Formación profesional requiere ajustarse a exigencias labourales", *El Comercio*, Lima, 24 June 2011, b4).

Internship

Internships take place at the employer's premises and help youth approach the world of work, by enabling them to apply, update and complement the skills they have acquired in vocational training bodies, while providing relevant information about job opportunities and production processes. This form of learning is addressed to young people aged 14 and over who want to put in practice and further increase the knowledge they acquired in training bodies. Those in technical schools established by the Ministry of Education, in vocational training centres, and training bodies for some specific industries set up by the Ministry of Labour and Employment Promotion can take part in internships. Students in upper secondary education who have to enter an internship as a mandatory part of their educational curriculum can take part in the programme too. The role of public and private schools is that of contributing to better matching labour demand and supply, helping students increase and develop necessary social skills. The agreement must be signed by the employer, the intern, and an authorised vocational training centre or school. Its duration cannot exceed three months[44] and, by signing the agreement, the company undertakes to assign working tasks on the basis of internship plans defined by the training provider. For their part, interns have to carry out the assigned tasks in compliance with company regulations and with what is stated in their plans. The training centres have to develop the "road map" of training, and to manage, assess and certify the skills supplied. In addition, a number of state-funded training programmes have been also set up[45]. In general, vocational training centres are issued authorisation if they meet certain qualification and eligibility criteria.[46] The internship agreement must include the above mentioned authorisation.

There are also some forms of internships for instructors who operate in vocational training bodies to help them gain better insight into socio-economic, technological and organisational changes occurring in productive

---

[44] Training for students of the final grade of secondary education cannot last more than 2 months.

[45] These are state-funded programmes for training to increase participants' employability.

[46] Technical education centres that supply vocational training are accredited by the Ministry of Education, provided that certain activities (e.g. internships) are included in the curriculum. The Ministry of Labour and Employment Promotion issues the authorisation in case of training centres of a more general nature, while it is down to organizations that operate at a sectoral level to authorize special training bodies.

sectors, updating training content, and introduce new teaching techniques and learning methods. For this purpose, teachers are called on to update and increase their knowledge to better match training activities with employers' needs. Internship agreements should be concluded by the employer, an instructor and a representative from the training provider, and cannot last longer than 3 months. The company undertakes to provide training by assigning working tasks as well as special research projects on the basis of the internship plan. The centre is in charge of defining training activities also providing for the remuneration of teachers during training. Working tasks must be closely related to the area of specialisation of the teaching personnel.

Retraining to Help Workers Re-enter the Labour Market

Retraining is thought to enable adult workers to acquire new skills to re-enter the labour market. To this end, participants gain practical experience while on the job, that is while receiving specific training and guidance. This instrument can contribute to increasing their employability, helping the long-term unemployed in the 45-65 age group, and those who have been unemployed for more than 12 months, to find new employment. According to the "retraining agreement", the company assigns participants practical tasks following a training plan. The company bears the costs of upgrading and is responsible for designing, managing, assessing and certifying training activities. For their part, workers carry out the assigned tasks in accordance with company regulations. The duration of the agreement cannot exceed 12 months and is extendable for a further 12 months according to the relevant provisions.

Participants are required to certify their unemployment status. In addition, they must produce a written statement indicating that they have not been in employment—neither as employees nor as self-employed—during the previous 12 months, and that they have never entered into a retraining agreement before. These documents should be submitted to and validated by the Labour Department.

The number of participants to the programme cannot exceed 20% of all the workers in a specific occupation or 10% of all the company's total workforce. This limit may be increased by a further 10%, provided that this is made up by workers with disabilities. In such cases, the disability status is demonstrated by inclusion in the National Register of Persons with Disabilities of the National Council for the Integration of Persons with Disabilities (*Conadis*) or through a disability certificate, pursuant to General Law No. 27050 on People with Disabilities. Companies with 3 to

10 employees can only hire one trainee. It should be noted that employers are not allowed to force employees into retraining. Furthermore, it is not permitted to conclude an agreement with people who already had an employment relationship with the signatory employer, unless at least a year has passed after the termination of the employment contract and provided that during that period the concluding parties were not engaged in so-called "service contracts".

As already said, participants must be unemployed. Consequently, no access to retraining schemes is allowed for people running a business, even though they had previously worked as employees in a company. Unemployed workers can engage in retraining only once. Retraining and upgrading plans are defined by the employer along with the participant. The plan is developed according to individual needs and must be drafted within 15 days of the start of the employment relationship. After this period, the company is under the obligation to notify the implementation of the plan to the Labour Department within 5 working days, with the latter that may subsequently verify the accuracy of the information gathered. Only one amendment to the plan is allowed during the first three months of training and it should be agreed upon by the parties. The tasks assigned to participants should be related to their qualification and work experience. The retraining plan should include at least the description of the job to be performed, the number of hours of training—at least 1,700 hours—a complementary retraining service including at least 300 hours of specialised training to be carried out either full time or as a combination of school and work, regular evaluation, the duration of the programme, criteria to be met to obtain the final certificate, the skills to be developed by the participant, and the qualification to be obtained at the end of training. The retraining plan for the reinstatement of workers should follow the guidelines defined in the national vocational training plan. Supplementary training and guidance can be provided by the company alone or in cooperation with third parties. In either case, they should guarantee the acquisition, update and improvement of specific skills and abilities. Further services include training, guidance and job counselling, and placement, skills certification, and special forms of internship. They may also provide guidance to the self-employed or to people who are about to start a business, especially to service providers or subcontractors.

Retraining for the reinstatement of workers should be supplied at the workplace. Supplementary training and guidance can be provided at the employers' premises or by specific bodies authorised by the Labour Department or centres that afford sectoral vocational training. Once the final certificate has been issued, participants are acknowledged an occupational qualification upon fulfilling the criteria established by the Labour Department.

4. Statistics

This section provides some statistical data concerning some interesting information about the recourse to vocational training schemes. On the basis of the statistical yearbook published by the Ministry of Labour and Employment Promotion (MTPE) on an annual basis, an analysis of the number of training agreements concluded in 2008, 2009 and 2010 at a national level is given.

Following on from the table above, one can argue that:

1) in the period 2008-2010, the number of training agreements concluded had been reported to increase stepwise every year;
2) over the same period, there has been a significant increase in the number of apprenticeship agreements, either for company-based and centre-based apprenticeship;
3) between 2009 and 2010, the number of internship agreements dropped significantly;
4) the most widespread forms of training arrangements include centre-based apprenticeship and vocational training, followed by youth training and internship (save for 2009, when internship was more extensively used than youth training schemes);
5) there has been low to no recourse to internship for instructors and retraining for unemployed workers.

Table 3-10. Peru: Type of Vocational Training Agreements Concluded Nationally in the Period 2008-2010

Year	Job Training Scheme							Total
	Apprenticeship		Vocational Training	Youth Training	Internship		Retraining for Reinstatement	
	Company-based	Centre-based			In-company Internship	Internship for Instructors		
2008	278	25,481	17,514	5,676	5,305	1	-	54,255
2009	920	27,944	18,008	6,389	7,160	-	1	60,502
2010	2173	30,834	18,992	6,868	3,244	2	1	62,114

Sources: Author's own elaboration on data provided by MTPE. 2011. *Statistical Yearbook 2010*. Lima: MTPE, Table No. 240, MTPE. 2010. *Statistical Yearbook 2009*, Lima: MTPE, Table No. 220, MTPE. 2009. *Statistical Yearbook 2008*. Lima: MTPE, Table No. 203.

In addition, vocational training agreements did not produce an increase in job insecurity for both adults and youth.

The total number of vocational training agreements concluded between 2008 and 2010 is significantly lower than the total number of employment contracts concluded with Peruvian and foreign workers and submitted to the Ministry of Labour.[47] More specifically:

1) in 2008, there were 54,255 training agreements, 2,470,417 employment contracts (Peruvian workers) and 3,332 employment contracts (foreign workers);
2) in 2009, there were 60,502 training agreements, 2,754,647 employment contracts (Peruvian workers) and 3,778 employment contracts (foreign workers);
3) in 2010: 62,114 training agreements against 3,524,844 employment contracts (Peruvian workers) and 3,961 employment contracts (foreign workers).

5. Conclusions

Vocational training arrangements discussed above play a significant role in supplying young people with practical training and real work experience, and appear to be more effective as compared to traditional forms of vocational training. Therefore, it seems of the utmost importance to promote cooperation between traditional vocational training institutions and employers, with a view to developing training activities that respond to companies' needs effectively. In many respects, vocational training in Peru is governed by ad-hoc labour legislation. Although labour laws regulate a variety of aspects concerning these training arrangements, trainees are generally not entitled to the same economic and social benefits as the other employees. Despite that, vocational training did not produce an increase in the rate of job insecurity—especially among young people—nor did it result in a downward trend in terms of employment quality, as a consequence of precarious work. On an annual basis, the number of training agreements concluded is considerably low if compared to the total number of contracts of employment—even if one counts fixed-

---

[47] MTPE. 2011. *Statistical Yearbook 2010*. Lima: MTPE, Table No. 78, MTPE. 2010. *Statistical Yearbook 2009*, Lima: MTPE, Table No. 73, MTPE. 2009. *Statistical Yearbook 2008*. Lima: MTPE, Table No. 68. These tables do not include the overall number of permanent contracts: in Peru, permanent contracts should not necessarily be submitted to the Ministry of Labour for information and registration.

term and part-time employment, telework, and so forth. Accordingly, these vocational training schemes can serve as a valuable tool to help youth enter the labour market.

By way of example, apprenticeship existed since the Middle Ages—e.g. in craftsmanship—and, in the building sector, the terms "helper" and "skilled workers" have long been attributed to those who perform the same job as "operators"—that is skilled workers in a particular occupation—but who have not yet achieved full qualification for the relevant job and who provide support to the "operators" who are in charge of the task.

The Law on Vocational Training attempts to prevent misuse of these instruments, by issuing special authorisations to training bodies to match labour supply and demand and requiring the drafting of detailed training plans. Furthermore, the parties involved need to conclude an agreement to be submitted to the Labour Department, while the Ministry of Labour and Employment Promotion keeps record of all the participants of vocational training and carries out inspections. These measures are aimed at responding to the concerns raised about potential misuse of these forms of training. Finally, it would be likewise necessary to define vocational training policies and programmes through social dialogue. Employers' associations and trade unions should agree on a number of different aspects related to vocational training, to boost training opportunities and workers' employability by meeting the needs of the labour market. Employment policies that aim at promoting vocational training should also grant employers who hire people who leave during the training period tax advantages and financial benefits.

References

Alexim, J. C. 1992. *Las nuevas fronteras de la formación profesional*, Lima: Organización Internacional del Trabajo—Oficina Regional para América Latina y el Caribe.

Boza Pro, G. 2011. *Lecciones de derecho del trabajo.* Lima: Fondo Editorial de la Pontificia Universidad Católica del Perú.

Briceño, H., 2011. *Remuneración diferenciada.* Newspaper El Comercio, Lima, 28 May, b9.

Camerlynck, G. H., and G. Lyon-Caen. 1974. *Derecho del Trabajo.* Madrid: Aguilar.

Campana, D., and Prelle, H. 2000. "La reforma normativa de la contratación laboural durante los noventa: ¿Flexibilidad o precarización?" in *Estudios sobre la flexibilidad en el Perú*, (Lima: Oficina Internacional del Trabajo), Working Paper No. 124.

Deveali, M. L. 1983. *El derecho del trabajo en su aplicación y sus tendencias*, Buenos Aires: Astrea.

Ministerio de Trabajo y Promoción del Empleo. 2009. *Anuario Estadístico 2008.* Lima: MTPE.

—. 2010. *Anuario Estadístico 2009.* Lima: MTPE.

—. 2011. *Anuario Estadístico 2010.* Lima: MTPE.

Neves Mujica, J. 2009. *Introducción al Derecho del Trabajo.* Lima: Fondo Editorial de la Pontificia Universidad Católica del Perú.

Pasco Cosmópolis, M. 2001. "Los contratos formativos," in *Advocatus*, No. 4.

Pizarro Posse, R. 2005. "Rol y función de la gerencia de recursos humanos," in *Relaciones Industriales y Recursos Humanos en América Latina*, eds. Aldao-Zapiola, C. M. and Hermida Martínez, D. (Buenos Aires: Federación Interamericana de Administración de Personal).

Plá Rodríguez, A. 1998. *Los principios del Derecho del Trabajo*. Buenos Aires: Depalma.

Real Academia Española. 2001. *Diccionario de la Lengua Española.* Madrid.

Rubio Correa, M. 1986. *Título Preliminar*, *Para leer el Código Civil. Vol. III*. Lima: Fondo Editorial de la Pontificia Universidad Católica del Perú.

—. 2007. *El Sistema Jurídico. Introducción al Derecho*. Lima: Fondo Editorial de la Pontificia Universidad Católica del Perú.

Saco Barrios, R. 1998. "Flexibilidad Laboural, Derecho del Trabajo y Administración de Personal" in *Análisis Laboural*, Lima: Aele, Vol. 22, No. 247.

—. 2009 *Derecho Laboural Empresarial.* Material de estudio del curso "Derecho Laboural Empresarial", Diploma en Derecho de la Empresa, Modalidad Virtual. Lima: Pontificia Universidad Católica del Perú – PUCP Virtual.

Von Potobsky, G. W. and Bartolomei De La Cruz, H. G. 1990 *La Organización Internacional del Trabajo*. Buenos Aires: Astrea.

CHAPTER FOUR:

FUTURE SCENARIOS FOR YOUNG PEOPLE

ALTERNATIVE PATTERNS OF DEVELOPMENT AS A RESPONSE TO YOUTH UNEMPLOYMENT AND SOCIAL EXCLUSION IN LATIN AMERICA

JUAN RASO DELGUE

1. Youth Unemployment and Poverty in Latin America[1]

In considering the economically active population (EAP) in Latin America, national statistics report that unemployment mostly concerns young people. If one examines the data from the Economic Commission for Latin America (ECLA), what emerges is that unemployment is a major issue in this area, even more so if taking into account that half of the population in Latin America is under 24 years old and the number of those not in employment is on the rise in all South American countries. As shown in Table 1-1, the unemployment rates for this age group in 2010 were twice—and sometimes three times—as high as the total unemployment rates:

Table 4-1. Unemployment Rates for the Year 2010 in Latin America

Country	Total Rate of Unemployment (%)	Unemployment Rate for the 15-24 Age Group (%)
Argentina	7.5	21.2
Bolivia	6.5	23.2
Brazil	6.7	19.7
Colombia	12.34	30.9
Ecuador	8.0	21.8
Paraguay	7.8	18.5
Peru	8.0	12
Uruguay	6.3	26.2

Source: Cepal 2010.

[1] Translation from Spanish by Pietro Manzella.

Of relevance is also the fact that the average rate of unemployment in Latin America for the year 2010 was 10.4, whereas the percentage of young people not in employment over the same time period was reported to be 19.4. In turn, unemployment did not affect people in this age group in a uniform manner, as it was higher among the poor (30%) and lower among the rich (10%). These preliminary data are significant as they demonstrate that unemployment in Latin America is closely connected to poor living conditions, with this aspect that is also reflected in the complex interplay between economic vulnerability, occupational and educational issues, as a number of studies on the school-to-work transition and labour market in this area have pointed out. In other words, the economic inequality that has always been a main feature of Latin America inevitably results in structural differences, particularly with regard to education, training and access to employment. As maintained by Abdala "young people from poorer backgrounds move through the main stages of poverty through a process of identification and socialisation which is typical of the precocious access to informal and precarious work".[2] They usually look for jobs that are precarious and of low quality, and this is a reflection of "a culture of work which is felt as absent or instable", and that causes the number of inactive young people to increase.[3] Accordingly, those from disadvantaged areas have less opportunities of reaching social inclusion by means of decent jobs, perpetuating the vicious circle of poverty and increasing the already sizeable number of those who are engaged in the informal economy and, what is worse, organised crime. As pointed out by the President of Uruguay, Jose Mujica Cordano "the imbalance between generations in terms of entitlements and social security is the expression of social inequality. As a consequence, the government should prioritise public policies that help future generations, by boosting the levels of education, reducing youth employment and making them the protagonists of the labour market".[4] In Latin America, the young not only face difficulty in accessing the labour market, but they usually work in the informal economy on a part-time basis. This aspect is relevant as it contributes to high levels of precariousness and job rotation for this category of workers, particularly when compared to their adult

---

[2] Abdala, E. 2005. "Nuevas soluciones para un viejo problema: modelos de capacitación para el empleo de jóvenes—Aprendizajes en América Latina," La inclusión laboural de los jóvenes. Montevideo: ILO-Cinterfor,185-186.

[3] Ibid.

[4] INJU/MIDES. 2011. *Plan Nacional de Juventudes 2011/2015*. Montevideo: INJU/MIDES, 9.

counterparts.[5] Of equal importance is that young people are increasingly making use of alcohol and other drugs, which obviously affect their health. This is particularly the case of Uruguay, as here alcohol is the most consumed drug, and young people tend to start drinking at the average age of 12.89 years old. Further, relative statistics reveal that 70% of students start drinking during the first year of secondary school on an occasional basis, with half of them having had a drink thirty days before being interviewed. With regard to smoking, 4 students out of 10 in junior high school smoke, and 28% of people in the same cohort make use of marijuana habitually, or have tried it at least once. Drugs might also have serious effects on younger users, although cocaine, and an inexpensive cocaine base product known as "pasta base", are not used as much as alcohol and cigarettes.[6]

2. The Education System and Access to Employment Programmes for Young People

On a general basis, it can be argued that governments in Latin America failed to develop an education system that meets the needs of the labour market. Indeed, public schooling is viewed as providing skills that are no longer required by employers, as priority is given to theoretical learning, rather than to the practical aspects of learning. This mismatch between theory and practice represents a serious problem in terms of sustainable development, all the more so because the programmes offered at school are ostensibly inadequate to keep up with ongoing changes in production and labour demand, where skills other than traditional ones are increasingly required. This point has been made in a cogent manner by Hernández Arroyave. In recounting that half the population in Latin America and the Caribbean is less than 24 years old, and that unemployment rates have been found to increase everywhere, he has argued that "the education system currently in place has failed to provide young people with necessary knowledge and skills to succeed in a fast changing labour market".[7] This issue is also confirmed by those supporting the project "Promoting Youth Employment in Latin America"—PREJAL—according to whom one of the reasons for young

---

[5] Ibid, 33.

[6] Ibid, 36.

[7] Hernández Arroyave, J. C. 2005. "Preparando a los jóvenes para entrar en el nuevo mundo del trabajo," La inclusión laboural de los jóvenes. Montevideo: ILO-Cinterfor, 30.

people having difficulty to access the labour market lies in the imbalance between skills gained through schooling and skills required in different industries. More specifically "there is usually a lack of communication and coordination between the education and the production system".[8]

To further complicate the picture, Latin America is diversified in terms of businesses and production systems, as here companies making use of cutting-edge technology and advanced management processes coexist with factories that still operate at a production rate that was typical of the Industrial Revolution. In this sense, Gallart recounts that "in the biggest countries such as Brazil and Mexico one can find technologically advanced companies—both in the manufacturing and retail sectors—and small businesses scattered through the country that still resort to outdated production methods".[9] The author goes on to point out that in medium-sized countries—e.g. Argentina and Chile—"outdated production techniques hamper the advent of modernity in the industry sector in a uniform manner, although in some sectors more modern production methods are widely used and well-established".[10] Another major issue is the share of workers who are not affiliated to a trade union "who are also called "unregistered", as failing to comply with collective bargaining provisions", which contributes to enlarge the informal economic sector.[11] According to data from 2005—they have not changed significantly since then—Peru is reported to have the highest rate of informal employment (54.9%), followed by Brazil (49.1%), Argentina (43.6%) and Chile (31.9%). On average, the share of the informal economy in Latin America amounts to 48.5%. From a gender perspective, the percentage of females working in the informal sector is higher than that of males—51.3% and 46.3%, respectively. This trend is widespread across the South American countries, also because domestic work is taken into account.[12] Accordingly, at the time of reviewing the education patterns in this geographic area, differences in the economic systems between countries and regions should not be overlooked.

In general terms, the mismatch between education, training and employment is usually experienced in the transition from primary to secondary school. By way of example, in Uruguay, a country with high

---

[8] Proyecto PREJAL. 2009. *Jóvenes y empleo: experiencias innovadoras en el mundo empresarial.* LIMA: ILO, 95-96.

[9] Gallart, M. A. 2008. "Competencias, Productividad y Crecimiento del Empleo," Trazos de la formación. Montevideo: ILO-Cinterfor, 17.

[10] Ibid.

[11] Ibid, 18.

[12] Ibid, 19, 79.

levels of education, progress of 86% of students in the 4th and 5th years of elementary school are monitored regularly, a figure which is reported to decrease steadily so that 13% of students do not complete the first year in junior high school, and 17.5% in the same cohort fail to succeed in the following years. On the whole, the percentage of young people in the 20-29 age group completing junior high school is 36.5%.[13] As pointed out by Cabella "education constitutes the key to better job positions, therefore enhancing access to employment. Inequality in educational attainment among different groups is one of the leading causes of social imbalance".[14] Further, young people who are not given access to schooling—or at least to a part of it—are inevitably forced out of the formal labour market. In this sense, Lasida maintains that "shortcomings in education, training and employment cause young people to face poverty. They encounter difficulty in finding decent jobs for lacking necessary skills and they are not adequately prepared because they rush to seek employment".[15] Finally, in addition to social segmentation, it is also important to highlight the role of the labour market and the impact of young people's cultural background, which can both be very diverse. Notwithstanding this diversity, the outcome is that young people inherit their parents' employment situation. If they have not been employed in the formal economy, neither will their children.[16]

3. Issues in the Transition from School to Work: Those Not in Employment, Education, or Training (NEETs)

The considerations above on the education system suggest that the transition from education to work is a complicated matter. As recently investigated by Filardo and Filguerais, the term "transition" indicates the main objectives individuals aim to fulfil in order to enter adulthood and place themselves in society. Suitable examples of such a transition are exiting school, entering the labour market, leaving one's place of origin,

[13] INJU/MIDES. 2011. *Plan Nacional de Juventudes 2011/2015*. Montevideo: INJU/MIDES, 28-29.

[14] Cabella, W. 2008. "Panorama de la infancia y la adolescencia en la población afrouruguaya," Proyecto Población afro descendiente y Desigualdades étnico-raciones en el Uruguay. Montevideo: PNUD, 103 et seq.

[15] Lasida, J. "El trabajo dentro la formación y la formación como parte del trabajo. Aportes y desafíos a partir de Projoven y otras experiencias uruguayas," La inclusión laboural de los jóvenes. Montevideo: ILO-Cinterfor, 96.

[16] Ibid.

starting a family, and having children.[17] Indeed, the ways these events take place in one's lifetime—that is the way social inclusion is fully achieved in adult life—can be varied. This stands in stark contrast with the past, when young people of earlier generations pursued avenues which were similar and well-established. Nowadays, the individual shift from school to work might be significantly different from one another, and so might be the level of vulnerability with regard to future employment. The research focus should be on how the passage from school to work is realised by young people, pointing out the role of institutions in smoothing—or in some cases hampering—such transition by means of public policies and measures of social protection, also considering the circumstances under which individuals operate.[18]

Filardo and Filgueiras have investigated the educational trajectories, characterised by a certain level of inequality that affects the transition under consideration in their work. The point of departure of their analysis has been the legislation concerning education enacted in Uruguay in 2008, which sets forth the compulsory nature of secondary education. In surveying young people in the 20 to 29 age group, it has emerged that 19% of students finished junior high school on time, 14% of them need more time than required to graduate, and 52% of them failed to complete high school.[19] As rightly pointed out by Abdala, requirements to enter the labour market are increasingly challenging and represent an additional barrier for young people from poor communities to compete for quality jobs. Such a situation "forces them out of the labour market, giving rise to a category of people which also comprises those who are unemployed because they lack the necessary education, are inactive (not in employment, education and training), poor women (mainly teenagers), people living in rural areas and members of ethnic groups".[20]

In contemporary society, the quality of work depends on individual knowledge and competence. Those poorly educated and with no special skills are doomed to perform unspecialised jobs. In this sense, local vocational training centres often attract criticism for prioritising

---

[17] Filardo, V., and Filgueira, F. 2011. "Transiciones a la adultez y educación," Fondo de Población de Naciones Unidad. Montevideo: UNFPA. See the interview to the authors at: //www.el.espectador.com/1v4_contenido.php?id=213392&sts=1, (Accessed April 13, 2010).

[18] Ibid.

[19] Ibid.

[20] Abdala, E. 2005. "Nuevas soluciones para un viejo problema: modelos de capacitación para el empleo de jóvenes—Aprendizajes en América Latina," La inclusión laboural de los jóvenes. Montevideo: ILO-Cinterfor,185-186.

qualifications over real educational needs (e.g. hairdressing, cooking, craftsmanship and so on), yet this state of affairs originates from the everyday reality that requires the promotion of young workers who often are not adequately prepared. High quality jobs, usually those performed in the high-tech and communication sectors can only be accessed by young students with average levels of education, who therefore are not regarded as vulnerable workers. As a consequence, there is a higher number of those not in employment, education and training—the result of fewer job opportunities and low to no educational attainment—which in Uruguay have been labelled "*ni-ni*" (the NEETs).

Table 4-2. Percentage of NEETs by Age (2010)

Age Group	NEETs
From 15 to 17 years	12.6%
From 18 to 19 years	12.5%
From 20 to 24 years	10.7%
From 25 to 29 years	11.8%

Source: Minister of Labour and Social Security/OMT - ECH[21].

In Uruguay, roughly 30% of young people aged between 12 and 27 years old are not in education, employment or training, and neither do they actively seek work. Further, 25% of them aim to attain social inclusion by way of employment, but this attempt is often unsuccessful. As maintained by Lasida "In both cases, the educational programmes promoted by public education and traditional vocational training bodies—which is provided free of charge in terms of direct costs—are not appealing, or young people in this age group cannot afford enrolling in such courses". This state of affairs is a further reflection of thc failure of education and training policies, particularly with regard to access-to-work opportunities.[22]

4. Youth Unemployment and Social Actors

Raising self-awareness of social actors as promoting entities for quality jobs is one of the main challenges to take up to improve youth

[21] Ministry of Labour and Social Security. 2011. *Diagnóstico sobre Empleo Juvenil - Empleo y Educación: pilares para la construcción de la trayectoria laboural de los jóvenes,* 29.

[22] Lasida, J. "El trabajo dentro la formación y la formación como parte del trabajo. Aportes y desafíos a partir de Projoven y otras experiencias uruguayas," La inclusión laboural de los jóvenes. Montevideo: ILO-Cinterfor, 97.

employability. As shown by Neffa, not only should employment policies be underpinned by legal provisions, but also by institutions. Experts of labour policies should focus on stemming the phenomenon of early school leaving, as people who drop-out of school are some of the most vulnerable in the labour market, due to their lack of either qualifications or vocational training. These measures are to be welcomed by social actors who—by means of tripartite consultation—should promote the involvement of workers, government and employers from the planning stages.[23] Clearly, making social actors aware of their role in devising strategies to enhance youth employability presents a number of obstacles. Employers and trade unions often have divergent views on how to devise programmes that facilitate the transition from school to work by way of training. Employers, who are usually from the wealthy parts of society, show more willingness to cooperate with private institutions, because they provide a wider range of educational strategies in terms of access-to-work and because trade unions are not exerting pressure to re-establish more disadvantaged individuals into formal employment. In most cases, the debate on the employability of young people narrows down to questioning the effectiveness of flexibility measures, without providing an in-depth study of how disadvantaged individuals can have access to quality jobs and formal employment, which is pivotal. Another barrier for them to enter into permanent jobs—which widens the gap with young workers in high quality positions—is the increasing need to obtain education and training. With regard to this issue, Ermida makes reference to a reform initiative—*Autorreforma Sindical*—put forward by the Trade Union Confederation of the Americas (TUCA-CSA), which also involves unions from Canada and the US. The reform plan was proposed by Uruguayan General Secretary of TUCA-CSA, Victor Báez, and offers a critical reflection of the role of trade unions in Latin America, in order to highlight their major shortcomings and provide solutions to deal with them. The remarks directed at the unions in this connection mainly concerned their failure to anticipate and satisfy collective needs, particularly those of the young people. [24] In this respect, union leaders in Colombia recall the address from representatives of International Trade Unions Confederation (ITUC) that was delivered in August 2010, according to whom the higher levels of youth unemployment represent "a

[23] Neffa, J. C. 2011. "Políticas de Empleo: una visión sintética de largo plazo (1989 - 2011)," in *Voces en el Fenix*, 6:77-81.

[24] Ermida Uriarte, O. 2010. "Dificultades del Movimiento Sindical con especiar referencia a su estructura en América Latina", a study commented on by the Trade Union Confederation of the Americas, 11-12.

social weapon that might compromise economic, political and social stability worldwide".

5. Education, Gender and Unemployment

Statistics show some very interesting outcomes—both positive and negative indeed—with regard to the relationship between education, gender and unemployment in Uruguay[25] (Table 1-3):

Table 4-3. Young People's Educational Attainment in the 20 to 29 Age Group by Gender[26]

Young People's Educational Attainment	Males	Females
With no formal education	0.3%	0.2%
Not completing primary school	4.2%	2.5%
Completing primary school	15.5%	12.4%
Not completing junior high-school	17.4%	13.9%
Completing junior high-school	11.6%	10.6%
Not completing high-school	23.7%	22.0%
Completing high-school	7.3%	9.0%
Not completing secondary education	16.8%	23.1%
Completing secondary education	3.2%	6.4%
TOTAL	100%	100%

Source: Ministry of Labour and Social Security OMT—ECH, 2010.

In general, the data above indicate that the share of males involved in primary and secondary education is higher than the corresponding figure among the females. The trend is reversed if one considers tertiary education. The majority of those obtaining a university degree are female, with the average female-male ratio which is 2:1. These figures are even more relevant if one takes into account the levels of poverty. Indeed, women are proportionally less active than men in the poorest segments of

---

[25] Although a relatively small country, Uruguay is regarded as the country with the lowest educational standards in Latin America. In this sense, statistics reflect a reality that would be considered more serious in other countries.

[26] Ministry of Labour and Social Security. 2011. *Diagnóstico sobre Empleo Juvenil - Empleo y Educación: pilares para la construcción de la trayectoria laboural de los jóvenes,* 23.

population, but this does not result from lower levels of qualifications, yet from the *machista* culture which is peculiar to Latin America. The gendered nature of society does not allow women—particularly those with low income—to perform jobs other than housework and caring. For this reason, women are not statistically relevant as they do not access the formal labour market in a strict sense. This point is made by Filardo and Figueiras, who highlight that this inactivity rate is not considered in surveys, and even disregarded in some cases, despite differences in terms of gender clearly exist. Compounding the picture is the fact that these women swell the ranks of NEETs, since they are forced out of the labour market.[27] In addition, they have settled down—in the sense that they leave their place of origin and have children—earlier than their male counterparts. They *de facto* work, yet without being remunerated, as they carried out a number of activities falling within the umbrella of housework.[28]

Table 4-4. Youth Unemployment Rates by Gender

Age Group	Males	Females
15—17 years old	20.3%	33.7%
18—24 years old	15.4%	24.8%
25—29 years old	5.6%	12.1%

Source: Ministry of Labour and Social Security OMT—ECH, 2010[29].

When not facing poor economic conditions, women have more opportunities to demonstrate their skills and knowledge, thus proving more successful than men in tertiary education.

6. Contractual Arrangements for Young People

In Latin America, the devising of contractual schemes targeted for young people and intended to promote access to employment for jobseekers under a certain age has been the subject of a lively debate. Those advocating for such reform in employment contracts hail this solution as being beneficial to young workers and society, more generally.

[27] Filardo, V., and Filgueira, F. 2011. "Transiciones a la adultez y educación," Fondo de Población de Naciones Unidad. Montevideo: UNFPA.

[28] Ibid.

[29] Ministry of Labour and Social Security. 2011. *Diagnóstico sobre Empleo Juvenil—Empleo y Educación: pilares para la construcción de la trayectoria laboural de los jóvenes,* 23.

Those arguing against the provision of special contractual arrangements for young people regard this proposal as a "Trojan horse" in the sense that it might produce higher levels of flexibility in labour legislation, making the entire workforce vulnerable. In addition, opponents also point out that less stringent legislation to promote youth employment might lead to lower levels of protection for all categories of workers. In addition, doubts can be cast as to whether more relaxed labour rules produce an increase in employability and more opportunities to access the labour market for youth, particularly without the training required by employers. In general terms, there are three categories of employment contracts for young people:

apprenticeship contracts: it is a fixed-term contract that usually provides dual training, with signatories that are obliged to fulfil some requirements in this connection. Apprenticeship schemes make provision for both theoretical and practical learning, with on-the-job training that takes place within the company. Apart from the employer and the young workers, a major role is played by the representatives of the educational bodies who are under the obligation to follow the apprentice's progress. The duration of this contract is laid down by law, and it usually ranges from 6 to 24 months;

training contracts: they are fixed-term contracts targeting young people, the aim of which is to allow students to practice what they have learnt at school. There is a slight difference between training contracts and apprenticeship contracts with respect to the provision of on-the-job training, as in the former it takes place at the end of the period of theoretical learning;

scholarships to access the labour market: these scholarships are usually granted to young people in poor economic conditions, with the aim of easing their access to work by providing them with a first job opportunity. Arguably, the need for recipients to gain experience is given priority over the learning process.

All the contractual arrangements discussed above envisage some form of remuneration—usually corresponding to the statutory minimum wage—and also provide social security benefits. In this sense, holders of these contracts must be included in registers to be signed in accordance to what is laid down by competent authorities, usually the Ministry of Labour. [30]

[30] For further information on the issue, see Vera, A., and Castioni, R. 2010. "Los jóvenes en Latinoamérica. La transición escuela-trabajo como objeto de las políticas públicas", in *Boletim Tecnico do Senac,* 36, No. 2:5-17, at

7. Alternative Programmes to Enhance the School-to-work Transition

With such bleak prospects, a number of alternative programmes have been put forward by different institutions—both secular and religious bodies in the public and private sector and at a national and international level (usually NGOs)—in order to deal with the issue of youth unemployment and improve the school-to-work transition. These projects are devised considering a dual training system that combines off-the job teaching with on-the job practice and learning, usually by means of scholarships, internships and special contractual schemes. In the context of this paper, mention should be made of the following programmes and institutions that provide training and can be further developed:[31]

- training programme set up by the Province of Cordoba, Argentina (*Programa de Formación Laboural de Gobierno de la Provincia de Córdoba*);
- the Ecuador Fund Populorum Progressio (*Fondo Ecuatoriano Populorum Progressio*);
- a number of initiatives in Uruguay, such as *Opción Joven, El Abrojo, Los Pinos, Gurises Unidos y el Movimiento Tacurú;*
- the Axé Project (Brazil)
- the Don Bosco Industrial in El Salvador
- the municipalities of México
- the CAPLAB project in Peru
- the Gaspar Melchor de Jovellanos de Cuba y Navegar School in the South of Argentina

However, the relevance of the foregoing programmes is not as such as to be considered alternative patterns of education, because they are devised for limited groups or because—as in the case of the Opción Joven project—they did not include training in the form of apprenticeship. For this reason, the research focus of the last section of the present study will be on those programmes that can be regarded as a real alternative to traditional education paths that are also implemented in other countries.

---

http://www.senac.br/BTS/362/artigo1.pdf. (Accessed April 13, 2010).

[31] Abdala, E. 2005. "Nuevas soluciones para un viejo problema: modelos de capacitación para el empleo de jóvenes—Aprendizajes en América Latina," La inclusión laboural de los jóvenes. Montevideo: ILO-Cinterfor,197.

- Programme "ENTRA 21" (18 countries in Latin America)

The aim of this programme is to provide training for young people in the 16 to 29 age group to help them find employment in those sectors—e.g. the ITC sector—that have developed within the new economy. The founding institutions are the International Youth Foundation (IYF), the Multilateral Investment Fund (MIF) run by the Inter-American Development Bank and the US International Cooperation Agency (USAID). The programme is available in 18 countries of Latin America and provides training opportunities and placement services by means of internships.

- Promoting Youth Employment in Latin America (PREJAL)

This initiative has been set up thanks to the commitment of the Youth Employment Network (YEN) with the support of the ILO. Supported by both public and private institutions, the main objective is to enhance young people's social inclusion particularly with regard to their involvement in public policies and activities. The PREJAL project carries out a number of initiatives in terms of training for the most disadvantaged groups in a number of countries (Argentina, Brazil, Chile, Colombia, Mexico and Peru) also counting on the support of employers and foundations that operate in Latin America.

- National Service for Industrial Apprenticeship—SENAI (Brazil)

This is a private service which operates at a national level. Over the years, it has become well-established and it is now a reference model with regard to the provision of apprenticeship, technical assistance and the dissemination of relevant information. The SENAI service is usually attended by 2 million students every year and has helped to train 34 million workers since 1942. Its main objectives are:

a) providing training to enhance workers' skills;
b) providing apprenticeship programmes in some specific IT sectors (food industry, vehicle manufacturing, building sector, power sector, telecommunications, textile and metalworking sector);
c) promoting social dialogue among the technical committees and the SENAI service itself;
d) certifying the skills acquired;

e) promoting the setting up of evaluation procedures within the labour market. In this sense, it should be said that 63% of graduates have access to high quality positions.[32]

f) National Service of Occupational Training in Industry—SENATI (Peru)

The main goal of this service is to provide a dual training system (theoretical learning and in-company training), according to the "learning by doing" approach. The SENATI service aims at giving workers vocational training in order to operate in the manufacturing sector and to specialise in several activities in some other industries (installation, maintenance, and repair among others). This programme is usually provided for young people in the 12 to 24 age group and it combines tasks to be carried out within a working unit and with practical assignments within the company. Traditional learning—200 hours of classroom study—is provided to further develop general knowledge. Learners who successfully complete this phase move on to the next stage—that is training in a strict sense—which consists of three levels:

- basic training to be carried out at the educational centres, for a duration of 552 hours;
- special on-the-job training, which usually lasts 920 hours each semester and also consists of 4 working days within the company and 1 day at the educational body.
- The National Apprenticeship Service - SENA (Colombia)

This service provided by a tripartite body has the goal to employ 250,000 young workers in the most vulnerable groups of the population.[33] Training programmes usually help learners to develop skills in the fields of electronics, telecommunications, industrial design, communication, innovative materials, nanotechnology, covering materials, logistics, transportation, animal, vegetal and industrial biotechnology, industrial design and production, environmental production and the building sector.

[32] Gallart, M. A. 2008. "Competencias, Productividad y Crecimiento del Empleo," Trazos de la formación. Montevideo: ILO-Cinterfor, 98-99.

[33] Vargas, F. 2009. "Colombia - Programa de Formación de Jóvenes: Plan 250 mil," ILO - Notas sobre la crisis, 3. Santiago de Chile: ILO Subregional Office.

8. Concluding Remarks

The following points summarise the main findings of the present paper:

- in Latin America, unemployment mostly affects young people, because of the link between poverty and unemployment rates. All of the studies investigating the school-to-work transition in this geographic area will cast light on the interplay between economic vulnerability, shortcomings in educational levels, and employment.
- The issue of youth employment is more serious if one considers the wide range of companies and productive systems in Latin America.
- In the formal sector, the phenomenon of early school-leaving, which is often accompanied by a situation of poverty, is regarded as the main obstacle to enhance access to decent work.
- At the time of dealing with youth employment, social actors often have divergent views on how to devise effective policies to improve employability.
- Unemployment—particularly among the youth—is often gender-biased. Statistics reveal that unemployment rates are higher among women and this does not depend on the fact that they are less qualified or unable to acquire necessary skills, but can be explained by the levels of poverty reported among them—they often have children while still teenagers—so they are involved in housework, also because of the *machista* culture in Latin America;
- One should be careful in highlighting the need to promote active labour policies targeted on young people as a tool to increase their opportunity to find employment. In this connection, the following points should be madc:

a) minors—that is those under the age of 18—should not be employed and should stay in education, unless in the cases laid down in ILO Convention No. 138 on Child Labour. Strangely enough, according to most statistics on youth employment in Latin America the minimum age for employment is reported to be 15 years old, whereas it should be 18 years old. Because of this aspect, these surveys should be handled with care as they might also include minors employed illegally;

b) in order to boost employment among those under the age of 18, priority should be given to their education, providing incentives and financial aid where necessary. In most of the cases, an employment relationship in a strict sense is not concluded between the employer and the minors performing such activities. Arguably, the financial support should be provided by private and public bodies;

c) governments, alongside social actors, should promote active labour policies to enhance the employability of workers under age. In doing so, however, a distinction should be made between school-leavers not in employment who are supported by their family and those who are in need of finding a job. In the first case, financial aid in the form of scholarships and subsidies should be provided to those who are willing to continue studying. In other words, tertiary education should be accessible to anyone, though in reality only students from wealthy families have access to higher education in Latin America, be it public or private.[34]

- Finally, an attempt on the part of social security to support young people and families with school-age children has been reported. On this point, it is worth pointing out that social welfare in Latin America is an important tool to obtain social achievement.

References

Abdala, E. 2005. "Nuevas soluciones para un viejo problema: modelos de capacitación para el empleo de jóvenes—Aprendizajes en América Latina," La inclusión laboural de los jóvenes. Montevideo: ILO-Cinterfor.

Arteta, M. 2007. "Educación y empleo juvenil en América Latina y el Caribe," Trabajo Decente y Juventud, Documentos de Base, 1. Lima: ILO.

Cabella, W. 2008. "Panorama de la infancia y la adolescencia en la población afrouruguaya," Proyecto Población afro descendiente y Desigualdades étnico-raciones en el Uruguay. Montevideo: PNUD, 103 et seq.

Ermida Uriarte, O. 2010. "Dificultades del Movimiento Sindical con especiar referencia a su estructura en América Latina", a study commented on by the Trade Union Confederation of the Americas, 11-12.

[34] Vera, A., and Castioni, R. 2010. "Los jóvenes en Latinoamérica. La transición escuela-trabajo como objeto de las políticas públicas", in *Boletim Tecnico do Senac,* 36, No. 2:6, at http://www.senac.br/BTS/362/artigo1.pdf. (Accessed April 13, 2010).

Filardo, V., and Filgueira, F. 2011. "Transiciones a la adultez y educación," Fondo de Población de Naciones Unidad. Montevideo: UNFPA

Filardo, V., and Filgueira, F. 2011. "Transiciones a la adultez y educación," Fondo de Población de Naciones Unidad. Montevideo: UNFPA.

Gallart, M. A. 2008. "Competencias, Productividad y Crecimiento del Empleo," Trazos de la formación. Montevideo: ILO-Cinterfor, 17.

Hernández Arroyave, J. C. 2005. "Preparando a los jóvenes para entrar en el nuevo mundo del trabajo," La inclusión laboural de los jóvenes. Montevideo: ILO-Cinterfor, 30.

Hernandez, J. C. 2006. "La pasantía laboural en los proyectos Entra 21: estrategias, aciertos y retos," in *Estudios y Reflexiones*, 4. Washington: IYF.

ILO. 2006. "Trabajo Decente en las Américas: Una Agenda Hemisférica 2006-2015," Informe del Director General, Décimo Sexta Reunión Regional Americana. Brasilia: ILO.

INJU/MIDES. 2011. *Plan Nacional de Juventudes 2011/2015.* Montevideo: INJU/MIDES, 9.

Lasida, J. "El trabajo dentro la formación y la formación como parte del trabajo. Aportes y desafíos a partir de Projoven y otras experiencias uruguayas," La inclusión laboural de los jóvenes. Montevideo: ILO-Cinterfor, 96.

Ministry of Labour and Social Security. 2011. *Diagnóstico sobre Empleo Juvenil - Empleo y Educación: pilares para la construcción de la trayectoria laboural de los jóvenes,* 29.

Neffa, J. C. 2011. "Políticas de Empleo: una visión sintética de largo plazo (1989-2011)," in *Voces en el Fenix*, 6:77-81.

Proyecto PREJAL. 2009. *Jóvenes y empleo: experiencias innovadoras en el mundo empresarial.* LIMA: ILO, 95-96.

Vargas, F. 2009. "Colombia - Programa de Formación de Jóvenes: Plan 250 mil," ILO - Notas sobre la crisis, 3. Santiago de Chile: ILO Subregional Office.

Vera, A., and Castioni, R. 2010. "Los jóvenes en Latinoamérica. La transición escuela-trabajo como objeto de las políticas públicas", in *Boletim Tecnico do Senac,* 36, No. 2:5-17.

Villamil, E. M. 2010. "Desempleo juvenil: Una bomba de tiempo social," *Boletín de la Escuela Nacional Sindical de Colombia,* Brussels: International Trade Union Confederation.

WORKING TOWARDS EMPLOYMENT POLICIES FOR YOUNG PEOPLE IN MEXICO

CARLOS REYNOSO CASTILLO

1. Overview

Attempts at studying young people at a given time and place pose many challenges because, among the many reasons, there are different angles from which to approach the issue. This complexity is even more evident in countries that have a large share of youth, as is the case of Mexico. Demographically, young people now represent a broad sector of the population and will be an important part of Mexico's population evolution in the near future. In a similar vein, the economic impact of young people is undeniable, due to their participation in national economic development, that is, their political importance as potential voters and as a focus point of programmes at all levels of decision-making. However, in addition to the foregoing areas in which social sciences centre their research focus on young people, there are a series of questions of both biological and psychological nature[1] that people face during this stage of their lives—such as their entry into the workforce[2]—which make the issue of young people even more serious. In a number of countries, this segment of the population feels highly vulnerable and unprotected, and it attributes this state of affairs to the legal framework

[1] See Hopenhayn, M. 2004. "El nuevo mundo del trabajo y los jóvenes," *Revista de Estudios sobre Juventud*, Year 8, No. 20:55.

[2] Some studies point at low level jobs and salaries, more violence-related deaths, increased teen pregnancies, drug use, discrimination and violence among the many problems young people face in countries like Mexico. See Rodríguez, L. 2010. Políticas Públicas para promover empleo juvenil y el emprendedurismo de los jóvenes en México," Proyecto PREJEL, 5, at: www.prejal.oit.org.pe/.../emp_juvenil_i_emprendedurismo_mexico, (accessed on June 16, 2011).

laid down to regulate labour issues.[3] The same holds for Mexico, where a bleak picture is painted with regard to young people. So much so that, when facing a job market that does not accept them, illegal activities like drug trafficking appear to be real options young people resort to.[4] Following on from these considerations, this paper provides an initial approach to the study of employment policies for young people in Mexico, with special attention given to the legal framework that—either directly or indirectly—has affected their implementation. The recent efforts the State has made to fight unemployment in this age group will also be investigated.

One of the first problems a survey like this has to deal with is the wide set of definitions put forward for the notion of "young people". Although this topic is highly debated, it mainly considers the age range between which people are regarded as being "young". Some studies at an international level affirm that adolescence is "the stage in the life cycle in which people go from childhood to adulthood, during which time important biological, psychological, social and cultural changes take place."[5] In some other cases, the concept of young people and youth requires taking account of cultural and historical aspects.[6] For example, in

---

[3] "The scenario is even more dramatic when dealing with the youth population that enters the job market at an early age. Within a context of few jobs and deregulation of labour relations, the young workforce is exposed to extremely precarious working conditions", see De Oliveira, O. 2006. "Jóvenes y precariedad en México," Papeles de Población No. 49. Mexico: CIEAP/UAEM, 37 et seq. (author's own translation).

[4] http://contralinea.info/archivo-revista/index.php/2011/03/06, (accessed June 5, 2011). "However, we are living in a period of history in which young people are seen as a social problem, a threat to public morals and family peace. Youth are associated with drugs and marginalisation. There is nothing more mistaken, on the other hand, than allowing this transmittable generation, because it distorts analysis and understanding and as a result, proposals for objectives and programmes. Youth are truly and increasingly a necessary participant in the family's economic endeavours", see Alexim, J. C. 2006. "Educación y Empleo Juvenil en América Latina," in *Relaciones de Trabajo, empleo y formación profesional* ed. Alexim, J. C. (Montevideo: Cinterfor/ILO), 148 (Author's own translation).

[5] Definition presented by the CEPAL in a study cited by Hernández Pérez V. 2007. "Panorama del empleo juvenil en México: situación actual y perspectivas," Centro de Estudios Sociales y de Opinión Pública, Conference Paper No. 21: 4.

[6] "The concept of youth is quite complex and cannot be simply addressed abstractly. Its definition requires taking historical and cultural factors into account. Youth indicates a period of life devoted to individuals preparing themselves to take on the responsibilities of adult life. In this sense, its duration can vary, depending on the culture and values of each country", see Alexim, J. C. 2006. "Educación y

the Convention on the Rights of the Child, the concept of "young people" includes those under the age of 18, while in 1985 the United Nations (UN) placed the age range between 15 and 24 years old to commemorate the International Year of Youth. As for Mexico, the Law on the Mexican Institute of Youth considers young people as those between the ages of 12 and 29. These differences often make it difficult to target the universe of young people that are referred to, and sometimes give rise to distortions in designing and applying public policies for this share of the population. In a similar vein, the different methodologies for measuring the scope of youth-related problems and the policies dealing with them show high degrees of uniformity. For instance, according to the United Nations, there are more than 1 million young men and women in the world. In other words, approximately one out of every five people is between the ages of 14 and 24 years old. Research carried out by a number of institutions—e.g. the ILO—estimates that by 2015, the number of young people between 15 and 24 years will be approximately 657 million. Moreover, it has been pointed out that in late 2009, there were 81 million unemployed young people, making this one of the problems that affects youth the most.[7] The rates of youth unemployment in most Latin American countries usually account for more than half of the average rate of unemployment. This situation, along with a wide variety of issues that have arisen in recent years, paint a disheartening picture of youth employment.[8] In Mexico, young people between the ages of 12 and 20

Empleo Juvenil en América Latina," in *Relaciones de Trabajo, empleo y formación profesional* ed. Alexim, J. C. (Montevideo: Cinterfor/ILO), 148, (Author's own translation).

7 http://contralinea.info/archivo-revista/index.php/2011/03/06, (accessed June 5, 2011).

8 "In a segmented job market in which employment grows at a slower pace than the economically active population, in which changes in the global productive scenario and the recurring financial restrictions take many employees through the drama of entering and leaving employment, in which the lack of State welfare for the unemployed, candidates to destitution, and in which the new policy demobilizes the workers themselves in defence of their interests, all of these question the way Latin America approaches the relationship between the new forms of work and new opportunities of social well-being. This presents young people with a series of tensions that, while already hinted at in earlier scenarios, gain even more strength today. Among these "tensions", we find that the more education, the fewer the jobs and more market segmentation is often the case, see Hopenhayn, M. 2004. "El nuevo mundo del trabajo y los jóvenes," *Revista de Estudios sobre Juventud*, Year 8, No. 20: 55 (Author's own translation).

years old represent little over 30% of the total population, more than half of which is employed in the informal sector or poorly remunerated.

According to the National Survey of Occupations and Employment and the CONEVAL, in the first quarter of 2010, 68% of young people did not have access to social security and 3.3 million live in conditions of extreme poverty. These figures have led researchers to speak of Mexico's "demographic bonus", understood as a large working age population. To this, we should add that there are more than 7 million young people according to the survey data who do not study nor work.[9] Nor are the problems of young people in Mexico the same. The 2009 National Population Council Report stated that unemployed young people with university degrees are estimated to have duplicated compared to those who did not finish elementary school. On the other hand, about 13% of young college graduates leave the country in search of job opportunities elsewhere.[10] Unemployment has a greater effect on young people, for whom the rate of unemployment stands at about 7%, compared to 3.5% of the EAP, which is largely due to requirements needed to perform a job (experience, availability, training, and so forth), and the conditions in which they enter the job market. One common factor that emerged in available data and studies on young people in Mexico is their lack of protection. For example, in 2005, 58.7% of employed young people did not enter into an employment contract—earning between 57% and 67% of the minimum wage—and were not usually entitled to benefits. Meanwhile, only 17% had healthcare services, 37% joined the retirement savings system (SAT), and 34% were granted housing assistance. This

[9] This broad sector of young people, who are now known as idle youth, face a very complex situation: "Por un lado los jóvenes enfrentan una frustración de expectativas sobre la oferta educativa que no corresponde con sus ilusiones o ambiciones; hoy en día la educación ha dejado de ser un mecanismo de movilidad social; y por el otro, está el problema del grave estancamiento económico, así como la creciente informalidad y precarización del empleo, situación en donde las empresas formales tratan de ahorrar costos a través de la subcontratación, condición que repercute en salarios reales más bajos y escasas o nulas prestaciones sociales. En consecuencia, los jóvenes experimentan una drástica caída en las oportunidades educativas y de empleo, con sus secuelas en salud y vivienda. Rodríguez, L. 2010. Políticas Públicas para promover empleo juvenil y el emprendedurismo de los jóvenes en México," Proyecto PREJEL, 18 at: www.prejal.oit.org.pe/.../emp_juvenil_i_emprendedurismo_mexico (accessed on June 16, 2011).

[10] Huerta, H. "Sin resultados las políticas para empleo de jóvenes", www.publimetro.com.mx/noticias/sin-resultados-las-politicas-para-empleo, (accessed June 5, 2011).

situation is even more serious for young people between 12 and 19 years old (Source: National Occupation Survey, third quarter 2007). According to the ILO standards, this state of affairs denotes a lack of decent jobs, and leads us to reflect on the role of legislation, and more specifically on labour legislation as a guarantee of the rights of both workers and employers. However, in the case of young people these labour laws are not always enforced, making it more like an unreachable paradise for them.

2. The Legal Framework

In Mexico, there are a set of laws and rules that—either directly or indirectly—concern young people. In this sense, a distinction can be made among those laid down at a national level and international provisions that are transposed into national law or are ratified. With regard to the latter group, the following should be mentioned: the Convention on the Rights of the Child adopted by the UN in 1989 and ratified by Mexico in 1990, and the Lisbon Declaration on Youth Policies and Programmes approved by the World Conference of Ministers Responsible for Youth celebrated in Lisbon in August 1998, with the latter that includes the commitment to ensure national youth policy and international development plans and programmes, and a special section on employment that affirms the goal of full employment. There are also the 1995-2000 Regional Action Programme for the Development of Youth in Latin America, a document adopted by the Heads of State and Government, in which the issue of young people holds an important place;[11] the Ibero-American Convention on Rights of Youth (signed by Mexico, but yet to be ratified) adopted by the Ibero-American Young Organization in 2008. Mexico has also concluded various bilateral treaties that address the issue of young people in one way or another. Some of these, among others include those celebrated with Russia, Bolivia, Costa Rica, Moldova and Japan.[12] It also should be noted that the International Labour Organization (ILO) labour standards, including Convention No. 111 concerning Discrimination (Employment and Occupation) were ratified by Mexico in 1961, as well as Convention No. 182 concerning the Worst Forms of

[11] www.cinterfor.org.uy/public/spanish/region/ampro/.../doc/.../libro111.pdf. (accessed June 5, 2011).

[12] For a better understanding of the international documents to which Mexico is party or has participated in some way, see: www.diputados.gob.mx/cesop/Comisiones/9_jyd.htm (accessed June 5, 2011).

Child Labour ratified by Mexico in 2000,[13] and Recommendation 136 concerning Special Youth Employment and Training Schemes for Development Purposes.[14] It should be recalled that the issue of productive work for young people is an important part of the ILO's advocacy for decent work, as part of its effort and proposals to attain the full integration of young people in society.[15] Meanwhile, within the national legal framework, the Political Constitution of the United Mexican States establishes a set of safeguards for young people, such as the prohibition of discrimination on grounds of age, the right to education, equality under the law, the right to health, children's right to nutritious food and to their full development in general, and among others the right to a nationality. More specifically, it is Article 123 of the Constitution that sets the grounds on which labour relations in Mexico are regulated. This article broadly sets forth that every person has the right to work in a dignified and socially useful way. The constitutional framework in Mexico has gained momentum only recently, which is in 2011, after reform that recognises international standards on human rights. This situation has attained particular notice since the above mentioned international norms form part of Mexican positive law and several of them focus on the rights and the protection of children and young people. It is often pointed out

---

[13] In addition to these Conventions and Recommendation No. 136, the ILO has stated that there are other international standards that should be followed in matters of youth employment, such as: Convention No. 87 concerning Freedom of Association and Protection of the Right to Organise, Convention No. 98 concerning the Right to Organise and Collective Bargaining, Convention No. 29 concerning Forced Labour, Convention No. 105 concerning the Abolition of Forced Labour, Convention No. 100 concerning Equal Remuneration, Convention No. 138 concerning Minimum Age for Admission to Employment, Convention No. 79 concerning the Restriction of Night Work of Children and Young Persons in Non-Industrial Occupations, Convention No. 122 concerning Employment Policy, and Convention No. 142 concerning Human Resources Development. Although Mexico has not ratified some of these standards, they form part of the international legal framework in this field.

[14] For the purposes of this Recommendation, special schemes are understood as "...schemes which meet needs for youth employment and training not yet met by existing national educational or vocational training programmes or by normal opportunities on the employment market," as well as "schemes that enable young persons, especially unemployed young persons, who have educational or technical qualifications which are needed by the community for development, particularly in the economic, social, educational or health fields, to use their qualifications in the service of the community."

[15] http://www.cinterfor.org.uy/public/spanish/region/ampro/cinterfor/temas/youth/doc (accessed June 5, 2011).

that in Mexico, labour legislation, and more specifically Federal Labour Law, does not encourage hiring young people and, if anything, deters it. This perception has been one of the principal arguments for putting forward reforms to the labour laws, a goal that is still to be fully achieved today. In this sense, there are two legislative areas that would be directly linked to youth employment: child labour and special arrangements for individual hiring. In the first case, the laws are intended to safeguard minors' health and development, as well as to lay down special rules concerning their working conditions. These rules consider under-age workers from the age of 14, since those younger than this age limit are prohibited from working. Therefore, minors between the ages of 14 and 16 must supply a medical certificate that states their ability to work and must undergo medical examination authorised by way of inspections on a regular basis. Among others, minors are not allowed to operate in workplaces where alcoholic drinks for immediate consumption are sold, or to take on jobs capable of affecting their personal or public morals, or work in itinerant jobs—unless special permission is granted. For those under the age of 18, the law prohibits them from taking part in industrial night work. The law also lays down a number of obligations on those who employ minors, such as requiring medicals certifying the minors' capacity for work, maintaining a special control of records with certain information and providing them with training, in addition to arranging the work so that minors can continue with their schooling. Concerning forms of individual hiring, it should be noted that while the law differentiates contracts on the basis of their duration (open-ended contracts, fixed-term contracts and contracts for a specific project), none of them specifically addresses young people or minors. Despite the need to establish new contractual arrangements directly aimed at young people that has been widely discussed, this attempt has been viewed with suspicion, since they can become a potential source of abuse by employers, who, by recruiting them, might simply try to reduce labour costs. The Mexican legal framework also has some provisions addressing young people on an exclusive basis, such as the Law on the Mexican Institute of Youth (IMJUVE),[16] which was established by a decentralised public agency with a high level of autonomy in order to define and implement a national youth policy through special programmes. Moreover, the agency supports the executive branch and other associated agencies, concluding agreements with the government at different levels, and carrying out

[16] Federal Official Gazette, January 6, 1999.

research on the problems that afflict young people.[17] However, the work this agency does in terms of employment is negligible, since other agencies at different government levels take care of the corresponding policies. Along with this policy space—as in the case of the IMJUVE Law—and in the absence of federal legislation to influence rules and policies aimed at young people, Mexican states have been developing some other provisions. The main goal of some of these laws is "to establish the guiding principles of public policies that contribute to the comprehensive development of young people, according to their general needs" (Nuevo Leon);[18] and "to facilitate and advance the comprehensive development of young people" (Nayarit).[19] Others put forward the setup of institutions to deal with this issue by coordinating state efforts, as in the case of Baja California through its Youth Institute[20] or the Nayarit Youth Institute. All of these laws propose the inclusion of young people in regional development, as well as the pursuit of equal opportunities. This regulatory landscape is complemented with the Official Mexican Standard for Labour Equality between Women and Men (NMX-R-025-SCFI-2009), which sets the requirements to certify companies on matters of equality at work based on certain indicators and specific methodology to be implemented voluntarily. This standard also tries to ensure compliance with aspects like equality, non-discrimination, social security, an adequate working environment, freedom and accessibility at work for both men and women. Although not directly addressing young people, the Official Mexican Standard for Labour Equality between Women and Men is important all the same, as it sets conditions of equality and to eliminate discrimination.[21]

3. Policies for Young People

For some authors, State employment guidelines can be divided into three categories: employment policies—usually forming part of the economic policies—work policies—which fall under the competence of

---

[17] www.imjuventud.gob.mx.(accessed on June 16, 2011).

[18] Law published in the Nuevo Leon State Official Gazette, on July 28, 2008.

[19] Law for the Young People of the State of Nayarit, September 10, 2009.

[20] The law that creates the Baja California Youth Institute, Official Gazette of June 22, 2001.

[21] See Rodríguez, L. 2010. Políticas Públicas para promover empleo juvenil y el emprendedurismo de los jóvenes en México," Proyecto PREJEL, 31, at: www.prejal.oit.org.pe/.../emp_juvenil_i_emprendedurismo_mexico (accessed on June 16, 2011).

the Ministry of Labour and Social Security—and job market policies—such as job market intervention mechanisms, which can be active or passive[22]. In Mexico, practically all these different methods have been resorted to in the youth sector.[23] Active government participation in job markets is relatively new. This distinct development is strongly influenced by international financial bodies that have tried to have some bearing on job markets since the 1970s, but the results have generally not met the expectations.[24] An important aspect is the creation of the National Employment Service in 1978, which stemmed from the national and international economic policies of the time and out of the concern that training should be considered a central aspect of employment policies, thus amending the Federal Labour Law.[25] More specifically, the 2007-2012 National Development Plan establishes a set of concepts, such as the "Competitive and Job-Creating Economy". Among other strategies, this one includes promoting employment, which should translate into creating formal jobs with benefits and social security, and motivating young people to enter the formal job market, especially for the first time. In this model, the National Employment Service is the agency in charge of coordinating federal government employment actions[26] across the country through its almost 150 offices, and each state can institute the coordinated

---

[22] See Samaniego, N. "Las políticas de mercado de trabajo y su evaluación en América latina," cited in Hernández Pérez V. 2007. "Panorama del empleo juvenil en México: situación actual y perspectivas," Centro de Estudios Sociales y de Opinión Pública, Conference Paper No. 21:12.

[23] In Mexico, these policies have encompassed practically all the active forms of support, such as: employment services, training the workforce and direct or indirect job creation. Save for social security – e.g. retirement and early retirement that have been in place in Mexico for decades – passive policies like unemployment subsidies are only starting to come into being", see Samaniego, N. "Las políticas de mercado de trabajo y su evaluación en América latina," cited in Hernández Pérez V. 2007. "Panorama del empleo juvenil en México: situación actual y perspectivas," Centro de Estudios Sociales y de Opinión Pública, Conference Paper No. 21: 13, (Author's own translation).

[24] See Jiménez Jiménez, J. A. 2005. "Las políticas de empleo en México y el desarrollo regional," *Revista de la Facultad de Economía*, Puebla, Mexico: BUAP, No. 29: 35 et seq.

[25] See Sánchez Castañeda, A. 2007. "La capacitación y el adiestramiento en México: regulación, realidades y retos," *Revista Latinoamericana de Derecho Social*, No. 5. Mexico: UNAM-IIJ, 191.

[26] The National Employment Training Service is regulated by Articles 537 to 539-F of the Federal Labour Law. Its objectives consist of studying and promoting job creation. It is an agency that works under the auspices of the Ministry of Labour and Social Welfare.

implementation of public policies for employment. Over the years, public employment policies will become part of a six-year plan of the administration in office. There have been many approaches to address the problems young people face, especially those referring to their entry into the workforce. There is now a diagnosis and a proposal for action guidelines that the federal government has tried to implement called the 2008-2012 National Youth Programme. This programme was presented in 2008 and includes not only the current administration's view of young people, but also the approaches to take and set of action of public policies aimed at this age group. It is based on the 2007-2012 National Development Plan, which establishes that it is necessary to "implement transversal public policies that guarantee the necessary conditions for the full development of young people," while expressly mentioning promoting their entry into the workforce. The general objective of the plan was to safeguard young people's right to work by making them part of the workforce under conditions of "decent work".[27] This objective would evolve through more specific objectives like increasing the number of certificates supplied at work training centres, lowering the rate of unemployment among young people, increasing the number of working young people with employment contracts and benefits, or even increasing the number of young people who can start their own business. Among the strategies adopted to revert the problems of young people entering the workforce, one proposal was to promote employability through various initiatives—in addition to generating statistical data and identifying successful efforts—such as designing distance training programmes to be implemented at several public agencies, offering flexible forms of training, assisting young people with disabilities through the Workforce Entrance Agency, promoting re-employment programmes for young people with illnesses, providing incentives to the private sector to fund training schemes, carrying out campaigns on liaison and training services, encouraging young people to do volunteer work and making public the Standardized Labour Skills System. Within this entire scope of actions put forward by the federal government, specific programmes aimed at attaining a higher rate of young people entering the workforce deserve

---

[27] The expression "decent work" first appeared in the 1999 Report of the ILO Director, which points out that "decent work" means productive work carried out in conditions of freedom, equality, safety and dignity, in which rights are protected, which generates adequate income and adequate social protection. See Reynoso Castillo, C. 2007. "La idea de 'trabajo decente'," in *El Derecho Social en México a Inicios del Siglo XXI, Una Visión de Conjunto*, ed. Ortega Solís, A., and G. Ruiz Moreno (Mexico: Universidad de Guadalajara), 95.

special mention, like the Promotion of First Employment. At the end of 2010, the federal government embarked on one of the most ambitious attempts to promote the creation of permanent jobs. The strategy consisted of sponsoring job creation by offering companies tax incentives and, to this end, modified certain Income Tax Law provisions.[28] Criticisms of this government policy usually concern the fact that this initiative inasmuch as legislative efforts were aimed at supporting and even lowering companies' tax contributions, and this way of approaching the issue affected one of the general principles embodied in Mexican labour legislation: a balance between production factors. Some experts have pointed out that the implemented policies did not produce the expected results because "their vision is pro-business to an extreme" since the progress or success of some programmes lies in the hands of companies, like that of hiring young workers or not. This idea has to do with the willingness of many companies to hire only young workers who have some experience and do not need training. The First Employment Programme begun in 2007, and by May 2008 15,037 employers enrolled and registered 26,176 workers. By the end of 2009, there were 1,900 employer registrations and 12,400 worker registrations, corresponding to a 60.1% decrease. The 2011 Federal Revenue Law incorporated certain amendments which would give way to what was named the Law to Promote First Employment, which absorbed the First Employment Programme. In 2011, the latest version of the programme—issued in the Federal Official Gazette on November 14 —was amended in an attempt to make the model more flexible. By way of example, its applicability was extended until 2012; a subsidy for IMSS quotas was granted to employers after three months after worker's registration and support was given to companies even though it was not necessarily the first time workers who had been registered in the said institution. Furthermore, procedures could be done online so as to speed up the process.[29] Even though the federal government has insisted that these changes to the model should not deter employers from participating as they will not be controlled or persecuted, part of management is fearful that once a worker is registered, for instance, with the Mexican Social Security Institute, they will become captive taxpayers and could be subjected to audits or other coercive measures. This employment programme can be seen as the first

[28] Decree by which various provisions are added to the Income Tax Law, December 31, 2010.

[29] Through a number of amendments made to the programmes, the government intends to create at least 50,000 jobs, which will provide subsidies for social security dues ranging from 10% to 100%, depending on the income.

and most important effort on the part of the government to create jobs for young people. According to the Ministry of Labour, the programme has produced unsuccessful results because the tax authorities were too involved in its implementation, and this deterred employers from participating in the programme. On the other hand, it has been stressed that it was a highly onerous programme in view of the administrative costs to be borne. Some organisations, like the Centre for Labour Thinking and Action, stated that this programme provided employers with more room to manoeuvre with regard to their obligations. Another criticism of the policies in this field concerned their disregard of social vision, as designed from a pronounced business point of view. The poor results in boosting youth employment in Mexico are now faced with different challenges. Without a healthy and growing economy, there are not enough positions to place the unemployed. Another aspect that requires special attention is the relationship between schooling and vocational training, on the one side, and on the other side the needs of the productive sector. Today, more than half of the young people between 14 and 17 years old are not in education. Moreover, a large share of them—estimated at 30 million—have not completed elementary school. This is a challenge the country needs to address, not only in an effort to attain equality and equal opportunities, but also to help these people, and young people in particular, to contribute to the country's development. However, employing young people—at least in Mexico—not only has to do with offering more opportunities, but also with the need for quality jobs and full compliance with labour laws and applicable benefits. This is necessary because youth employment, where available, is often found to have high levels of non-compliance with labour laws, which means that the State must push for the legal framework to be brought up-to-date. In view of these issues, there are at least two legislative channels that should be explored to modify, update and strengthen the legal framework. First of all, the chapter on child labour included in the Federal Labour Law should be reviewed to increase the protection measures for working children, grounded in the legal proposals already stated in international standards like those of the ILO. Secondly, the bodies in charge of verifying compliance with the standards for modes of production in Mexico should be reinforced, specifically labour courts or conciliation and arbitration boards, the operations of which need to be reviewed in important respects, but particularly in those that have to do with compliance with applicable laws in force on child labour. Finally, with reference to the legislative measures that are currently being used to address the different problems young people face in Mexico, it should be mentioned that several legal reforms have been presented to the Federal Chamber of Deputies, among which are the following:

a) initiatives for the General Youth Law, presented by the Institutional Revolutionary Party in 2009, that seek recognition of the fundamental rights of young people between the ages of 14 and 29, as well as moving towards a comprehensive development policy for young people.
b) Initiatives for the Federal Mexican Youth Law, presented by the Institutional Revolutionary Party in 2010, that aim at guaranteeing full recognition and enjoyment of young people's rights and obligations and proposes mandatory medical insurance for students and the creation of a National Young People's Potential System.
c) Initiatives to reform several articles in the IMJUVE Law and that of the National Women's Institute, presented by the National Action Party in 2010, that aim at the IMJUVE's designing and coordinating policies, plans and programmes for young people that encourage access to cultural events and develop their artistic abilities and cultural policies.
d) Initiatives for the Law to Promote Education, Vocational Training and Employment for Young People, presented by the Labour Party in 2010, that aim at:
- setting the working conditions for young people between the ages of 14 and 29 years old; stem school dropouts by granting scholarships;
- seeking the creation of the National Council to Promote Education, Vocational Training and Employment for Young People, as well as an Advisory Forum of the Council with authorities from different levels of government; and
- establishing a National Programme and Fund to promote education, vocational training and employment for young people.
e) Initiatives for a provision that would amend a number of statutes, such as the General Education Law, the Organic Law of Federal Public Administration, the Law on Prizes, Civil Incentives and Rewards, and the General Law for Physical Culture and Sports, among others, presented by the Party of the Democratic Revolution in 2011, in order to address the various problems that now affect young people, such as discrimination, education, employment, and so forth.[30] As seen, there is a variety of legislative proposals that at

[30] For further information and dates on which these initiatives were issued in State Official Gazettes, as well as a brief summary of each of them, see: http//sitl.diputados.gob.mx/LXI_leg/iniciativaslxi.php. accessed on June 18, 2011.

first glance seem to largely collide in their attempt to address the concerns of young people from various angles. The differences seem to lie in the public policy instruments to be used to put in place policies for this sector, and here lies the importance of reaching appropriate consensus so as not to further postponing the necessary action on the part of the State and government.

4. Conclusions

International experiences on matters of policies and projects for youth employment are wide-ranging. However, most of them have approached the issue from two different angles: the education and vocational training needed to enter the job market, and employers' specific needs to attract young people, with more emphasis often given to one or the other. In recent years, some studies have pointed at two successful experiences in Latin America: the Young Chile project (*Chile Jóven*) and the internship project carried out by the Brazilian Youth Institute.[31] In the case of Mexico, analyses on youth employment have been carried out considering different perspectives. In this paper, the focus has been on the legal aspects of the issue, and in this field we believe future Mexican decision-makers should direct their efforts on at least two aspects. First of all, there is the issue of coordinating the various government agencies (at federal, state and local level), particularly those bodies dealing with employment, so that the programmes and projects aimed at young people can be systematically carried out under a single, federal system. This objective could be achieved, by pursuing at least two avenues: concluding necessary political-administrative agreements—for example, by means of coordination agreements based on a legal mandate—or setting-up a legal and structural framework that would make it possible to reach this end. This is the way in which a decentralised public entity of a federal nature could be established to formulate policies on this issue, with the participation and representation of the different agencies involved—e.g. the Ministry of Public Education, the Department of Treasury and Public

[31] See Alexim, J. C. 2006. "Educación y Empleo Juvenil en América Latina," in *Relaciones de Trabajo, empleo y formación profesional* ed. Alexim, J. C. (Montevideo: Cinterfor/ILO), 152 (Author's own translation).
This programme is "a training and vocational training package" aimed at certain principles like the relevance of training to the job market, coordinated State efforts in the sector, the identification of beneficiaries, and so on.
www.cinterfor.org.uy/public/spanish/region/ampro/cinterfor/publ/sala/poldev/v.htm (accessed July 7, 2011).

Credit, the Ministry of Labour and Social Welfare, the Ministry of Social Advancement, as well as state representations, and so on.[32] In passing, it is fitting to point out that the overall design of a policy aimed at young people should include a variable regarding the area where young people live. Evidently, the best way to attend to young people will differ whether they live in cities or in the countryside, a situation that should result in more focalised strategies.[33] Meanwhile, there is the issue of the legal regulation that facilitates and promotes employment for young people. From this standpoint, there are at least two ways of bringing this about:

- on the one side, tax incentives would make employing young people attractive to companies, and not an obstacle to them. As mentioned above, the strategies on this issue that have been carried out have not produced the expected results. Therefore, before embarking on a programme that entails lowering taxes for employers that hire young people, it would be advisable to design strategies based on past experiences in order to directly influence this age group.
- on the other side, there are the reforms to the legal labour framework regarding individual hiring in general. The scope of reforming the forms of individual hiring contained in the legal labour framework

---

[32] Mention should be made of further attempts that have been made in Mexico recently to address the problems young people face, such as the agreement reached by the National Public Security Convention, which decided to establish a fund from the National Governors' Conference to guarantee a scholarship system for Young people between the ages of 15 and 20 years old to offer young people employment. This is a plausible effort on behalf of those overseeing this agency. While it should be welcomed and hoped that it will have good results, it is an example of a strategy the Mexican State has used many times for local purposes and not structural ones. See Breach, M. 2011. "Pactan gobernadores abrir un fondo para becar a jóvenes en educación y empleo," *La Jornada* Newspaper, July 12.

[33] Some experts have already insisted that the changes to which young people are exposed to vary and have a different impact depending on several variables, such as access to education, the place they live, access to new technologies, etc. Some politicians have also pointed out that approximately 1.5 million jobs a year would be needed to attend the young people who join the workforce every year. See Xantonilla, G. 2011. "Políticas públicas más efectivas para poner fin a la desocupacion juvenil," in the Newspaper *El Sol de México*, 3. Therefore, for example. "Las tasas de desempleo y subempleo son mucho más altas en jóvenes de minorías étnicas, jóvenes con bajos niveles de educación, jóvenes en zonas rurales dispersas, jóvenes con distintos niveles de discapacidad [...]". See Hopenhayn, M. 2004. "El nuevo mundo del trabajo y los jóvenes," *Revista de Estudios sobre Juventud*, Year 8, No. 20:41.

have been widely discussed. The arguments in favour of widening the forms of individual contractual schemes centre on seeing these changes as a mechanism for job creation. This is risky because it gives rise to expectations that based on the experiences of countries that have implemented this type of change have not necessarily led to job creation as hoped for, because it has been proven that a series of factors are involved in creating a job position, and one of them is the legal framework for hiring, yet it is not the only one. In this sense, we believe that mechanisms that offer companies options for hiring in general and for hiring young people in particular which should be developed. In this way, the employer would have periods in which the new recruits either show their professional qualities and capabilities or the company offers them the knowledge and skills needed to perform their duties adequately. To the extent to which these periods are subject to rules and discretionary powers regarding the type of activities to be carried out are eliminated, as well as ways to terminate or continue in employment under these circumstances, we would be offering a legal framework suitable for employment, one that does not sacrifice workers' rights. In addition to the above, it is important to move towards standardising the national regulatory framework aimed at young people in general and at employment in particular. Since standard regulations give rise to the public policies intended for young people that are not always homogenous, they should be more suitably implemented and coordinated by the various public agencies involved in this matter, either directly or indirectly. Along this same line, there are those who have expressed the need for coordinated effort of public policies aimed at young people and specifically at their employment, which could be implemented with a set of provisions envisaging these objectives, where the rights of young people are given priority. All of these actions do not exclude reinforcing other strategies and lateral approaches that could influence in improving young people's employability. By this, we refer to the educational policies in general, as well as work-related education policies, in addition to the efforts made to encourage an entrepreneurial spirit in young people through appropriate means and mechanisms, both public and private.

References

Alexim, J. C. 2006. “Educación y Empleo Juvenil en América Latina,” in *Relaciones de Trabajo, empleo y formación profesional* ed. Alexim, J. C. (Montevideo: Cinterfor/ILO).

Breach, M. 2011. “Pactan gobernadores abrir un fondo para becar a jóvenes en educación y empleo,” *La Jornada* Newspaper, July 12.

De Oliveira, O. 2006. “Jóvenes y precariedad en México,” Papeles de Población No. 49. Mexico: CIEAP/UAEM, 37 et seq.

Hernández Pérez V. 2007. “Panorama del empleo juvenil en México: situación actual y perspectivas,” Centro de Estudios Sociales y de Opinión Pública, Conference Paper No. 21: 4.

Hopenhayn, M. 2004. “El nuevo mundo del trabajo y los jóvenes,” *Revista de Estudios sobre Juventud*, Year 8, No. 20:55.

Huerta, H. “Sin resultados las políticas para empleo de jóvenes”, www.publimetro.com.mx/noticias/sin-resultados-las-politicas-para-empleo, (accessed June 5, 2011).

Jiménez Jiménez, J. A. 2005. “Las políticas de empleo en México y el desarrollo regional,” *Revista de la Facultad de Economía*, Puebla, Mexico: BUAP, No. 29: 35 et seq.

Reynoso Castillo, C. 2007. “La idea de ‘trabajo decente’,” in *El Derecho Social en México a Inicios del Siglo XXI, Una Visión de Conjunto*, ed. Ortega Solís, A., and G. Ruiz Moreno (Mexico: Universidad de Guadalajara), 95.

Rodríguez, L. 2010. Políticas Públicas para promover empleo juvenil y el emprendedurismo de los jóvenes en México,” Proyecto PREJEL, 5, at www.prejal.oit.org.pe/.../emp_juvenil_i_emprendedurismo_mexico (accessed on June 16, 2011). Samaniego, N. “Las políticas de mercado de trabajo y su evaluación en América latina,” cited in Hernández Pérez V. 2007. “Panorama del empleo juvenil en México: situación actual y perspectivas,” Centro de Estudios Sociales y de Opinión Pública, Conference Paper No. 21.

Sánchez Castañeda, A. 2007. “La capacitación y el adiestramiento en México: regulación, realidades y retos,” *Revista Latinoamericana de Derecho Social*, No. 5. Mexico: UNAM-IIJ, 191.

Xantonilla, G. 2011. “Políticas públicas más efectivas para poner fin a la desocupacion juvenil,” in the Newspaper *El Sol de México*, 3.

READING INSTRUCTIONS

All volumes of the *ADAPT LABOUR STUDIES BOOK-SERIES* comprise of an online resources section (available at www.bollettinoadapt.it), set up for documentary purposes with the aim to implement and update the content of our publications on a regular basis, which includes:

a) sources of law,

b) relevant EU and international documentation,

c) memoranda of understanding, agreements and collective agreements,

d) monographic works,

e) studies and research reports.

ONLINE RESOURCES

1. APPRENTICESHIP
(Apprendistato)

EU DOCUMENTS *(Documentazione comunitaria)*

European Centre for the Development of Vocational Training, 2011
Skills for Green Jobs: Country Report United Kingdom

European Commission, July 2011
Midterm Review of the Lifelong Learning Programme, COM(2011) 413 final

European Youth Forum, 2011
Interns Revealed: A Survey on Internship Quality in Europe

INTERNATIONAL DOCUMENTS *(Documentazione internazionale)*

ILO, January 2012
Upgrading Informal Apprenticeship: a Resource Guide for Africa

OECD and Germany Federal Government, March 2012,
Partnerships for Youth

REPORTS AND RESEARCH *(Studi e ricerche)*

BIS Research Paper Number 18, February 2011
National Learner Satisfaction Survey: Young People in FE and Apprenticeships

Hilary Steedman, December 2011

Apprenticeship policy in England: Increasing Skills versus Boosting Young People's Job Prospects

Ofsted, April 2012
Apprenticeship for the Young People

O'Toole, R., December 2011
Apprenticeships in Wales and the UK

2. EDUCATION, TRAINING AND LABOUR (*Istruzione, formazione, lavoro*)

EU DOCUMENTS (*Documentazione comunitaria)*

European Commission, March 2012
UEAPME Contribution to the "Youth Opportunities Initiative"

INTERNATIONAL DOCUMENTS (*Documentazione internazionale)*

ILO, April 2012
Better Job for Better Economy: World of Work Report 2012

ILO, June 2011,
Regulating for Decent Work: New Directions in Labour Market Regulation

ILO, June 2011
Equality at Work: The Continuing Challenge

ILO and European Union, 2011
Building a Sustainable Job-rich Recovery

ILO and OECD, September 2011
Promoting Policy Coherence for Decent Work and Full, Productive Employment

ILO and OECD, September 2011
Short-term Employment and Labour Market Outlook and Key Challenges in G20 Countries

The International Bank for Reconstruction and Development/the World Bank, 2012
Putting Higher Education to Work: Skills and Research for Growth in East Asia

World Bank, November 2010
Active Labour Market Programs for Youth, Employment Policy Primer

REPORTS AND RESEARCH (*Studi e ricerche)*

Bell, D. N. F., and D. G. Blanchflower, April 2011
The Crisis, Policy Reactions and Attitudes to Globalization and Jobs

Leibniz Information Centre for Economics, 2012
Challenges Facing European Labour Markets: Is a Skill Upgrade the Appropriate Instrument?

Nelson, J., and L. O'Donnell, 2011
Approaches to Supporting Young People Not in Education, Employment or Training: a Review. Slough: NFER.

Quintini, G., 2011
"Right for the Job: Over-Qualified or Under-Skilled?" OECD Social, Employment and Migration Working Papers, No. 120, Paris: OECD Publishing.

Schmitt, J., May 2011
Labour Market Policy in the Great Recession: Some Lessons from Denmark and Germany

World of Work Report, October 2011
Making Markets Work for Jobs

DATA AND STATISTICS (*Statistiche e note economiche*)

OECD Indicators, September 2011
Education at a Glance 2011

OECD, 2011
Country Note: ITALY, Priorities Supported by Indicators

3. YOUNG WORKERS (*Lavoratori giovani*)

EU DOCUMENTS *(Documentazione comunitaria)*

European Commission, December 2011
Youth Opportunities Initiative, COM (2011) 933 final

European Youth Forum, December 2011
Youth Employment in Europe: A Call for Change

INTERNATIONAL DOCUMENTS *(Documentazione internazionale)*

ILO , January 2012
Global Employment Trends 2012, Preventing a Deeper Jobs Crisis

ILO, January 2012
Work Inequalities in the Crisis, Evidence from Europe: Executive Summary

ILO, June 2011
Youth Employment in Eastern Europe: Crisis Within the Crisis

ILO, March 2012
Decent Work for Youth – the EU Dimension

ILO, November 2011
Increasing the Employability of Disadvantaged Youth

ILO, 2011
The Global Crisis: Causes, Responses and Challenges

International Labour Conference, 101st Session, March 2012
The Youth Employment Crisis: Time for Action

OECD, December 2010
Off to a Good Start? Jobs for Youth

OECD and ILO, September 2011
Give Youth a Better Start

The World Bank, 2011
More and Better Jobs in South Asia: South Asia Development Matters

REPORTS AND RESEARCH *(Studi e ricerche)*

Bell, D. N. F., and D. G. Blanchflower, April 2011
Youth Unemployment in Europe and the United States

Bell, D. N. F., and D. G. Blanchflower, April 2011
Young People and the Great Recession

Cunningham W., July 2010.
Youth at Risk in Latin America and the Caribbean

Miller, S., June 2011
Achieving Full, Productive and Freely Chosen Employment for Young People

Scarpetta, S., A. Sonnet and T. Manfredi, 2010
"Rising Youth Unemployment During The Crisis: How to Prevent Negative Long-term Consequences on a Generation?" OECD Social, Employment and Migration Working Papers, No. 106, OECD Publishing.

Schulz, N., C. Lahusen and P. R. Graziano, August 2011
Promoting Social Europe: The Emergence of a European Youth Unemployment Policy Regime?

DATA AND STATISTICS (*Statistiche e note economiche*)

ILO, April 2012
Global Employment Outlook

ILO, October 2011
Global Employment Trends for Youth: 2011 Update

ILO, January 2012
Global Employment Trends 2012; Preventing A Deeper Jobs Crisis

OECD, December 2011
Young People Not In Education or Employment

OECD, 2011
Off to a Good Start? Jobs for Youth

OECD, 2010
Off To A Good Start? Jobs for Youth Spain

4. SCHOOL-TO-WORK TRANSITION *(Transizione scuola lavoro)*

INTERNATIONAL DOCUMENTS *(Documentazione internazionale)*

OECD, September 2011
Transition from School to Work: Where are the 15-29 Year-olds?

OECD, October 2010
Learning for Jobs, The OECD International Survey of VET Systems: First Results and Technical Report

REPORTS AND RESEARCH *(Studi e ricerche)*

Cunningham W., and B. Salvagno, January 2011,
Youth Employment Transitions in Latin America, Policy Research Working Paper 5521, World Bank

Brodmann, S. E. P. Cuadra, M. I. Allouche, and S. A. Hilli, January 2012

From Education-To-Work: Opportunities and Challenges in the West Bank and Gaza

CONTRIBUTORS

Héctor-Hugo Barbagelata, Professor Emeritus, The University of the Republic, Uruguay.

Helena Carvalho, Assistant Professor, University Institute of Lisbon, Portugal.

Gordon Cooke, Assistant Professor, Memorial University of Newfoundland, Canada.

Sérgio Estevinha, Junior Researcher, University Institute of Lisbon, Portugal.

Francesca Fazio, PhD. Student, University of Bergamo, Italy.

Jong-Sung Kim, PhD. Student, Chung-Ang University, South Korea.

Byoung-Hoon Lee, Professor, Chung-Ang University, South Korea.

Janusz Łyko, Professor, Wroclaw University of Economics, Poland.

Gabriela Mendizábal, Professor, Autonomous University of Morelos (UAEM), Mexico.

María Ascensión Morales Ramírez, Professor, National Autonomous University of Mexico, Mexico.

Boaz Omori Munga, PhD. Student, University of Nairobi, Kenya.

Luísa Oliveira, Assistant Professor, University Institute of Lisbon, Portugal.

Eldah Onsomu, Policy Analyst, Kenya Institute for Public Policy Research and Analysis, Kenya.

Carlos Reynoso Castillo, Professor, National Autonomous University of Mexico, Mexico

Raul Saco Barrios, Professor, Pontifical Catholic University of Peru, Peru.

Alfredo Sánchez-Castañeda, Mexico National Autonomous University, Mexico.

Lavinia Serrani, ADAPT Research Fellow, Italy.

Irina Soboleva, Researcher, Institute of Economy, Russian Academy of Sciences, Russia.

Francesca Sperotti, ADAPT Research Fellow, Italy.

Maria Tuttobene, PhD Student, University of Bergamo, Italy.

Luísa Veloso, Researcher, Centre for Research and Studies on Sociology, University Institute of Lisbon, Portugal.

Patricia Vendramin, Research Director, Fondation Travail-Université, Belgium.

INDEX